D0535597

65

THE DOCTRINE OF CORRECTNESS
IN ENGLISH USAGE
1700-1800

THE DOCTRINE OF CORRECTNESS
IN ENGLISH USAGE
1700-1800

BY

STERLING ANDRUS LEONARD

NEW YORK

RUSSELL & RUSSELL · INC

1962

FIRST PUBLISHED IN 1929 AS NUMBER 25
IN THE UNIVERSITY OF WISCONSIN STUDIES IN
LANGUAGE AND LITERATURE
REISSUED, 1962, BY RUSSELL & RUSSELL, INC.
L. C. CATALOG CARD NO: 62-13838

PRINTED IN THE UNITED STATES OF AMERICA

CONTENTS

NOTE

The topic of this study was suggested by Dr. Krapp, with a reference to the valuable notes published by Dr. W. F. Bryan in the *Manly Anniversary Studies*. Dr. Bryan's article on Campbell, the rhetorician, appeared after the completion of this manuscript, but is referred to in the relevant places. The collection of sufficient material in this country would have been impossible without the courteous helpfulness of the library officials of Columbia University, Harvard University, and the Library of Congress, and the facilities of the Inter-Library Loan generously accorded by these institutions and by Princeton, Yale, Cornell, and Michigan Universities.

In addition to the unfailing guidance and criticism of Dr. Krapp, helpful counsel has been given by Professors F. T. Baker, C. S. Baldwin, H. M. Ayers, and Allan Abbott, and by Mr. George Genzmer, of Columbia University; and by Professors B. S. Monroe, Charles C. Fries, James R. Foster, and George McKnight. I appreciate the courtesy of my colleague Professor H. B. Lathrop and of the Publication Committees of the Department of English and the University of Wisconsin Studies, who have made possible the publication of this study, and of Professors W. E. Leonard and Miles Hanley, who read the entire manuscript and gave valuable criticisms and encouragement. I am indebted to Miss Inez Richards, of the same department, for the interesting quotation from Walpole's Letters concerning the English of Lord Chesterfield. The glossary and index would have been impossible to complete without the careful work of Miss Frances Wagner and Miss Mildred Hergenhan.

The material here presented is of course only a sampling of a large mass of writing about the English language, and particularly about the idea of correctness in the use of English, during the eighteenth century. Further references casting new light on these problems will be gratefully received and acknowledged.

S. L.

Ben Jonson's posthumous "English Grammar" came out in 1640. The titlepage declares that it is "made . . . . out of his observation of the English language now spoken, and in use," and contains also a golden utterance of Quintilian calling *custom* "the surest mistress of speech" and making an apt comparison between current language and current coin. The lesson of this passage seems very hard to learn. Scholars have always consistently averred that good usage is the only conceivable criterion of good English, but most people still clamor for a heaven-sent "standard" to measure their words by. The best established idioms are continually put upon their defence merely because, since they *are* idioms, they differ from somebody's preconceived notion of what ought to be correct.

George Lyman Kittredge, *Some Landmarks in the History of English Grammars,* 1906.

CHAPTER I

INTEREST IN PROBLEMS OF LANGUAGE IN THE EIGHTEENTH CENTURY

I do here, in the Name of all the Learned and polite Persons of the Nation, complain . . . that our Language is extremely imperfect; that its daily Improvements are by no means in proportion to its daily Corruptions, that the Pretenders to polish and refine it, have chiefly multiplied Abuses and Absurdities, and that in many Instances, it offends against every part of Grammar.

Swift, *Proposal for Correcting,* 1712.

I found our speech copious without order, and energetic without rules.

Johnson, Preface to the *Dictionary,* 1755.

CHAPTER I

EIGHTEENTH-CENTURY INTEREST IN PROBLEMS OF LANGUAGE

1. *Earlier views of English.* The materials on the theory of language, and on English grammar in particular, in the seventeenth century and earlier, are interestingly presented in several studies.[1] These writings show that while interest in problems of language was keen, little or no attention was given to questions of grammatical correctness; criticism previous to the eighteenth century seems to have been concerned with matters of vocabulary chiefly. Fitzedward Hall notes that *its* was a "neoterism" in Queen Elizabeth's day, and states that it had "a weary struggle" for acceptance,[2] but he cites no protest against it. The critical attitude in the eighteenth century is shown by contrast in the "very levanter of ire and villification"[3] aroused by the form "is being built," which apparently was first devised and condemned after 1750. Richard Mulcaster's *Elementarie*, 1582,[4] states the need of bringing "our tung to Art and form of disapline" and says that "our *Sparta* must be spunged"; but Mulcaster's "Grammer" was apparently never completed and nobody seems to have taken up his challenge.

Dr. Fries cites a remarkable quotation from George Fox's "A Battle-Door for Teachers and Professors to Learn Singular

---

[1] J. L. Moore, "Tudor-Stuart Views of the Growth, Status and Destiny of the English Language." *Studien zur Englischen Philologie*, Volume II, Halle, 1910.

George H. McKnight, *Modern English in the Making*, Appleton, 1928.

B. S. Monroe, "An English Academy," *Modern Philology*, VIII, 107-22.

Richard Morris, *Historical Outlines of English Accidence*, 1872.

Henry Cecil Wyld, *History of Modern Colloquial English*, Unwin, 1920.

C. C. Fries, "Rules of the Common School Grammars," *P. M. L. A.* XLII, 221-37, and "The Periphrastic Future in Modern English," *P. M. L. A*, XL, 963-1024.

[2] *Modern English*, p. 354.

[3] *Ibid.*, p. 334.

[4] *Op. cit.*, pp. 30 and 271.

and Plural; *You* to Many, and *Thou* to One; Singular One, *Thou;* Plural Many, *You"* (1660):

"Do not they speak false English, false Latine, false Greek . . . . and false to the other Tongues . . . . that doth not speak *thou* to *one,* what ever he be, Father, Mother, King, or Judge; is he not a Novice and Unmannerly, and an Ideot and a Fool, that speaks *You* to *one,* which is not to be spoken to a *singular,* but to *many?* O Vulgar Professors and Teachers, that speaks Plural when they should Singular. . . . Come you Priests and Professors, have you not learnt your Accidence?"[5]   This is one of the few citations of a grammatical correction of usage previous to the eighteenth century.

2.   The demand for correct English was specifically stated early in that century, and it grew rapidly in volume and specific emphasis.   Perhaps the first suggestion is to be found in Richard Johnson's *Grammatical Commentaries*: ". . . . our Language . . . . for want of Rule is subject to uncertainty, and the Occasion of frequent Contentions.   And upon this account, it has been the practice of several wise nations, such of them, I mean, as have a thorough Education, to learn even their own Language by stated Rules, to avoid that Confusion, that must needs follow from leaving it wholly to vulgar Use."[5a]

Dean Swift, in his proposal for the establishment of an Academy, was more specific in calling attention to the offences "against every Part of Grammar" of which the language was in his opinion guilty.[6]   And even Swift's major emphasis was upon problems of wording and pronunciation.   A few of Bentley's emendations of Milton and Warburton's of Shakespeare were grammatical.   But not until Dr. Johnson and Bishop Lowth took up Swift's challenge with a bill of particulars, in the second half of the century, was much attention paid to grammatical correctness.   Johnson himself devoted but

---

[5]C. C. Fries, *The Teaching of the English Language*, Nelson, 1927, p. 6. Dr. McKnight has other references, particularly to Dryden's emendations of Johnson. *Mod. Eng. in the Making*, pp. 266-270.

[5a]*Op. cit.*, 1706, preface n. p. Dr. McKnight finds the same suggestion in Lane's Grammar (1700) *Mod. Eng. pp.* 291 f.

[6]*A Proposal for Correcting, Improving and Ascertaining the English Tongue,* in a letter to the Earl of Oxford, 1712, p. 8.

twelve lines of the "English Grammar" in his *Dictionary*, 1755, to presentation of syntax.

3. *The urgent need for reform of English.* Everyone in the eighteenth century, however, appears to have noted the imperfection of the language and the necessity for remedial measures. Philip Withers expressed a commonly accepted idea, that grammatical Construction is the "first Excellence of style";[7] and though Campbell admitted it is a negative virtue, nevertheless it was given precedence and elaborate attention in the period after 1700. Only precision in choice of words ranks with it in consideration by writers on the language during the eighteenth century.

Following Swift at a long interval, Dr. Johnson wrote in the preface to his *Dictionary*, 1755, "I found our speech copious without order, and energetic without rules," and in the "English Grammar" which followed, he remarked that ". . . . in a language subjected so little and so lately to grammar, [such] anomalies must frequently occur."[8]   In about the same year John Ward wrote, ". . . . much remains yet to be done, for bringing it [the language] to a regular and compleat system in all its parts."[9]

Lowth's *Short Introduction*, 1762, was devoted to the proposition that the English language is capable of refinement by grammar, whose purpose is "to teach us to express ourselves with propriety."[10]   Elucidating and supporting Swift's statement, he maintained that "the English Language, as it is spoken by the politest part of the nation, and as it stands in the writings of the most approved authors, often offends against every part of grammar."[11]   In Buchanan, following him, we find, ". . . it is hoped, that Men of Learning, who are studious to correct Composition, will for the future, be exemplary in rejecting such Barbarisms [as he has cited]; otherwise the few

[7]*Aristarchus*, [1788], p. 136.
[8]*Op. cit.*, preface, n.p.
[9]*Four Essays upon the English Language*, 1754 (1758 edition, preface, p. iii).
[10]*Op. cit.*, p. x.
[11]*Short Introduction*, 1762, p. ii.

traces of Analogy that are to be found in our language will, in a little Time, be utterly annihilated."[12]   In his preface Buchanan writes, "considering the many grammatical Improprieties to be found in our best Writers, such as SWIFT, ADDISON, POPE, etc. A Systematical English Syntax is not beneath the Notice of the Learned themselves."[13]

4. *The flood of English grammars.*   The remarkable inundation of books on language problems during the last half of the eighteenth century was devoted mainly to producing this "Systematical Syntax."   Lowth filled the notes of his *Short Introduction* with lists of errors by "standard authors," and the interest aroused was remarkable.   Whereas fewer than fifty writings on grammar, rhetoric, criticism, and linguistic theory have been listed for the first half of the eighteenth century, and still fewer for all the period before 1600, the publications in the period 1750-1800 exceeded two hundred titles.[14]   And most of these were concerned in whole or in part with solecisms, barbarisms, improprieties, and questions of precision in the use of English.

5. *Basic assumptions about language.*   In order to understand the mass of prescriptions about English usage which piled up amazingly in the eighteenth century, and which has indeed continued in increasing volume ever since, it seems necessary to find out if possible why such prescriptions became prevalent and popular, and especially, upon what assumptions about language, and the English language in particular, they are based.   For this purpose more than ninety works, ranging from articles, reviews, and pamphlets to the six volumes of Lord Monboddo, were examined for this study.   In each, the writer's prescriptions and rules, and especially his statements of the theoretical bases of these in grammar, logic, or whatever he appealed to, were tabulated and analyzed.

[12]*A Regular English Syntax*, 1767, p. 90. This quotation has its humorous aspect when one recollects the "annoyance at the ravages of analogy"—i. e., popular etymologies, back-formations, and the like—felt by nineteenth-century linguists. See Vendryes, *Language*, (English translation, Knopf, 1925, p. 49).
[13]*Op. cit.*, p. ix. The sentence division is Buchanan's, or his printers'.
[14]See Kennedy, *Bibliography, passim.*

6. *Two contrasting theories of usage.* In dealing with problems of language, one of two basic and contrary principles is generally adhered to; in the eighteenth century the two are clearly differentiated. The one assumes the power of reason to remold language completely, and appeals to various principles of metaphysics or logic, or even makes pronouncements on mere individual preference posing as authority, in the endeavor to "correct, improve, and fix" usage. The other, while admitting the usefulness of purism in recommending what may be regarded as improvements, recognizes language —even cultivated language—as a vastly complicated and often haphazard growth of habits stubbornly rooted, the product of great variation in social soil and climate, not more readily changed by fiat into clipped and formal garden pattern than is any vast area of swamp and jungle and timber-line vegetation. Adherents of this second principle are primarily interested in studying the facts of usage, determining as much as possible of their history and causes, and attempting to classify them according to valid criteria of their social effects in communication.

As will appear in the following chapters, a sufficient basis for beginning a scientific study of English on this second principle was actually available to eighteenth-century scholars. Quite perspicuous statements that usage is the "sole arbiter and norm of speech," in the classical writers and later, were generally known and indeed often quoted. Moreover, the philosophy of John Locke furnished an ample reinforcement of this fundamental principle. And grammars of Anglo-Saxon and texts in this and other Germanic languages were already available.

But the eighteenth-century grammarians and rhetoricians were mainly clergymen, retired gentlemen, and amateur philosophers like the elder Shandy, with an immense distaste for Locke's dangerous and subversive doctrines. Though more or less conversant with classical texts, they had little or no conception of the history and relations of the classical or other languages, and of course no equipment for carrying on linguistic research or even for making valid observations of contemporary usage. One or two like Dr. Johnson and Horne Tooke made forays of some brilliance and did useful work, but none consolidated any position. Frequently they quoted with approval the Horatian dictum about usage, or an equivalent, but always they destroyed its entire force in application. As we shall see in the following chapter, their fundamental difficulty was in philosophy. They built in general upon the neo-Platonic notion of a divinely instituted language, perfectly mirroring actuality but debased by man, and they labored to restore its pristine perfection.

Only one writer, Joseph Priestley, appears to have held to a clear conception of the force of usage, as presented by Horace and Quintilian and by Locke and his followers. His work, marred of course by his lack of training for specifically linguistic research, is, almost alone in the eighteenth century, a precursor of modern study of these problems. It was, however, so remote from the general trend of thought in his time that it was without important influence. It did not often figure in the ireful combats in which the other grammarians, engaged, but was obscured by the brilliance of Lowth's completely logical grammar, published only a month after Priestley's, and was completely buried under Lindley Murray's eclectic productions.

The prevailing view of language in the eighteenth century was that English could and must be subjected to a process of classical regularizing. Where actual usage was observed and recorded—even when the theory was promulgated that usage is supreme—this was, in general, done only to denounce and reform the actual idiom.

7. *The divisions of this study.* The present investigation has been for convenience divided into the categories discussed in the following chapters. All were expressed or implied as basic considerations in writings about the English language in the eighteenth century:

Chapter II. The contrasting ideas (1) of language as an entity or an originally perfect instrument, needing only logical and authoritative restoration to its pristine state, and (2) of language as a product merely of convention or compact. These are traced to their origin in earlier and contemporary philosophic views of language.

Chapter III. The appeal to authority, whether that of the writer or of another theorist whose *ipse dixit* was assumed to have sway. This extremely common mode of judgment was used by most of the writers here discussed, from Swift to Webster, and of course is still employed.

Chapter IV. The appeal to norms of "universal grammar" to which individual problems of usage could be referred for settlement, developed by Bishop Lowth, Anselm Bayly, and James Harris chiefly. As the only grammars studied to any extent in the eighteenth century were those of the classical languages, this meant in practice an appeal to supposed parallels in Latin, and more rarely in Greek. Occasional resort was had to French, and still less often to the Anglo-Saxon and the other even less comprehended Germanic languages.

Chapter V. The appeal to "reason and analogy" in the language itself. This led to proposing (1) parallels and (2) differentiae in form as altogether essential in deciding problems of inflection and syntax in English. As these two principles were often contrary in application, this is a most involved story of contradictions and mutual recriminations in which all the grammarians took part.

Chapter VI. Appeals to considerations of logic in dealing with problems of syntax and word order.

Chapter VII. Similar application of logic to nice discriminations of the meanings of words.

Chapter VIII. Appeal to the etymology or the earlier meanings of words to determine what their present use should be, and to language history for justification of opinions as to structure. Dr. Johnson, Horne Tooke, George Campbell, and Noah Webster are interesting figures here. In the prevailing state of ignorance of both etymology and the history of languages, this principle naturally introduced further confusion.

Chapter IX. The explicit appeal to custom—variously interpreted as cultivated speech, the usage of the best writers, and "what sounds best"—and its actual repudiation in practically all cases. The elaborate treatment of the subject in Campbell's *Rhetoric* in an amazing instance of attempted adherence to the principle and its utter betrayal.

Chapter X. The attack upon regional and class dialects as opposed to an assumed national and reputable usage.

Chapters XI and XII give examples of various particularly confused attempts to settle points of inflection and of syntax by all these categories of logic.

Chapter XIII is a summary of the study and an interpretation of the effect and value of doctrines of correctness.

A glossary exhibiting the contrast between the facts of usage and the contradictory mass of eighteenth-century dogmas about it, and a bibliography particularly of eighteenth-century publications consulted, are given in the appendix.

CHAPTER II

THE PHILOSOPHICAL BASIS OF EIGHTEENTH-CENTURY LANGUAGE THEORIES

Those parts of speech unite of themselves in grammar, whose original archetypes unite of themselves in nature.

Harris, *Hermes*, 1751

Words having naturally no signification, the idea, which each stands for, must be learned by those who would exchange thoughts. This should teach us moderation, in imposing our own sense of old authors.

John Locke, *Essay on the Human Understanding*, 1688

CHAPTER II

THE PHILOSOPHICAL BASIS OF EIGHTEENTH-CENTURY LANGUAGE THEORIES

1. *Theories of the origin of language.* The idea that language was instituted by the deity directly was held during a great part of the eighteenth century, and is explicitly stated as late as 1824 in Thomas Martin's *Philological Grammar of the English Tongue.*[1] It was understood that the perfect primitive language was much affected by the dispersal at Babel, which Lord Beattie said "solves all difficulties" as to the origin of various languages.[2] And hence arose the necessity for grammarians to remold languages, especially so remote and barbarous a dialect as English, nearer to the original perfectly logical pattern.

2. *Language mirroring nature.* A natural corollary to the idea of a language divinely instituted is the belief that such a language is formed by God or its Genius to a consistent and logical plan, so as perfectly to mirror actuality or the precise reasoning processes assumed for the mind of man. All this springs apparently from the notion of language as an entity. For example, in speaking of the necessary use of prepositions for showing the relations between substantives, whereas attributes can be united to substantives without their aid, Harris wrote in *Hermes,* 1751 :

> Those parts of speech unite of themselves in grammar, whose original archetypes unite of themselves in nature.
>
> *Hermes* (1771 edition), pp. 263-4.

He shows here no indication of recollecting the relation of substantives by inflection in Greek, or in English the sur-

[1]*Op. cit.,* preface and chart (Plimpton Collection).
[2]*Theory of Language,* 1787 ed., p. 103.

viving genitive case and particularly relation by apposition. If he had thought of these, he could no doubt have found their archetype in Nature; for from his elaborate doctrine of "Time Definite, Indefinite, and Universal," Harris derives twelve necessary tenses. But he admits here, "be the language upon the whole ever so perfect, much must be left, in defiance of all analogy, to the harsh laws of mere authority and chance."[3]

Again Harris says, even more clearly:

> All these MODES have this in common, that they exhibit some way or other the SOUL and its AFFECTIONS.
>
> *Hermes*, pp. 146-7.

> It is equally absurd in Modes for a person to request or give a command to himself, as it is in Pronouns for the speaker to become the subject of his own address.
>
> *Ibid.*, p. 154.

> Number and ɔerson, attributes of substance, are merely affixt to verbs for conveɪience.
>
> *Ibid.*, pp. 170-1.

Further quotations can serve only to re-enforce the statement that this idea of language as an entity was prevalent among many different sorts of writers and entered into quite various conceptions of the structure of language:

> Words must be joined together according to the nature of the things they stand for.
>
> Monboddo, *Origin and Process,* 1773 (II, 343).

> When we pronounce Judgment on a Plurality of Objects, the Affirmation ought to be plural, in Conformity to the Plurality of Ideas in the Mind. The Analogy is natural and Elegant. [Here the difficult problem of the -*s* in the plural of substantives in English and the want of it in the plural of verbs, with the precise analogy suggested, is not treated.]
>
> Withers, *Aristarchus,* 1788, p. 68.

> But whence comes it that—AND—may be omitted, and the verb gracefully used in the singular Number after TWO or more IN-FINITIVES, if a similar Construction with NOUNS be inelegant and absurd? From *Nature,* the Source of real Elegance. For several Actions, perfectly distinct, may be resolved into the Energy of

Op. cit., pp. 122-3. See pp. 95-139 for the whole discussion.

ONE Agent, and considered as ONE Effect. . . . Action is measured by Quantity, as well as enumerated in it's Effects.

Ibid., pp. 123-4.

Words then are the names of particular ideas, and are consequently as various in their structure, as the ideas themselves.

Willich, *Philological Essays,* 1798, p. xciv-v.

Anselm Bayly, who considered himself an unrelenting foe to the solution of linguistic problems by the appeal to language as an entity, nevertheless speaks in his *Introduction to Languages* of their necessary divine origin.[4] That this influenced Bayly's ideas about language problems is suggested by a remark in his later grammar, that "In nature there is no occasion for these moods [the subjunctive, potential, etc., in English]; because they are determined by particles and verbs subjoined"—for example "modesty, politeness, and submission" shown by the auxiliaries *should* and the like.[5] Similar to Withers' "natural and elegant analogy," above, but directly contrary to his logic on other plural subjects, is Bayly's comment that, since a verb expresses one action though the agents be many, "it may stand singular with a nominative case plural."[6]

These instances are perhaps sufficient to show that in the eighteenth-century writers there is clearly evident a tendency to substitute remotely metaphysical explanations for the difficult and necessary scientific processes of observing and recording the facts of language.

3. *Language as convention.* But the assumptions so far considered did not escape attack in the eighteenth century. The materials for their complete demolition were already at hand in the philosophical views of John Locke and in the recurring clear statements about usage in classical and later authors. Although Locke's rational views of language did not gain much credit or acceptance in this period or indeed much later, it is

---

[4] *Op. cit.,* 1758, II, 26. A note in pencil in the Columbia Library copy, Johnson Collection (possibly by the first president of the College) remarks caustically that it were as sensible to argue an immediate divine origin of watches, "because two children suckled by Goats could not make one."

[5] *Plain and Complete Grammar,* 1772, p. 35.

[6] *Ibid.,* pp. 31-2. See Chapter XII, § 6, below.

important to review his work and that of the eighteenth-century philosophers who followed him, to find the basis from which the notion of language as an entity was attacked and finally destroyed.

4. *The philosophy of John Locke.* Locke's *Essay on the Human Understanding,* 1688, provides the basic philosophy for an objective and scientific study of linguistic problems. Proceeding from his demonstration that "ideas are not innate in the mind," he devotes his third book to considering the nature of language. In summary, his position is as follows:

"Articulate sounds . . . . words . . . . came to be made use of by men, as the signs of their ideas; not by any natural connection that there is between particular, articulate sounds and certain ideas . . . . but by a voluntary imposition, whereby such a word is made arbitrarily the mark of such an idea."[7]   Again, "Words, properly and immediately signify nothing, but the ideas that are in the mind of the speaker; yet they, in their thoughts, give them a secret [unconscious?] reference to two other things: First, they suppose their words to be marks of the ideas in the minds of other men, with whom they communicate. [This is one of the roots of misunderstanding through failure to define, treated fully in Chapter X of Book III.]   Secondly, ... they often suppose their words to stand also for the reality of things . . . . that is a perverting of the use of words, and brings unavoidable obscurity, and confusion into their signification.[8]

". . . . there comes, by constant use, to be such a connection between certain sounds, and the ideas they stand for, that the names heard, almost as readily excite certain ideas, as if the objects themselves . . . . did actually affect the senses.

"Because of familiar use words are often used with no meaning . . . . Words . . . . come to excite in men certain ideas so constantly and readily, that they are apt to suppose a natural

---

[7]*Works of John Locke,* Fifth Edition, 1751, Volume 1: *The Essay,* Book III, Chapter II, § 1, p. 184. Locke's views are usefully restated and developed in Ogden and Richards' *The Meaning of Meaning.* American Edition, Harcourt, 1923.

[8]Locke, *op. cit.,* § 4, p. 185.

connection between them. But that they signifiy only men's peculiar ideas, and that by a perfectly arbitrary imposition, is evident in that they often fail to excite in others (even that use the same language) the same ideas we take them to be the signs of. And every man has so inviolable a liberty, to make words stand for what ideas he pleases, that no one hath the power to make others have the same ideas that they have in their minds, when they use the same words that he does. . . . It is true, common use, by tacit consent, appropriates certain sounds to certain ideas, in all languages, which so far limits the signification of that sound, that unless a man applies it to the same idea, he does not speak properly: and . . . . unless a man's words excite the same ideas in the hearer, which he makes them stand for in speaking, he does not speak intelligibly. But, whatever be the consequences of any man's using words differently, either from their general meaning, or the particular sense of the person to whom he addresses them, this is certain, their signification, in his use of them, is limited to his ideas, and they can be signs of nothing else."[9]

5. Locke's chapters IX-XI, on the imperfections of words and on remedies, are admirable accounts, still of clear relevance. In Chapter X he defines the "ends of language, in our discourse with others . . . .: first, to make known one man's thoughts and ideas to another; secondly, to do it with as much ease and quickness, as possible; and thirdly, to convey thereby the knowledge of things. Language is either abased or deficient, when it fails in any of these three."[10]

The imperfection of words preventing this is "the doubtfulness of their signification. Words having naturally no signification, the idea, which each stands for, must be learned by those who would exchange thoughts. This should teach us moderation, in imposing our own sense of old [or any] authors."[11] The abuses of words are: using them without any clear ideas, with unsteady application, by the use of new and

[9]Locke, *op. cit.*, § 4-8, pp. 185-6, *passim.*
[10]*Op. cit.*, 1751 ed., Ch. X, § 23, pp. 235-7.
[11]*Ibid.*, § 4-5 and 22 (pp. 221 and 227f.) *passim.*

ambiguous terms [elsewhere called "learned gibberish"][12] by taking words for things, and by supposing that words have a certain and evident application. Failure also arises from want of exact words, especially for complex ideas.[13]

Locke's remedies for these difficulties with words are clearly given and illustrated: "to use no word without an idea annexed, and to have distinct ideas annexed to words; to apply words to such ideas as common use has associated with them; to make known their meanings by synonymous terms, by showing, or defining; and to observe constancy in the significations of words."[14]

6. *Eighteenth-century followers of Locke.* The philosophers of the eighteenth century seem to have added but one new idea, relevant to language problems, to these complete and valuable notions of Locke's. Bishop Berkeley appears to attempt expressing, but with less clarity, some of Locke's ideas, and to mingle them with mystical notions, when he writes: "There are some grounds to think, that, if there was one invariable and universal language in the world, and that men were born with the faculty of speaking it, it would be the opinion of some, that the ideas in other men's minds were properly perceived by the ear, or had at least a necessary and inseparable tie with the sounds that were affixed to them."[15] He uses Locke's wording almost, but with a strange application: "the arbitrary use of sensible sounds which have no similitude or necessary connection with the things signified" is proof of "an intelligent, thinking, designing cause."[16]

He reëmphasizes the peril of words, adding that they are frequently used to raise some passion—clearly an important observation, not developed by Locke—and the neces-

---

[12]". . . he that applies the words of any language to ideas different from those, to which the common sense of that country applies them . . . without defining his terms, . . . wants propriety in the language . . . and speaks gibberish." *Ibid.*, § 31, p. 236.

[13]*Ibid.*, Ch. X, § 1-22, pp. 228 ff.

[14]*Ibid.*, Ch. XI, pp. 241 ff., *passim.*

[15]*Works*, Oxford, 1881 ed., "Commonplace Book," pp. 435 and 64.

[16]*Ibid.*, "Alciphron, or the Minute Philosopher, Fourth Dialog," pp. 146-7.

sity of dissecting words from ideas if possible, so as to consider the idea only. He speaks particularly of the danger arising from our necessity to speak of the operations of the mind in terms borrowed from sensible ideas, as the phrase "the motion of the soul" carries inevitably a suggestion that the mind is a ball rolling.[17] So "It is scarce possible to deliver the naked and precise truth without great circumlocution, impropriety, and . . . . seeming contradictions. I do, therefore, once and for all, desire . . . . that [the reader] would not stick in the expression, but candidly collect my meaning from the whole sum and tenor of my discourse, and laying aside the words, as much as possible consider the bare notions themselves."[18]

Finally, he has the following really noble passage: "Whoever therefore designs to read the following sheets, I entreat him that he would make my words the occasion of his own thinking, and endeavor to attain the same train of thought that I had in writing them. By this means it will be easy for him to discover the truth or falsity of what I say. He will be out of all danger of being deceived by my words. . . ."[19]

Butler appears to have only one passage in the "Analogy," and that of no particular importance, on the imperfections of language.[20]

Hume has a clear analogy for the origin of language in compact, which helped to exorcise the false conceptions of divine fiat or deliberative process in making language.[20a] "As two men pull oars together by convention, though they have never given promises to each other . . . . the sense of interest common to all our fellows gives us a confidence of the future regularity of their conduct. . . . In like manner are languages gradually establish'd by human conventions without any promise."[21]

---

[17]*Ibid.*, "Principles of Human Knowledge" (1st ed., 1710), p. 231.

[18]*Ibid.*, "Theory of Vision," (1st ed., 1709), p. 90.

[19]*Ibid.*, Introduction to "Principles of Human Knowledge," pp. 139 ff.

[20]*Works*, Gladstone's edition, Oxford, 1896, Vol. I, "Analogy" II, iii, 15. The first edition was 1736.

[20a]See Ch. IV, § 1, and *note* 1, below.

[21]*A Treatise of Human Nature*, Oxford, 1896 ed., p. 490. The first edition was 1739-40.

The following passage, though very "general," says much the same thing: "General language . . . . being formed for general use, must be molded on some more general views [than every man's interest, peculiar to himself] and must affix terms in conformity to the sentiments which arise from the general interest of the community."[22]

7. *Attacks upon the entity theory.* In the work of Locke and his followers in eighteenth-century philosophy, then, appeared clear statements that language is solely "a form of behavior" originated by compact and determined in form and meaning by convention. Here was a thoroughly adequate basis for the destruction of theological and mystic notions and for beginning a sound and scientific study of language problems.

At least the conception of language as an entity was vigorously attacked, even by the logical grammarians themselves, and pretty completely discredited before the end of the eighteenth century. The first pronouncement against the idea appears in Anselm Bayly's *Grammar,* which shows some realization of historical fact in its remark on "the difficulty of writing a grammar for any language, especially a living, which is subject to continual variation."[23] He remarks also, "It is not absolutely necessary in language to vary its [the adjective's] terminations to the gender and number of its substantive."[24] Horne Tooke's *Diversions of Purley.* 1786, an attempt at comparative linguistics, is a surprising mixture of fairly clear views of the nature and history of language and of completely absurd ideas. Tooke ridicules Harris' notion that certain words—particles—"have no signification." But when he states that "Articles supply the Place of Words which are not in the Language," he deserves, and suffers, the fire of Philip Withers' heavy sarcasm.[25]

8. Withers, author of *Aristarchus,* is a sworn enemy to the

---

[22]*Principles of Morals.* Open Court, 1900, pp. 63-4. See a similar passage from Priestley, below, Chapter IX, § 3.

[23]Anselm Bayly, *Plain and Complete Grammar,* 1772, p. v.

[24]*Ibid.,* p. 18. See also his comments on the genius of the language, below, § 9.

[25]*Aristarchus,* 1788, pp. 225f.

metaphysical ideas of the other grammarians. He notes that
Adam Smith "continually speaks of the *'metaphysical Abstrac-*
tion and profound Discernment of the Inventors of Speech' "
and remarked "the word—OF—expresses a Relation so mysterious and abstruse" that it would take " 'a WEEK to give a tolerable account of it's real import.' " Says Withers, "Degrading
Idea! Did 'SAVAGES' invent what PHILOSOPHERS cannot investigate? Had Dr. Smith consulted common Sense on
the Occasion, he must have been convinced that the Hypothesis
is *visionary.*"[26] And again, "From this Propensity in the Soul
of Man to have Recourse to occult Causes and other incom-
prehensible Influence, I attribute the Ignorance which universally prevails concerning the Origin and present Structure of
SPEECH."[27]

Withers scoffs at the notion of a divine inspiration
of language; he observes very acutely that cases and
genders represent no archetypes of nature, but are conventions
purely for convenience in language—however inconvenient
they actually may be. But "polite authors," says he, "begin to
appropriate WHOM—in the 'oblique Cases' to the rational
creation, and WHICH to the irrational Creation. I approve
the Distinction, and recommend the Observance of it to the
Student. But if any future * * * * *,[28] should compose a metaphysical Grammar, and inform the World that—WHOM—
is *rational,* and—WHICH—*irrational,* I hope he will be chas-
tized for his Insult to COMMON SENSE."[29] Lowth, he
adds elsewhere, "being more conversant with the metaphysical
Institutes of Grammar than with the Origin of Languages, has
made prodigious Havock with the 'PARTICLES' of
Speech."[30] Again, he says, "Words are Combinations of Symbols. They have no more Influence on each other than
Figures."[31] As "a globular Form obscurely painted in the

[26]*Ibid.,* pp. 219-20.
[27]*Aristarchus,* 1788, p. 388.
[28]Withers' five asterisks undoubtedly mean Lowth
[29]*Aristarchus,* p. 330.
[30]*Aristarchus,* p. 395.
[31]*Aristarchus,* p. 336.

back Ground of a Landscape might be accepted as a Stone falling, an Air Balloon just liberated, or a large Stilton Cheese," so "any Ideas might have been originally annexed to WORDS, and even now they must be ANIMATED by the Omnipotence of FANCY."[32]

Yet, after a passage of great vigor, strewn with words in capital letters, which informs us that Withers is "a decided enemy to CONJECTURE" and riddles with sharp fire the theories of correspondence between language and nature and of derivation of alphabets from the Hebrew—after all this Withers devotes over a hundred pages to an account of the original "fourteen plain Letters . . . . in Use before the Deluge," as he is "FULLY PERSUADED," and to symbolic meanings of these letters and of numbers.[33] Johnson, too, gives several pages of his grammar to similar passages from Wallis's *Grammatica linguae anglicanae* (1674) on the signification of *sn, sw,* and the like.[34] This sort of occupation was very common in the eighteenth century.

Withers is careful to distinguish his metaphysics, "having its Foundation on SENSE" and "in *Conjunction* with Nature," from that of other thinkers. "The Metaphysics, which I take the Liberty to censure, are founded on *metaphysical Data,* the Offspring of the IMAGINATION, and so repugnant to the Dictates of Common Sense, that INSANITY is the only Apology that can be offered for it's Advocates."[35] In his clear perceptions of the determination of meaning by compact or usage, and in his clouded metaphysics, Withers is an especially instructive example of what results from mixing abstruse preconceptions with the practical business of collecting and evaluating data of observation—particularly in dealing with so complex a subject as language. To this danger the eighteenth-century grammarians, in their ignorance of the safeguards of linguistic study, were peculiarly liable.

[32]*Aristarchus*, 1788, p. 259.
[33]*Ibid.,* pp. 231 and 242 ff.
[34]*Dictionary,* 1755 "English Grammar" (no paging).
[35]*Aristarchus,* pp. 378-80. Whether *it's* refers to Sense or Insanity is not apparent. *Metaphysics* he has made plural.

9. *"The genius of the language."* A sense of the eighteenth-century confusion between metaphysical terms and fairly specific, concrete notions is provided by current references to "the genius of the language." The word "genius" in certain of the quotations following meant sometimes an effective principle in the language itself, concerned with its logical and accurate mirroring of nature. This view is vigorously attacked by Anselm Bayly in a comment on Bishop Lowth's grammar:

> "Adjectives," says the Short Introd., p. 156, "are sometimes employed as adverbs improperly and not agreeably to the genius of the English language." What the custom and usage of a language may be, it is easy to determine, but not what is the *genius* of any language. . . . Certainly the ear, which will overrule judgment and theory, taught the use of some adjectives as adverbs without the adverbial termination, and custom hath introduced others, as . . . excessive good; mighty great; right honorable; exceeding fair; prodigious cold: it is observable that *exceedingly* is always joined with a verb, and *exceeding* with adjectives. What now has genius to say?
> *Plain and Complete Grammar,* 1772, pp. 60-61.

On the other hand, it is equally clear that this apparently mystical term genius had sometimes a fairly objective meaning. Thus, when Swift wrote, "I do not reckon that we want a genius more than the rest of our neighbors,"[36] or Webster,[37] "I deny that the genius of the language requires" a subjunctive mode, they may have intended the following sense of the word, defined in the 1775 (first) edition of the *Encyclopaedia Britannica*:

> The genius of a language is "the particular set of ideas which the words . . . either from their formation or multiplicity, are apt to excite in the mind of any one who hears it [the language] properly uttered," as idiom is "the general mode of arranging words into sentences which prevails in any particular language."
> *Encyclopaedia Britannica.* first (1775) edition, article "Language."

Campbell uses the word genius apparently as a synonym for grammatical form; ". . . . familiar relations . . . . expressed similarly . . . . by similar inflections, derivations, compositions,

---

[36]*Proposal for Correcting, etc.,* 1712, p. 27.
[37]*Dissertations,* 1789, p. 257.

arrangement of words, or juxtaposition of particles, according to the genius or grammatical form of the particular tongue,"[38] and again, ". . . . the genius of the tongue permits that all these [passive participles] may be construed as nouns in certain occurrences."[39]

Two final quotations, one early and one later in the eighteenth century, illustrate further what is suggested by Swift's expression above, the conception of a particular genius or character of each language. This idea is cleared of its mystical associations when it appears later as the doctrine of "national usage" in Campbell's *Philosophy of Rhetoric*.[40]

> "To perfectly understand the Custom of a Language, we must inform ourselves of the genus [sic], and observe the Idioms or peculiar Manner of Speaking which belong to it. The Genius of a Language consists of certain qualities, which those who speak do affect to give to this Stile," as that of the French is "perspicuity and liveliness," etc.
> *The Art of Speaking*, (tr. from the French, London, 2nd ed., 1708)

> . . . Every one who is master of the language he speaks . . . may form new words and form new phrases, provided they coincide with the genius of the language.
> Michaelis, *Dissertation*, 1769, p. 79 (See Locke's Essay, Book III, Ch. VI, 851: 1751 ed., p. 218).

The word "genius" then, was frequently used to indicate particular characteristics of a language, as shown objectively by its effects in use. But the metaphysical associations of the word and the false ideas of language still widely prevalent in the eighteenth century made this term peculiarly dangerous to use at a time when the history of languages was so incompletely

[38]*Philosophy of Rhetoric*, 1776, II, 101.
[39]*Ibid.*, I, 510. Cf. p. 380, and this study, Ch. XI, § 15.
That the shell of expression in which such mystical ideas were expressed persists in use, even by men of wholly enlightened view upon the history and the scientific observation of language, is illustrated by the following passage from Jespersen's *Philosophy of Grammar* (p. 350): "The form *whom* is used [in the construction 'Children whom we think are hungry'] because in 'who we think' the *speech instinct* would be bewildered by the contiguity of two nominatives, as it were two subjects in the same clause." The italics are not Jespersen's. This, of course, means simply "the hearer might be bewildered."
[40]See below, Chapter IX, § 9.

observed and so misunderstood. Similar ideas, though not intended in any mystical sense, nevertheless influence pronouncements on usage today.

10. *In summary.* The view expressed by Locke, followed by Berkeley and Hume, is sharply contrasted with the usual conceptions of language in the eighteenth century. Locke presented with special clarity the idea that language is an affair of compact or convention; that it has no inherently necessary form or any correspondence with reality; that words and forms can mean nothing whatever but what they are actually understood to mean; in short, that usage is the sole arbiter and norm. Hence, he continued, the only safety in discussion is a common understanding as to meaning and an intelligible agreement as to forms. Here was material to demolish completely all views of what words "ought to mean" or what any form or construction "ought to be."

Needless to say, the views of Locke were profoundly distasteful to his contemporaries and to most writers of the following century.[41] Just as the students of that day had access to many of the documents of the Germanic languages, but lacked scientific training for dealing with them, so they were by no means prepared to turn to account the ideas of the philosophers. To be sure, we find Aristotle quoted to the effect that meaning of words is determined "only by institution . . . . that is, convention or agreement,"[42] and there is frequent repetition of Horace's and Quintilian's statement to a like effect. In nearly every important writer, indeed, there will be found an occasional passage showing apparently clear perception and acceptance of this fundamental principle.

Throughout the eighteenth century, then, the opposing views of language as an entity, with a "genius" or inherent power of mirroring actuality, and of language as a result of convention or compact, are found represented. Indeed, the history of theories of language, in the eighteenth century in particular,

---

[41] As was his basic philosophy. An interesting specimen of the attack upon him is preserved in *Characteristicks, or a Specimen of the worth and integrity of . . . favourite authors* (1734) pp. 21-31.
[42] Monboddo, *Origin and Progress of Language*, 1774, II, 194.

may be interpreted as a truceless struggle between the logical school of grammarians and rhetoricians represented by Lowth and Harris, and the scientific school best exemplified in that time by Priestley. The entity theory greatly influenced thought and writing on English usage throughout the nineteenth century, and controls popular views of the subject today. Even when we have got clear of the belief in a divine institution of language and a mysterious entity or principle governing its forms, so long as the belief in a "genius and right nature of English" prevails, every one is altogether free to set up any criterion he pleases of this essential form, and none can disprove his contention. He can be met only by counter-assertion, and downed by nothing less than superior weight of authority. This authoritarian method of controversy will be discussed in the following chapter.

CHAPTER III

IPSE DIXIT PRONOUNCEMENTS

A multitude of errors committed by writers, evidently from their misapprehending the import of words, are cited as authorities by Johnson, instead of being noticed with censure. . . . thousands of instances . . . of a misapplication of terms . . . are clearly ascribable to the negligence and mistakes of that lexicographer.

Noah Webster, *Letter to Dr. Ramsay,* 1809.

CHAPTER III

IPSE DIXIT PRONOUNCEMENTS

1. *Authoritarian pronouncements.* As will be amply illustrated later,[1] every attempt to follow Locke and the classic writers in accepting the authority of custom, encountered in the eighteenth century insuperable obstacles. Whereas the critics of the sixteenth and seventeenth centuries objected to expressions chiefly which they regarded as newly coined, or imported, or obsolete, the eighteenth-century critics found a thousand positions in logic and grammar to use as points of sortie against the usage of their time. And, being seized of the "rage for emending," where they found no other sort of basis of attack, they quite naturally took to setting up their own opinions, without any assigned reason, as law and gospel of the language. This position is taken constantly in the famous editions of Milton by Bentley and of Shakespeare by Warburton, and in the acrimonious discussions which these aroused. The first writer to codify his preferences into a book, the ancestor of those handbooks of abuses and corrections which were so freely produced in the nineteenth century, appears to have been Robert Baker in his *Remarks on the English Language* (called *Reflections* in the [1770] edition), 1779. While he says his book is "in the nature of Vaugelas's on the French,"[2] he apparently did not read Vaugelas' preface with any care, for the French writer insists that we must follow usage blindly, usage which is "sometimes without, sometimes against reason." Though Vaugelas circumscribes his dictum so as to leave all authors open to his censure, in the usual manner of rhetoricians and grammarians, he nevertheless pays the principle full reverence to the end.

[1]Chapter IX, pp. 137 ff.
[2]*Remarques de M. de Vaugelas sur la Langue Françoise, Paris, 1647, 1687,* etc.

35

2. Many of the English critics, however, observe no such restraint of theory. Baker attacks briskly with the mere comment, "There is no such word," "This expression is wrong," and "used improperly by the greatest part of our writers." *Government* for "the Government" is "an Expression of great Barbarity."[3] Barbarous was a term used in earlier centuries, as in the eighteenth, to censure foreign importations,[4] but here it seems to have no such reference. Again, he says that *is lain down,* "used by most of our writers," offends him, but *is risen* does not. Why, he adds frankly, would be "perhaps no easy matter to tell." As Professor Scott well remarks,[5] the actual root of many such prescriptions is a mere personal dislike of an expression; a missionary zeal common to human nature leads us to propagate our idea and give it, if possible, a rational basis.

Baker himself expressly disclaims any appeal to authority, and often suggests for his proscriptions logical or grammatical bases which will be examined in their turn. He says, emphatically, "It will be easily discovered that I have paid no regard to authority. I have censured even our best penmen, where they have departed from what I conceive to be the idiom of the tongue, or where I have thought they violate grammar without necessity. To judge by the rule of *Ipse dixit* is the way to perpetuate error."[6] We find constant evidence, nevertheless, that actually Baker and his followers judged as often by that as any other rule. This appears to be the whole basis of a long succession of proscriptions, beginning long before the eighteenth century, but growing to formidable volume in its course and developing into such encyclopedias of absolutist censure as those of Richard Grant White, Moon, and the like in the nineteenth. No reason is assigned, but simply the statement "This is not English," "a deformity in the language." Less often the condemnation is given a milder but more persuasive force by this phraseology of a more polite so-

[3]Condemned as Scotch in the *Oxford Magazine* I, 216.
[4]J. L. Moore, *Tudor-Stuart Views* (Halle, 1910), p. 15.
[5]F. N. Scott, "Verbal Taboos," *School Review* 20 (June, 1912), 361ff.
[6]*Remarks*, 1779, preface p. vii; *Reflections*, 1770, p. iv.

ciety: "I can't conceive it to be English." Thus, Baker remarks, Swift's *"to commute to* I look upon not to be English"[7] —in itself surely a difficult phrase for the genius of the language to digest.

3. *Counter-attack.* The openness of this procedure to *tu quoque* attack, difficult to repel, is illustrated fully in Baker's case. In a copy of his 1779 edition in the Library of Congress, a pencil note, in handwriting apparently of the same century, reads "penmen—nonsense! Writer is the proper word. He might as well call him bagman as penman." There is no signature of the original owner of this copy; he, however, listed on the fly-leaf some forty numbers of pages or remarks which he considered interesting; at the back he referred to Michaelis, and commented on the "slovenly writing" of Warburton's *Divine Legation,* which Baker had attacked. Here was a commentator of Baker's own kidney.

Another sort of person owned a copy of this edition now in the New York Public Library. On the contents page he wrote in ink, "Every one of these amendments are incorrect . . . ."; on p. 2, opposite the censure of the omitted relative, "All these intended amendments are equally erroneous . . . . the omissions he noticed as wrong are all useless . . . . more than that better omitted, in point of correct application"; on p. 3, "All these alterations are equally waste paper which never should be wasted in Syllables Words or Letters." On p. 5 we find, "What has induced the writing of this Book at all. The author has not nor can not acct. for unless he had produced fatal consequences from the want of his queer explanations . . . . and this also may suffice for a final remark on the whole of this Book, by Readers fraught with mother Wit." From this point on the pages are unmarked and fresh, save p. 109, where the reader, apparently in turning hastily and irascibly through, lighted on the censure of "whom would you say passed." He added, "Alass poor Lockes book on Human Understanding was wrote by a Man who did not Love Waste Paper."

[7]*Reflections,* 1770, p. 60.

Baker's sentiments on the ideas of form and concord of this anonymous critic, if he had seen his strictures, can be conjectured. But the man had at least a principle of criticism; he favored terseness and vigor of style, and had no sympathy with the circumlocution, elaborate logical subtlety, and elegance which seem to be the basis of Baker's predilections.

4. The meeting of authority with authority is most dramatically presented, however, in the notice of Baker's 1770 edition (anonymous) in the *Monthly Review*.[8] The writers, because they have concurred in his general design of reforming the language, "hope he will accept" their chastisement as a necessary supplement to his book,[9] and proceed to list his gross violations of proper standards. "He uses the word *as* with *also* for *and* or *as well as*" (p. 95). "After a long period he repeats the words that began [a sentence] with *I say*, which is making one inelegance necessary by another." He "uses *whatsoever* when it is a mere expletive, and not only useless, but inelegant—'sold to any painter or sculptor whatsoever.' " They would allow him nothing for emphasis. They accuse him of vulgarism in writing, "as I take it," "I look upon it," "pitching upon" for "choosing,"[10] and "hammering their brains" "to express perplexed and difficult application," *hold* for *continue*, and "without any more *to do*." *'Tis* they call "a barbarous contraction of *it is*," and the phrase "a mistake many people lie under" they label, in quotation marks, "a vile phrase."

In the preface to the second edition (1779) Baker replies with spirit, setting authority once more against authority. Of *'tis* he makes, indeed, some attempt at being logical in defence. "It may be so [barbarous] in general," he writes; but . . . . "It was I that killed her (Othello) would be poor and spiritless. Where we are supposed to speak hastily and with passion, the contraction is necessary and the *it* would be un-

---

[8] Vol. XLV, (August 1771), pp. 87-96.
[9] *Op. cit.*, p. 96.
[10] Withers condemned Blair for this same phrase. They make no comment on Baker's almost invariable use of *it's* for the possessive, apparently at least equally common then with *its*.

natural."[11]   However, since Baker's *Remarks* were not supposedly written "hastily and with passion," it seems he might
have found a less feeble defence. For the rest he contents himself with replying, somewhat majestically, that *some few* is
"by no means a barbarous phrase," *"As also* is another expression which displeases them; and without any just reason.
The expression is a good one, and unexceptionable.

"About half a score more of their strictures appears to me
as injudicious as these; but to cite them all would take me up
too much time and would be no entertainment to the reader."[12]

In his first edition Baker had written, "I shall only say, that
I firmly believe these Observations are, in general, just, and . . .
may be of some use . . . wherever I am convinced of a Mistake, I will not fail to recant, should my Book pass through a
second Edition[13] . . . .though I were even *infallible,* it were to
be wished we had Performances of this kind by different Hands.
Every just Observation does not[14] occur to any *one* Mind."
But though he quietly altered some criticized phrases and defended others, like a stanch authority he never admits an
error.

That this simple procedure of denial would serve any author
in answer to almost any one of his remarks indeed troubled
Baker. He notices, as did Lowth and Murray and other
grammarians, that wrong uses were made of prepositions
"even by Swift, Temple, Addison, and other writers of the
highest reputation; some of them, indeed, with such shameful
impropriety as one must think must shock every English ear,
and almost induce the reader to suppose the writers to be

[11]*Remarks,* Preface, p. xxiv (1779 ed.) See, below, Ch. X, § 2.
[12]*Ibid.,* Preface, p. xxiv.
[13]*Reflections,* 1770, Preface, pp. iii-iv; repeated in the preface to the second
ed., p. vii.
[14]Neither Baker nor the Monthly Reviewers were consistent in following
Baker's and other current writers' rules for placing modifiers like *not* and
not only; the sentence above violates Baker's rule. So does the following,
from the *Monthly Review* criticism: "men who have not only been distinguished for genius, but learning." (See Chapter VI, § 2.) Here was a cat
ready to Baker's hands for a famous swingeing of his foes, but unfortunately he failed to note it.

foreigners."[15]   But he himself shocks the Monthly Reviewers
at least as sharply by writing, "I hope a school may be established upon a something-like principle with what I have here
gone upon."[16]

5. *Authority erected into an Academy.* To meet such difficulties, Baker notes elsewhere: "*One* man alone, who opposes a
whole nation, by persisting in what is in itself ever so right, for
the most part makes himself ridiculous. But such a respectable
body as this [the French, Academy,] would have a great
weight."[17]

And so we come out to the logical issue of the appeal to
authority, a favorite with the seventeenth century, and repeated
by numerous writers from Swift and the authors of *Many
Advantages* onward: a body legally empowered for "Correcting, Improving, and Ascertaining" or "fixing forever" the
English language.[18] The scheme was in favor also with the
theorists who argued for the rules of analogy, of logic, and
even of custom, but perhaps its essential idea was the codification of individual feelings into laws binding upon all writers.

6. *Moderation in ipse dixits.* That Robert Baker was capable of clearer observation and better psychology than his prescriptions so far cited would indicate, is shown by a number of
his remarks. He notes[19] that *either* for *each* in "sat either on
his throne" reprehended by Lowth, is quite allowable since
"numberless words are used in different senses without any
inconvenience."[20] He accepts the rule of custom in the usually
censured forms *from hence, from whence,* and so on, "it seeming in many places to add strength to the expression."[21] Again,
of a passage in Warburton's *Divine Legation of Moses,* which
he used as a storehouse of improprieties, he says in one in-

[15]*Remarks*, 1779, p. 109.
[16]Quoted in *Monthly Review XLV* (August, 1771), p. 95.
[17]Preface to *Remarks* 1779, p. xiii.
[18]Swift, *Proposal for Correcting,* pp. 6 and 31. Interestingly treated in
B. S. Monroe "An English Academy." *Modern Philology VIII,* 107-22 (July
1910).
[19]*Remarks*, 1779, pp. 86-7.
[20]But see his inconsistent comment in Ch. VII, § 13, below..
[21]*Remarks*, p. 67.

stance, "*It is very true what he says* . . . . is certainly very ungrammatical. Yet . . . . frequently used by the learned, and
having a certain air of ease, it cannot be condemned as bad
English."[22] Here he accepts Quintilian's *consensum eruditorum,*[23] but with the codicil that the expression be not unpleasing
to himself. So of *on't,* used "even by the correctest speakers"
where logically *of it* is required. In his passage on *different to*
he is less angry and perturbed than most of his successors, ...
"often used by good Writers. Yet I can't help thinking it to be exceptionable . . . . Is not the Word *From* here more
natural than *To*? And does it not make better Sense?"[24] And
nothing surely could be more reasonable than his note upon *sort
of a* and *kind of a*: "Would not the *a* or *an* be better omitted?
and is not 'a strange sort of man' . . . . a more correct, as well as
a more elegant, way of speaking?"[25] Of *sowed* or *sown* as the
past participle, he says, "I don't insist upon it that this expression [sowed] is the best"; the superlative here is interesting. But these moderate expressions are exceptional. Most
often he is authoritatively dogmatic, the true intellectual ancestor of the makers of purist handbooks. His attitude toward
custom is shadowed in his Remark on "upon the contrary"
which "frequently occurs in the Parliamentary Debates,"[26]
"*upon the contrary* is certainly not English, it not being an expression used."[27]

Trusler, the author of *The Distinction between Words Esteemed Synonymous,* is frank in stating his reliance upon
no other authority than his own opinion: he says, "I
know not how much I may differ from the rest of my country-
men, but the verb *appear,* in my opinion, relates more to the
eye, *seem* more to the imagination."[28]

[22]*Ibid.,* p. 102.
[23]*Institutes* I, 6, 45.
[24]*Reflections,* 1770, pp. 7 and 8.   See Chapter VII, § 12, below.
[25]*Remarks,* 1779, p. 66.
[26]Query: Had he read Johnson's accounts?   Potter censures Johnson for
use of *upon* where *on* is sufficient and simpler. (*Art of Criticism,* 1779.)
[27]*Remarks,* p. 78.
[28]*Distinctions,* 1783 ed., p. 188.

7. *Webster's authoritarian censures.* Noah Webster professed with repetition and italics that the "two points .... the basis of a standard in speaking, are .... *universal undisputed practice* and the *principle of analogy.* But since practice rarely, if ever, prevails universally and undisputed, and thus analogy or "the rules of the language" must "always decide the controversy," there is God's plenty of room for an authority here. Thus he says, "The best authors have erred in the use of the word [*attain*]. Thus the passage cited by Johnson from Swift to illustrate his definition, is not English. 'All the nobility here could not attain the same favor as Wood did.' It ought to be *obtain* or *procure.*" He states positively that "if *to* cannot be supplied, [*attain*] is improperly used... Dr. Johnson himself, not discriminating between the two words, or misled by the mistakes of others, used the word in the same inaccurate manner."[29] Again, Johnson's definition of this same word, "to gain, procure, obtain—founded on the errors of authors, has been the means of propagating this use of *attain*—a use at which the ears of scholars cannot but revolt"; and "who can read it without regretting the miserable state of philological criticism?"[30] Shakespeare is patronized: he "was a man of little learning, and although, when he wrote the popular language of his day, his use of words was tolerably correct, yet whenever he attempted a style beyond that, he often fell into the grossest improprieties." Among the examples are *patient* as a verb, "pelting rivers," "compunctious visitings," and *corresponsive*—"barbarisms which every correct ear instantly condemns and for which he certainly could plead no authority, even in the pedantic age in which he lived."[31]

Again, on want of discrimination between synonyms, ". . . a multitude of errors committed by writers, evidently from their misapprehending the import of words, are cited as authorities by Johnson, instead of being noticed with censure .... thousands of instances .... of a misapplication of terms

[29]Cited to Johnson's *"Letter to Drummond,* 1766." *Letter to Dr. Ramsay,* 1807, p. 16.
[30]*Letter to Dr. Ramsay,* 1807, pp. 16 and 17.
[31]*Ibid.,* p. 19.

. . . . are clearly ascribable to the negligence and mistakes of that lexicographer."[32]   In each case Webster would doubtless have appealed to a "principle of analogy," or perhaps the aid of etymology, which apparently he nowhere expressly invokes, to defend his dogmatic pronouncements.   But, essentially, he is constituting himself alone an Academy, and correcting usage without even a pretence of determining what it is.

8. *Summary.* So far we have found solely individual proscriptions, set down without stated grounds for objection, of offenses against the nature and genius of the language.   So much for authority.   It has been treated here at large, with examples which the authorities themselves might in some cases, perhaps, have justified by appeals to grammar, or logic, or etymology, or the like.   For even when explicitly made, such appeals are often, in the phrase of today, instances of "rationalization."   Whoever dislikes a word, or discovers that some one else has disliked it, is not content merely with using a preferable expression himself; and indeed, as will be discovered in many instances of authoritative dicta in the following chapters, a zeal to legislate in this fashion is by no means always accompanied by observance of the principle. In the *Regular English Syntax* (1767), for instance, Buchanan gives the conventional rules for the formation of the possessive of nouns, with many examples of False Syntax expressly manufactured.   But this was needless trouble, since the author himself writes the *readers judgment, childrens time,* and *for forms sake,* in the preface and text of his grammar.[33]   Moreover, not being scholars in linguistics, these men were quite unaware that scholarship is a condition precedent to intelligent judgment, to paraphrase Professor Matthews, and their legislation was "emphatic in exact proportion to their ignorance."[34]

Hence the prevalence and the hopeless contradictions of their "normative view of language."   It remains in the following chapters to discuss the proposals which they specifically

---

[32]*Letter to Dr. Ramsay,* 1807, p. 18.
[33]See Chapter XI, § 11, *infra.*
[34]Brander Matthews, *Parts of Speech* (Scribner, 1901), p. 132.

referred to principles of grammar, to norms of general logic in choice of words and structure of sentences, and to etymology. But the instances are very similar, and many of the principles adduced in the following chapters may be regarded as various ways of justifying and maintaining positions originally taken upon a point of feeling merely.

CHAPTER IV

"UNIVERSAL GRAMMAR" AND THE CLASSICAL ANALOGY

GRAMMAR UNIVERSAL; *that Grammar,* which without regarding the several Idioms of particular Languages, *only respects those principles, that are essential to them all.*

Harris, *Hermes*

CHAPTER IV

"UNIVERSAL GRAMMAR" AND THE CLASSICAL ANALOGY

1. *Reason building languages.* The search for a universal grammar, based on universal reason and settling once for all every question of usage, was based on a different assumption about the origin of language from that of its divine creation. It had been proposed in the seventeenth century that languages were in certain cases made, to fit men's needs, by a popular assemblage for discussion and legislation.[1] Lord Monboddo, more than a century later, has a serious account of the Pelasgi at work modeling the Greek language out of their own speech with some admixture of native materials.[2] To be sure, Beattie contends seriously that the Greek language was not made complete before it was used.[3] But this view is quite reconcilable with the other, since there was always the grammarian, "the greatest of all artists, and next in rank and dignity to the philosophers,"[4] to come in afterward, bring the language into form, and reconcile all anomalies.[5]

Robert Baker shows clearly how he conceived this ordering by reason or grammatical logic to have come about: "Why,"

---

[1] This is naively put in Bishop Wilkins' *Essay toward a Real Character, and a Philosophical Language,* published by order of the Royal Society in 1668, concerning "the Malayan Tongue, the newest in the World": "It was invented or occasioned by a Concourse of Fishermen from Pegu, Siam, Bengala, and other nations at Malacca, where they built the Town of that Name, and agreed upon a distinct Language made up of the easiest Words belonging to each Nation." (Bishop Wilkins' *Works,* Part V. pp. 175-6. London, 1706 ed.)

[2] *Origin and Progress,* 1774, II, 498-500.

[3] *Theory of Language,* 1787 ed., I, 202.

[4] *Ibid.,* II, 510.

[5] A rational account of the relation of Greek grammar to the development of the language, as a mere business of codification after the fact, is given in Gildersleeve's *Essays and Studies,* (Baltimore, 1890), pp. 137 ff.

he asks, "was Grammar invented, but that for want of it, Men were unable to convey their thought to each other in a clear and distinct Manner? . . . If we neglect those [few rules] we have already, we shall come in Time to understand one another no better than our Ancestors did before the Language was brought into any Form."[6] This. is clearly a similar notion to the Parliament of Pegu which Bishop Wilkins conceived for legislating the Malay language into being.

2. *Grammar universal.* The idea of a universal grammar, following upon these notions, was of course shaped by them. Such a grammar was to be grounded in "Universal Reason," of which Harris speaks confidently:

> It may afford perhaps no unpleasing speculation, to see how the SAME REASON has at all times prevailed; how there is ONE TRUTH, like one Sun, that has enlightened human Intelligence through every age, and saved it from the darkness both of Sophistry and Error.
>
> *Hermes,* 1781 ed., Preface, p. x.

And so he defines "GRAMMAR UNIVERSAL; *that Grammar,* which without regarding the several Idioms of particular Languages, *only respects those principles, that are essential to them all.*"[7]

Thus, the article "Grammar" in the first edition of the *Encyclopaedia Britannica,* "supposing a language introduced by custom," defines "grammar as an art" as a just method of furnishing "certain observations called rules, to which the methods of speaking used in this language may be reduced." But there follows this enlightening definition of "grammar as a science": It "examines the analogy and relation between words and things; and thus furnishes a certain standard by which different languages may be compared, and their several excellencies and defects pointed out." This is "Philosophic or Universal Grammar."[8] In the pursuit of this chimera no pains were spared, and its domestication was considered accomplished when Bayly "printed in a larger letter . . . general rules,

---

[6] Robert Baker, *Reflections on the English Language* (1770) p. 94.
[7] *Hermes,* p. x.
[8] *Op. cit.,* p. 728.

in which all languages agree, . . . to distinguish particulars, called idioms."[9]

These views are further illustrated by the following quotations from Harris' *Hermes* (1751):

> The Authors of Language have contrived a method to retrench these Comparative Adverbs, by expressing their force in the Primary Attribute. . . . This Practice however has reached no farther than to *Adjectives,* or at least to *Participles, sharing the nature of Adjectives.* Verbs perhaps were thought too much diversified already, to admit more Variations without perplexity.
> Harris, *Hermes* (London, 1771 ed.), pp. 199-200.

> It is perhaps due to the imperfect manner in which the Article (A) defines, that the *Greeks* have no Article correspondent to it, but supply its place, by a negation of their Article.
> *Ibid.,* p. 217.

3. *Reverence for the classical languages.* This last illustrates also another point of importance. By the eighteenth century the Greek, from being merely one of the seventy-two languages which had sprung up at the dispersion of men from Babel, was given general pre-eminence. In Harris we read that "the *Greek* language . . . is of all the most elegant and complete," and even Latin, upon which Ben Jonson and other writers on grammars drew so heavily, "but a Species of *Greek* somewhat debased."[10] The Romance Languages are naturally held far below even that, being merely vulgar dialects or corruptions of Latin, and "the modern languages, particularly those of Gothic extraction, . . . not near so accurate, and . . . the sound of them . . . much more unpleasant than that of the Greek." On the contrary, a dead language "exists after it ceases to be a living language; and perhaps in greater purity, and with less hazard of corruption, than while it continued to be spoken."[11] Swift gave as one reason for the inferiodity of English that "the Latin tongue in its purity was never in

---

[9]Anselm Bayly, *Plain and Complete Grammar,* 1772. Preface, pp. vi-vii.
[10]*Hermes,* pp. 147-8.
[11]Monboddo, 1774, I, 688-72—rather a mixed figure. Moore gives interesting quotations, both praise and blame of English, in *Tudor-Stuart Views,* Chapters I-III.

the Island."[12]   Dr. Johnson is quoted by the *Monthly Magazine*, 1800, as having said, in defence of his Latinisms, " . . . It is, seriously, my opinion, that every language must be servilely formed after the model of some one of the ancient, if we wish to give durability to our works."[13]   In keeping with this is Walpole's vigorously expressed opinion of the utter barbarity of the Saxon tongue: " . . . never did exist a more barbarous jargon than the dialect, still venerated by antiquaries, and called *Saxon*. It was so uncouth, so inflexible to all composition, that the monks, retaining the idiom, were reduced to write in what they took or meant to be Latin."[14]

4. *Analogy with Latin*. As was inevitable with these views of the origin and nature of language prevailing in the eighteenth century, universal grammar was formed to a purely classical pattern.   More than half of Harris' *Hermes* is filled with quotations from Latin and particularly from Greek grammars and rhetorics, and his examples are more frequently from the classics than from English.   As a natural result, no English construction is accepted save as it represents, or departs only slightly from, a classical prototype; the only instances of such departure that were tolerated are the use in English of the indefinite article, absent from the Greek—admitted, but given no particular value—and the "natural genders" of English, which are praised by Harris and Lowth as offering scope for personification in noble poetry. Otherwise, only classic patterns and analogues prevail.   Dryden's method of testing a doubtful passage in his own writing by turning it into Latin is frequently cited in the eighteenth century.[15]   Of the argument that Swift, Addison, and Pope "had scarcely a single rule to direct them," Buchanan writes, "Had they not the Rules of Latin Syntax to direct them?"[16] Lowth requires that in the verb following subjects of various

[12]*Proposal for Correcting*, 1712, p. 9.
[13]Cited by Fitzedward Hall to *Monthly Magazine*, vol. 9, p. 150. *Recent Exemplifications of False Philology*, 1872, p. 111, n 2.
[14]Walpole, *Historic Doubts on the Reign of King Richard the Third*, 1768, preface, p. x.
[15]Dedication of *Troilus and Cressida*, Scott ed., 1883, vol. 6, p. 251.
[16]*Regular English Syntax*, 1767 ed., preface, p. ix.

persons "the second Person takes place of the third, and the first of both";[17] and this rule is repeated by grammarians down to the 1800 edition of Murray and later.

Bayly, inconsistent as usual, is scornful of Lowth's justification of a phrase "by having recourse to the Saxon; which I should apprehend there is no occasion to do any more than to the Hebrew . . . or to the Latin";[18] yet he himself uses the analogy of the classics in defence of a point: He overrules Lowth's objection to "awaiting messengers, who if they come, I shall then be able to judge how to act" by saying that the expression is "purely Grecian and Roman"—he quotes Cicero— "And if the phrase is neat and correct in Greek and Latin without a pleonasm, certainly that figure cannot make it improper and mean in English."[19]

As late as 1793, John Shaw justified "John and I was . . ." on the Latin principle of "Zeugma," and applied the same rule for the "conjunction disjunctive" with singular subjects.[20] It is probable that the same principle, though not specifically invoked, lay behind defences of this structure by Greenwood and others earlier.[21]   Because it was more commonly known, Latin, not Greek, was alone appealed to in settling such problems as the proper expression of the negative.[22]

As to the case of interrogative pronouns with a preposition following, Webster proposed an analogy with Latin that is inconsistent with his position on other questions: ". . . 'whom do you speak to?' was never used in speaking, as [i. e., so far as?] I can find, and if so, is hardly English at all.   There is no doubt, in my mind, that the English who and the Latin qui are the same word with mere variations of dialect.   Who in the Gothic and Teutonic, has always answered to the Latin nominative, qui; and dative cui, which was pronounced like

[17]Short Introduction, 1762, p. 105.
[18]Plain and Complete Grammar, 1772, p. 71.
[19]Ibid., p. 82-3. He appears again inconsistent in marking the same redundant in "This Moses, whom they refused, the same God did send." (p. 84.)
[20]Methodical English Grammar, pp. 130-1.
[21]See Chapter XII, §§ 1-10.
[22]See below, Chapter VI, § 14.

qui, and the ablative *quo;* in the same manner as *whose* has answered to *cujus,* in all genders; *whom* to *quem, quam,* and *what* to *quod.* So that *who* did he speak *to? Who* did you go *with?* were probably as good English, in ancient times, as *cui dixit? Cum quo ivisti?* in Latin. Nay, it is more than probable that *who* was once wholly used in asking questions, even in the objective case; *who* did he marry? until some Latin student began to suspect it bad English, because not agreeable to the Latin rules. At any rate, *whom* do you speak *to?* is a corruption, and all the grammars that can be formed will not extend the use of the phrase beyond the walls of a college."[23]

5. *Reaction against Latin analogies.* But the reaction, as with most of the immutable principles and rules we are to consider in this study, was almost equally strong. Wallis in his *Grammatica linguae anglicanae* (1653) had "apparently led the way in discarding the framework of Latin grammar when treating English,"[24] and there were in the eighteenth century a number of complaints of the uselessness of the "various distinctions of the learned Languages, which have no Existence in our own,"[25] the "needless perplexities" which it is "only ignorance or parade . . . to teach or pretend much advantage therefrom to a mere English scholar."[26] William Ward[27] emphasized the difference between Latin and English grammar. He stated specifically that we are "freed in English, so far as the verb is concerned, from the Latin rule, 'The first person is more worthy than the second, and the second than the third,' "[28] and allowed that the "noun of multitude" might be either singular or plural. Priestley also complained that technical Latin terms in English grammar are "exceedingly aukward and absolutely superfluous," and noted that there is no future tense inflection in English.

[23]*Dissertations,* 1789, pp. 286-7.
[24]Moore, *Tudor-Stuart Views,* p. 68-9, *note.*
[25]Ash, *Easiest Introduction to Dr. Lowth's Grammar,* 1763, preface.
[26]"Mrs. Slack" (A. Fisher), *The Pleasing Instructor,* 1795 ed., p. ix.
[27]*Essay on Grammar,* 1765, pp. iv (preface) and 2.
[28]*Ibid.,* p. 455-6. See his remarks on *than whom,* Chapter XI, § 8, below.

Lowth sharply criticized Bentley's emendations of a half-dozen passages in *Paradise Lost* on the following pattern:

> Lest thou not tasting, different degree
> Disjoin us . . .   (IX 883)

which Bentley revised to "thee not tasting," on the model of the Latin ablative absolute. Lowth repudiates the Latin analogy as "forcing the English under the rules of a foreign language" and says Bentley himself spoke of such forcing as "an *ugly and deformed fault.*"[29]   Lowth notes in the same passage that where Milton had used the objective or accusative case, "him destroyed," Bentley, "very inconsistently with himself," corrects it to "he destroyed. . . His Latin Grammar Rules were happily out of his head, and by a kind of *vernacular instinct* (so, I imagine, he would call it) he perceived that his author was wrong."

Lowth indeed speaks specifically against patterning English after an ideal of universal grammar:

> . . . whatever other Metaphysical Modes there may be in the theory of Universal Grammar, there are in English no other Grammatical Modes than those above described [the indicative and subjunctive.]
>
> *Short Introduction,* 1763 ed., p. 50 note.

Withers, in defence of his principle that the singular verb is never correctly used with a compound subject, adds: "I am not ignorant, that the Practice may be supported by the Syntax of ancient Languages. But what have we to do with foreign Idioms? It is Wisdom to enrich our Vocabulary with *Words* from every Quarter of the Globe; but an Indignity to suffer any Nation to controul our Style."[30]

The battle for independence from Latin in the matter of construction seems to have been pretty clearly decided in the eighteenth century, though occasional rules still repeated derive from it; but mistaken ideas of the structure of English, based in a preoccupation with classical grammar, are still strongly evident today. More examples of this dispute will appear under the later discussions of the case after *as* and

---

[29] *Short Introduction,* 1762, pp. 107-8, *note,* 1763, p. 116, *note.*
[30] *Aristarchus,* 1788, p. 41.

than, of the negative, and of the subjunctive mood (Chapters VI and XI, below).

6. *The analogy with French* was less often invoked by grammarians to justify departures from the usual rule of pronoun case, especially in the predicate. Campbell disposes of this briskly: "The argument drawn from the French usage (which, by the way, hath no authority in our tongue), is not at all apposite . . . " and, in a footnote, "The oblique cases of their personal pronouns are . . . an indefinite form which serves indifferently as occasion requires, for either nominative or accusative, and to which there is nothing in our language that exactly corresponds. . . . Let this serve also as an answer to the plea for these vulgar, but unauthorized idioms, *It is me, it is him,* from the *C'est moi, c'est lui,* of the French."[31]

Priestley writes in his preface: "If I have done any essential service to my native tongue, I think it will arise from my detecting in time a very great number of *gallicisms,* which have insinuated themselves into the style of many of our most justly admired writers; and which, in my opinion, tend greatly to injure the true idiom of the English language, being contrary to its most established analogies.[32]

Priestley is for the native idiom, and stands against foreign constructions. Thus, he objects strongly to "told my lord and I," and "my father and him have been . . .," quoted from contemporary novels, and observes, "This last is a French construction."[34] He remarks that the type of phrase illustrated by "repenting him of" is a French idiom, "so foreign to the idiom of the English tongue, that I think it can never take generally." He was probably right at least in his prophecy.[35] He notes without objection, however, "We sometimes use the pronoun *one* in the same sense in which *on* is used in the French," quoting Addison and Atterbury.[36]

[31]*Philosophy* I, 438 and *note.*
[32]*Rudiments,* 1769, p. x.
[33]*Ibid.,* p. 108.
[34]*Ibid.,* p. 103. See a comment on Chesterton's use of this, below, Chapter XI, § 5.
[35]*Ibid.,* pp. 108-9.
[36]*Ibid.,* p. 94.

Robert Baker suspects the influence of the French Language in the English misuse of *lay* for *lie,* since the French have here one verb only, *coucher,*[37] and comments sharply on the stupid imitation of French wigs and fashions.

7. *Universal grammar abandoned.* With the falling off of this appeal to analogies with foreign and classical languages, we may note the abandonment of the ideal "universal grammar," in this quotation from Campbell's *Philosophy of Rhetoric* :[38] "In propriety there cannot be such a thing as an universal grammar, unless there were such a thing as an universal Language. The term hath sometimes, indeed, been applied to a collection of observations on the similar analogies that have been discovered in all tongues, ancient and modern, known to the authors of such collections. . . . But it is my purpose to observe, that as such collections convey the knowledge of no tongue whatever, the name *grammar,* when applied to them, is used in a sense quite different from that which it has in the common acceptation; perhaps as different, though the subject be language, as when it is applied to a system of geography."[39]

The foreign analogies have perhaps been sufficiently illustrated. It is impossible to overestimate their force in all discussions of English, not alone in the eighteenth century, but even now. In the remainder of this study, we shall be concerned chiefly with attempts to regulate English after an ideal of English grammar; but classical patterns run throughout the weave of that grammar as it was understood in the period here considered. The following chapters consider the pronouncements made by writers observing the state of English speech and attempting to "churn it into form" by means of analogy or grammar (Chapter V), general logical considerations (Chapters VI and VII), considerations of etymology and the history of the language (Chapter VIII), and a carefully hedged view of "custom" (Chapters IX and X).

[37]*Reflections,* 1770, pp. 33-36, 44-6.
[38]*Op. cit.,* vol, I, pp. 100-101.
[39]See further quotations below, Chapter IX, § 6.

CHAPTER V

ANALOGY AND DIFFERENTIATION IN GRAMMATICAL FORMS

In doubtful cases regard ought to be had in our decisions to the analogy of the language.

Campbell, Canon the Second, *Philosophy of Rhetoric*, 1776.

As the *paucity of inflections* is the greatest defect in our language, we ought to take advantage of every variety that the practice of good authors will warrant.

Priestley, *Rudiments*, 1769.

CHAPTER V

ANALOGY AND DIFFERENTIATION IN GRAMMATICAL FORMS

1. *The appeal to "Reason and Analogy."* The metaphysical conceptions of language were thus in theory repudiated, and analogies with foreign languages specifically disclaimed, by many of the grammarians of the eighteenth century. It remains to discuss the success of their constant and laborious efforts to make the English language a complete and consistent whole by application of what the grammarians frequently term "reason and analogy." Analogy was a term freely employed in the period as synonymous with grammatical regularity of whatever kind; it will be here used, however, only for the attempt to find in the language itself parallels for regularizing it and bringing it into form.

2. *Differentiation sought.* At the same time that this process was being furthered, it must be noted that a directly contrary application of reason was seeking to multiply differentiae, as for example in the attempt to keep separate the various parts of speech and the preterites and past participles of verbs. This attempt was based in a belief that multiplication of forms is always an aid to expression; and no doubt it had its ultimate root in the reverence for the inflected classical languages. But in the cases presented in this chapter, no specific appeal was made to the classical analogy. Indeed, the search for differentiae was not frequently described or acknowledged; the necessity for distinct forms and categories was simply assumed, and earnestly followed.

3. *Applications of the principle of analogy.* Campbell specifically makes the appeal to analogy as his second Canon:[1]

---

[1] *Philosophy*, I, 378 ff. For explanation of these Canons, see below, Chapter IX, §§ 12-15.

"In doubtful cases regard ought to be had in our decisions to the analogy of the language." By this he prefers *backwards* and *forwards, afterwards,* and *homewards* to the forms without *s,* though he does not tell us with what in the language they are analogous; but "Of the two adverbs *thereabout* and *thereabouts* . . . " the former alone is analogical, there being no such word in the language as *abouts.* Of course analogy leads him to declare for *dares* and *needs* in the third person singular present. He decrees "Would God" strictly analogical with "Would he but ask," and says he here subscribes to the decision of Dr. Johnson, as also in stating that "Of the two phrases *in no wise* . . . and *nowise* . . . the last only is conformable to the present genius of the tongue." Here Campbell means genius in a quite objective sense apparently, as synonymous with idiom, since he adduces analogues like *sidewise.* Finally, of "Whether he will or *no*" and "Whether he will or *not,*" "it is the latter only that is analogical," since "when you supply the ellipsis, you find it necessary to use the adverb *not, 'Whether* he will *or* will *not.'* "[2]

Lowth notes that *"himself, themselves,* seem to be used in the Nominative Case by corruption instead of *his self, their selves;* as, 'he came *himself';* 'they did it *themselves';* where *himself, themselves* cannot be in the Objective Case. If this be so, *self* must be in these instances, not a Pronoun, but a Noun."[3] In a note he cites Sidney and the Statutes of Edward VI to show that *"his self* and *their selves* were formerly in use, even in the Objective Case after a preposition." Other appeals to anology are made by J. Johnson, author of the *New Royal and Universal Dictionary,* 1762: Of *ten pound* and *five year* he says, "It should be observed that *ten pounds* and *five years* is better English on the modern analogy."[4] His verb-agreement in the sentence follows many contemporary analogies, as will be shown later.[5]

False analogies opposed. Baker, on the contrary, opposes

---

[2]*Ibid.,* I, 381.
[3]*Short Introduction,* 1762, p. 39.
[4]"English Grammar," prefixed to the *Dictionary, n. p.*
[5]See Chapter XII, §s 1-14.

certain false contemporary analogies, ridiculing the "extra-ordinary correctness" of saying "a twenty-guns Ship," "a four-wheels Chaise," "the Degrees of Doctors of Divinity" con-ferred on several candidates, and "several Hues and Cries" for Hue-and-Cries."[6]

4. *Comparative and superlative inflections.* The double comparative and superlative, found chiefly in writers of pre-ceding ages, was generally censured as anomalous by eighteenth-century grammarians. Lowth's defence of "most highest" as eminently proper for the Almighty was roundly abused. Jon-son had praised this type of inflection as "a kind of English Atticism."

No one in the eighteenth century seems to have taken as a serious anomaly the use of the superlative for comparing two persons or things. Priestley says it is "very common" and "very pardonable."[7] Campbell concludes, "We say rightly, 'This is the weaker of the two' or—'the weakest of the two.' If, however, we may form a judgment from the most general principles of analogy, the former is preferable, because there are only two things to be compared."[8] He does not tell with what the analogy is to be formed. It looks rather like a mystic "correspondence with nature."[9]

5. *Reasoning in favor of differences in form.* The contrary tendency, leading directly away from the establishment of analogies to the retention of whatever variations in form English possesses, and even to the creation of new forms, is more elaborately represented in eighteenth-century grammar. Whether or not this is due to the grammarians' notion that highly inflected languages are best, no direct appeal was made in these cases to the Latin analogy; in fact, such differences were most carefully cherished by men like Priestley and Web-ster who, in theory at least, altogether repudiated the classical pattern for English grammar.

[6]*Reflections,* 1770, pp. 14, 37, and 59. See also the "apostrophe plural" problem, Ch. XI, § 12.
[7]*Rudiments,* 1769, p. 78.
[8]*Philosophy,* I, 436.
[9]See further discussion on this point in § 16, below.

6. *Differentiations in irregular verbs.* Johnson is perfectly definite in his stand here, noting that "a distinct participle [i.e., different from the preterite] is more proper and elegant" ;[10] and Priestley, though stating in his introduction, "It is possible I may be thought to have leaned too much from the Latin idiom,"[11] says quite unequivocally, "As the *paucity of inflections* is the greatest defect in our language, we ought to take advantage of every variety that the practice of good authors will warrant; and therefore, if possible, make a *participle* different from the *preterite* of a verb; as, a book is *written,* not *wrote;* the ships are *taken,* not *took.*"[12] He admits, "This rule, however, has, by no means, been sufficiently attended to by good writers," and cites the usual list of eminent offenders. The "rule" appears to have been a rather impromptu invention of writers who professed to be fighting free of classical models but constantly followed them. Mennye, attempting the same reform, notes that "more blunders, than are to be found, among all the other parts of speech, put together," are made with these irregular verbs, and, largely copying Lowth, instances *have got,* with *have beat, broke, eat,* as examples in which the *en* is almost hopelessly lost.[13] A few illustrations follow of attempts to hold to such differences in form in these verbs— most of them, no doubt, found in actual use somewhere :

> cling, clang, clung, in which "the original and analogical form of the Past Tense in *a* is almost grown obsolete."
> > Lowth, 1762, p. 89.

> help, holp, holpen
> strike, stroke, strook, or struck, stricken
> > Bayly, 1772, pp. 45 ff.

> catch, catched or caught, caught
> win, wan, won
> wring, wrang, wrung
> eat, ate, eaten or eat; ([ɛt] as a Preterite was commoner in use)
> the participles writhen, washen, wreathen
> > Hornsey, pp. 34 ff.

[10]*Dictionary,* "English Grammar" section, *n. p.*
[11]*Rudiments,* 1769, p. ix.
[12]*Ibid.,* pp. 123-4.
[13]Mennye, 1785, pp. 82-7.

slidden, sitten, and spitten, holden (alternative), and loaden
Webster, *Institute*, 1804 ed., pp. 62-5.

Lowth also gives *beaten, bursten,* but in a footnote as additional forms, *stridden, bounden* (alternative to bound), *lien,*
with *lain,* and commends Dr. Middleton for restoring "the
true Participle *sitten.*"[14] Of the Spectator's "my studies having
laid very much in churchyards," Campbell says, "Properly *lien*
or *lain.*"[15]

Practically every verb here given is to be found with one or
more different forms in at least one other grammarian, and
even the proponents of the principle were by no means consistent themselves in carrying it through; thus, Lowth gives
only *swing, swung, swung,* and *wrought* alone for the two
forms of *work,* where a difference might conceivably have been
set up by confining *worked* to the participle. All grammarians
appear to have been agreed on *gotten.* Of this Wyld remarks
"The American use of the suffix -*en* in the uncompounded
form goes back to the current English of the sixteenth and
seventeenth centuries."[16]   In spite of the censures of grammarians, *have wrote* was used from the beginning to the end
of the century. Buchanan lumped "has spoke, was drove, was
stole, am took, was bore" with the participle *wrote* as all used
by "'writers of Note,"[17] and Webster comments that "*have
wrote, have drove* have become so familiar to our ears, that
we can every hour hear them uttered by some of our best
grammarians without a smile of ridicule."[18]

7. *Differentiation in gender.* Greenwood's *Essay* (1711)[19]
notes the lack of distinction of gender in English as an equal
advantage with its lack of case forms.   Harris, quoted by

[14]*Short Introduction,* 1762, pp. 74-9.
[15]*Philosophy,* I, 473, from *Spectator No. 518.* Campbell, though he ridicules the analogists for *sitten,* as against Present Use, writes *have slidden
into* (I, 433.)
[16]*Modern Colloquial English,* p. 352.
[17]*Regular English Syntax,* 1767, p. 90.
[18]*Grammatical Institute,* 1784 ed., pp. 56-60. It is not clear whose smile—
ours or the grammarians'.
[19]*Op. cit.,* p. 55.

Lowth, adds that this opens the way for personification by the poets, since the language in which Milton wrote imposed no necessity upon him of adhering to grammatical genders, "and he was too wise a Writer to impose it on himself. It were to be wished, his Correctors had been as wise on their parts"[20]—a sharp reference to a number of passages in which Bentley's "New Edition" of *Paradise Lost* (1732) had amazingly restored the genders which, according to Bentley, Milton "gave" but his careless "first editor" and publisher had deranged.

Of the phrases, " 'Tis these, 'tis they, 'tis one or two . . .," which will be discussed under agreement later, Campbell remarks that if they are to be censured, it should be on the ground of gender. "The distinction of genders, especially with us, is as essential as the distinction of persons or that of numbers. I say, especially with us, because, though the circumstances be few wherein the gender can be marked, yet, in those few, our language, perhaps more than any other tongue, follows the dictates of pure nature."[21]

8. The gender of nouns thus offering little ground for grammatical differentiation, attention was turned to the pronouns, particularly *that, whose,* and *which.* Lowth writes, "That is used indifferently both of persons and things; but perhaps would be more properly confined to the latter."[22] Buchanan is more positive: "*That* is often used, but inelegantly, for *who, whom* and *which.*"[23] Hornsey[24] more broadly states: "*That* is perhaps better expressed with *who* and *which.*" Agreement was general among the grammarians that *who* referred in their time only to "an object considered as endowed with the powers of speech and intelligence." Ward added, "In all the English writers, which flourished above a hundred years ago, 'which' is applied to both persons and things,"—perhaps

[20]*Hermes,* 1771 ed., p. 60.
[21]*Philosophy of Rhetoric,* I, 497.
[22]*Short Introduction,* 1762, p. 134.
[23]*Regular English Syntax,* 1767, p. 74.
[24]*Short English Grammar,* York, 1793, p. 24, *note.*

using *which* of former writers by a conscious archaism.[25] But Webster uses the same construction in the *Letter to Dr. Ramsay*.[26] The substitution of *who* for *which* in the Lord's Prayer seems to have been a matter of particular concern to the grammarians. Beattie spoke of *who* in this place as an "extreme modern delicacy" and preferred the old use, like *pardoneth*, as giving "an air of grandeur."[27] But John Clarke will have no such paltering with logic: "How ridiculous must it appear in many Clergymen, undoubtedly Men of Education, who continually use false English when they repeat the Lord's Prayer, 'Our Father, which art . . . ,' 'Spare thou them . . . which confess their faults.' "[28]

9. *Gender of whose.* About *whose* the opinion was even more varied. Dr. Johnson considered it "rather the poetic than the regular genitive of *which*."[29] Lowth quotes Dryden and Addison as using this form, "I think improperly," but makes no attempt to paraphrase.[30]

Priestley is quite inconsistent on this point. He is severe in restricting *who*; "A term which only implies the idea of persons . . . will hardly authorize the use of it," so that Mrs. Macaulay, Smollett, Hume must be censured for applying it to *faction, family,* etc. He adds, "We hardly consider children as persons. . . . A child, who . . ." he comments, "seems to be harsh."[31] But on page 122 he uses the pronoun *he* for his horse, quite naturally. In the grammatical catechism with which the *Rudiments* begins he states that *which, what,* etc., are indeclinable, "except *whose* may be said to be the genitive of *which*."[32] But on page 99 he notes, "The word *whose* begins likewise to be restricted to persons, but it is not done so

[25]William Ward, *Essay on Grammar*, 1765.
[26]*Op. cit.*, 1807, p. 18.
[27]*Theory of Language*, 1787 ed., p. 158 *n.*
[28]*Rational Spelling Book*, 16th ed., 1796, p. 83.
[29]*Dictionary*, "English Grammar," 1785 ed., *n. p.*
[30]*Short Introduction*, 1762, p. 38, *note.*
[31]*Rudiments*, 1769, pp. 97-9.
[32]*Ibid.*, p. 12.

generally but that good writers, and even in prose, use it when speaking of things. I do not think, however, that the construction is generally pleasing." He gives no clue to his reasoning, but proceeds to censure Hume, James Harris' *Hermes,* and Swift. He also makes no attempt to "express by circumlocution" the ideas given and to test how pleasing the result would be.

Buchanan states that *whose* is wrong save for persons, "in the lower kind of poetry and prose," and corrects Addison by substituting "a doctrine, the followers of which . . ."; but he makes the usual exception for personification as adding dignity to "solemn poetry."[33] Bayly, on the contrary, accepts either "a book whose paper, or the paper of which."[34] Mennye follows Priestley even to his examples, but adds that after adjectives *"that* is preferable to *who* or *which."*[35] Hornsey says, *"Which* properly speaking is indeclinable," and writes "That is the horse, the actions of which please me."[36] Murray, after copying Priestley almost verbatim, even in his discourtesy to children, surprises us by recording without any stricture that *whose* is "sometimes used as the possessive of which," with examples from Milton to Blair, and even adding, "By the use of this license, one word is substituted for three."[37] In this matter, then, the eighteenth century ends with a temporary check to the differentiators.

10. *Differentiation of parts of speech.* It was generally understood in the eighteenth-century grammars that the same word may appear as more than one part of speech, many of the authors giving lists of "derivations of substantives from verbs," and the like, often without change of form. But the feeling that there should be differences in terminations for the various parts of speech led to careful scrutiny of all cases that presented themselves to attention. Thus Lowth notes, "the Substantive becomes an Adjective or supplies its place; being pre-

[33]*Regular English Syntax,* pp. 74-5.
[34]*Plain and Complete Grammar,* 1772, p. 84.
[35]*English Grammar,* New York, 1785, p. 78.
[36]*Short English Grammar,* 1793, p. 49.
[37]*English Grammar,* 1800 ed., p. 95.

fixed to another Substantive and linked to it by a mark of conjunction: as, "sea-water. . . ."[38] He notes no other possibilities. But Webster is clear that "adjectives frequently become nouns," and instances *evil, the good.*[39] Campbell noted a "want of correctness in using *everlasting* as a substantive" in a familiar passage from the Bible. "It should be eternity."[40] And *plenty* as an adjective, to be found in "works of considerable merit," he nevertheless brands as a gross vulgarism.[41] J. Johnson's *Dictionary* says *"Notice* should not be used as a verb [since it is a noun]; the proper expression is *take notice.* Yet Lord Shaftesbury used *noticed,* the participle, and *unnoticed* is very common."[42]

The expressions *had rather, had better,* after being condemned heartily by Johnson, Lowth, Campbell, and others, and riddled through twenty-five pages of logic and analogy by Salisbury,[43] are gallantly rescued in eleven pages of rejoinder by Withers,[44] who concludes by crushing Dr. Johnson's objection under the weight of his own citation, in the *Dictionary,* of "I had rather be a doorkeeper . . . " We shall find Campbell rejecting the phrase, though admitting it is established in usage.[45] Webster contests the usually accepted derivation of the construction, since he finds a weakness in Salisbury's parsing of *would rather,* and adds, "At any rate, the phrases have become good English."[46] Priestley noted as an anomaly, but without censure, *had as lief,* which Salisbury writes *had as lieve* and includes in his condemnation, and which Campbell cites as obsolete under his eighth canon.[47]

Lindley Murray and others insisted always on *but* as a con-

---

[38]*Short Introduction,* 1769 ed., p. 158.
[39]*Grammatical Institute,* 1784 ed., p. 73. At the foot of the page in the NYPL (autograph) copy, apparently Webster himself added in ink "the aged, the young, the wise, the foolish, the great."
[40]*Philosophy of Rhetoric,* 1776 I, 463-4.
[41]*Ibid.,* pp. 473-4.
[42]*Royal and Universal Dictionary,* 1762, pp. 19-20.
[43]*Two Grammatical Essays,* 1768.
[44]*Aristarchus,* 1788, pp. 194-204.
[45]Chapter IX, § 14.
[46]*Dissertations,* 1789, p. 266 n.
[47]See Chapter IX, § 14.

junction followed by the nominative case: "but thou and I," etc.[48] Tooke notes that Dr. Johnson "makes *without* a preposition, an adverb, and a conjunction, but under the head of a Conjunction says, . . .—'Not in use.' " What Johnson wrote in the 1785 edition was "Not in use except in conversation."[49] Tooke concurs, but notes, "It is however used as a *conjunction* by Lord Mansfield, in *Horne's Trial,* p. 56. 'It cannot be read, *without* the Attorney-General consents to it.' "[50] Webster demurs, "I do not see the propriety of discarding *without* [as a conjunction]. The best writers [he cites Chaucer, Congreve, etc.] use *without* in the sense of *unless.* . . . The best speakers use the word in this manner, in common discourse, and I must think with propriety."[51]

The problem of *like* as a conjunction is not discussed in the texts examined. George Harris, the Observer, says it "ought never to be used when it cannot be translated into Latin by the Word *Similis,*" but he is objecting to "had like to have perished."[52]

11. *Differentiating the kinds of verbs.* The separation of transitive and neuter verbs caused a great deal of concern. The authors in the eighteenth century, as always before it, were very free in this kind of transference, as in Zachary Grey's "sneering you," Nash's "sneering Sir Kenelm Digby," "resembled them to the ten horns," and Monboddo's "may stumble him." But such freedom, and also the use of neuter verbs in passive senses, came to be closely questioned. Lowth begins the attack, including in his censure the use of "Active Verbs improperly made Neuter," like Swift's "I must premise with three circumstances," though he acknowledges that in general Neuter Verbs "admit in many instances the Passive form, retaining still the Neuter signification."[53]

---

[48] *Grammar,* 1800 ed., p. 119.
[49] *Dictionary,* 1785 ed., art. *without.*
[50] *Letter to John Dunning, Esq.* By Mr. Horne, Printed 1778. Included in vol. II of *Diversions of Purley,* Richard Taylor's 1829 edition, p. 549 and note.
[51] *Dissertations,* 1789, p. 387.
[52] *Observations,* 1752, pp. 20-21.
[53] *Short Introduction,* 1769 ed., pp. 83-4 and note.

One or two of Priestley's cases of "neuter verbs . . . used
as if they were active and transitive, without being used in a
reciprocal construction," surprise us, they are so usual today:
"parliament forfeited all those who . . . " and "all causes
. . . are appealed ultimately to the magistrates."[54]   Priestley
does not condemn these uses.   Dogmatic objection to cross-
ing the boundary line of transitive and neuter verbs set in
more strongly with Mennye's *Grammar*.   He notes that "intransitive verbs don't admit the passive," and condemns
phrases which Lowth had accepted as having "the Passive
Form," but "retaining still the Neuter signification," like "are
infinitely swerved," "was now amounted to" (Swift), and
others merely noted by Priestley: "repent him," "forfeiting
ships," "premise with," "ingratiate with him" (from Bentley).[55]   Caleb Bingham has "I am done" for "I have done"
in a list of miscellaneous improprieties ranging in seriousness
from "Is it true or no" and "Who did you speak to?" to "The
wessel lays at the voff" and "I cotch a werry bad cold."[56]

Lowth has a long discussion of the problem whether "the
rock was split upon by the ship" is grammatically allowable.[57]
Campbell replies that, as Lowth notes, prepositions sometimes
determine both "the meaning of the verb and the propriety of
the phrase" and that Lowth himself writes "is acted upon,"
which is logically parallel.   Campbell very properly concludes
that the difficulty is one of ready grasp of the sense, and not of
grammatical propriety at all.[58]

12.   Lowth continues Johnson's attack on "the Active Present Participle . . . vulgarly used in a Passive Sense; as, *beholding* for *beholden, owing* for *owed*" (Dryden).   *Wanting*,
in a sentence from Addison, he does not attempt to translate
out of the vulgar.   " 'I mistake'; or 'I am mistaking' means, 'I
misunderstand,' " he writes, but, " 'I am mistaken,' means

---

[54]*Rudiments*, 109-10.
[55]*Grammar*, 1785, p. 81.
[56]*Young Lady's Accidence*, 1794 ed., p. 49. Webster says *am done* is "nonsense." See below, Chapter X, § 9.
[57]*Short Introduction*, 1763 ed., pp. 110-11.
[58]*Philosophy I*, 489-91.

properly, 'I am misunderstood.' "[59] This follows Johnson's:
" 'The grammar is now printing,' 'brass is forging,'—in my
opinion a vitious expression, probably corrupted from a phrase
more pure, but now somewhat obsolete, *a printing, a forging,*"
in which the verbal noun is object of a preposition.[60]
The phrase "is being built" as a way of escape from this
dogmatic muddle of differentiation is recorded toward the end
of the eighteenth century,[62] and was itself subjected to furious
attack in the nineteenth.

Hornsey writes that "*a* is improperly used as a preposition"
in phrases like "*a bed, a fishing* for on bed, on fishing."[61]

13. *Differentiating adverbs and adjectives.* The utmost
confusion attended the efforts of grammarians to unscramble
the adverb and the adjective. This problem, also, was a somewhat late discovery; Greenwood noted, in 1711, that "Adjectives of the Comparative and Superlative Degree, do like other
Adjectives often take the nature of Adverbs,[63] and he and
other writers were quite free in interpreting this. Johnson
appears to have no remark on this point—curiously enough,
since he is apparently first responsible for creating or credit-
ing *lowlily* and even *soonly* (cited to More) and lists words
like *slow* as adjectives only.

Lowth attacks briskly with the general charge that adjectives are used for adverbs "improperly, and not agreeably
to the Genius of the English Language"; he adds the usual
list of famous violators.[64] Priestley says briefly, " . . . the
practice is hardly to be approved, except in cases where long
custom has made the examples quite easy; as *exceeding* for
exceedingly, near for *nearly* . . . The following examples are
not so easy . . . *miserable poor, extreme jealous* . . . The

[59]*Short Introduction*, 1769 ed., p. 142 *note*. See Withers' reply, below,
Chapter VI, § 23.
[60]"English Grammar," in the *Dictionary*, 1755.
[61]*Short Grammar*, p. 43, *note*. See Monboddo (*Origin* IV, 125): "*in
building*, or as we express it without propriety, *a-building*".
[62]Joan Platt, "Development of English Colloquial Idiom during the Eighteenth Century, I." *Review of Language Studies*, January, 1926. (II, 72).
[63]Greenwood's *Essay*, 1711, p. 99.
[64]*Short Introduction*, 1762 ed. p. 125 *note*. See Bayly's reply to this reasoning, above, Chapter II, § 9.

word *exceeding* makes a worse adjective than it does an adverb." *Exceeding honesty,* from Shenstone, he would read "exceeding great honesty."[65]

The problem of adverbial use of adjectives ending in *ly* is apparently first faced by Campbell; he prefers *heavenly, silly, godly, lowly, homely,* and so on as adverbs to forms manufactured from them according to the supposed analogy of the language, and censures Dr. Johnson for giving us *lowlily,* "but without quoting authorities"; for "when a short or unaccented syllable is repeated, or followed by another short or unaccented syllable very much resembling . . . this always gives the appearance of stammering to the pronounciation."[66]

Webster writes, "When this termination [*ly*] is added to a noun, it forms an adjective, as God, *Godly* . . . and these words are also used adverbially; for they will not admit the addition of another *ly*. *Godlily,* which has been sometimes used, that is *Godlikelike,* and other similar words, are not admissible, on any principle whatever."[67] Sufficient evidence that Webster reported the reputable usage of the period may be collected from the lists presented for censure in the grammars of Mennye, Alexander, and the rest, as of course for the use of such words as *slow, high, clear, quick,* and many others given without question as adverbs by the *New English Dictionary,* but still frequently censured in this use by handbooks.

14. The phrase *previous to* and its kind were argued very fully by Baker and Webster, among others. Baker in his first edition remarks that a number of these are "used improperly by the greatest part of our writers."[68] In the second edition he attempted a subtle distinction. Of " . . . practiced . . . previously to my dressing myself," he says, "There being no relation between [the actions], I should imagine the word *previously*

---

[65]*Rudiments,* 1769, pp. 80-81.
[66]This comes under his sixth canon, including cases in which exception should be taken to actually established usage on the ground of euphony See below, Chapter IX, § 14. *Philosophy* I, pp. 393-4.
[67]*Dissertations,* 1789, pp. 196-7 *note.*
[68]*Reflections,* 1770, p. 65-6.

to be here wrong"; and "It seems a wonder that we have
no such word as *priorly*. It would be naturally formed
from *prior*, and would be very useful."[69]

Webster rejoins upon Baker and other critics, "The criticism on these expressions must have been made on a very
superficial view of the subject . . . *previous* refers to the word
time or something equivalent implied . . . This is the strict
grammatical resolution of the phrase; and the usual correction,
previously, is glaringly absurd; *during the time previously to
the establishment;* into such wild errors are men led by a slight
view of things, or by applying the principles of one language
to the construction of another." Webster suspects another
false Latin analogy. A footnote adds that "PREVIOUS may
be vindicated . . . by considering it as qualifying the whole subsequent member of the sentence . . . But the other is the real
construction."[70]

But Bayly had already gone further, after giving substan-
tially the same interpretation: ". . . this amply justifies the
use of the adjective form rather than the adverbial, even
though it should be urged, that the adverbial form is usual and
preferred by good writers. The phrase suitably to—inconsistently with—would introduce into grammar an unknown
construction, that of adverbs governing a dative and ablative
case."[71]

Instances of adverbs as adjectives are often the result of
overlogical care, as Harris' *look apishly, leoninely, sound
somewhat harshly,* the last used also by Murray, and Withers'
"Only ought to be placed as *nearly* as possible to the Word to
which it is related." Of a similar case, "arrived safely," Baker
says, "this is wrong, because the Mischance is in the *Journey.*
In the Arrival there is none at all."[72] Thus over-care is met
by still nicer logic.

Other natural and common uses sometimes censured

[69]*Remarks*, 1779, p. 94.
[70]*Dissertations*, 1789, pp. 284-5 and *note*. Withers makes this point more
briefly in *Aristarchus*, p. 404.
[71]*Plain and Complete Grammar*, 1772, pp. 74-5.
[72]*Reflections*, 1770, p. 66.

in the eighteenth century are: "Their then Writings" (Baker), "The then government," "the above discourse" (Harris), "The manner of it was thus" (Swift, censured by Baker). Murray has no criticism to offer on these uses, and notes that the adverb may be used as adjective in the phrase "were there," and as substantive, "better than yesterday's."[73] The adverb as adjective did not apparently greatly exercise the eighteenth-century grammarians.

15. *Differentiation of Shall and Will.* As the notable points in the theory and practice of using *will* and *shall* have been adequately explored, it is sufficient here to refer to Dr. Fries' study and that of Dr. Krapp.[74] These accounts are amply clear in proof that the rule stated by Wallis, elaborated by Lowth and Ward, and copied by almost everybody since, has at no time represented universal cultivated usage. Even Lowth did not, perhaps, observe the rule that *"Will* in the first Person singular or plural, promises or threatens," when he wrote in his introduction, "I will not take upon me to say, whether we have any Grammar, that sufficiently instructs us by use and example."[75]

Withers is perfectly clear and correct on this phase of the controversy, "Dr. Priestley observes, that some Authors use WILL instead of SHALL in the Beginning of Chapters and Sections. E. G. I WILL *now demonstrate* instead of, I SHALL *now demonstrate.* The Doctor condemns without *assigning a Reason.* I add, with Reluctance, he condemns, on the present Occasion, in *Contradiction* to Reason. The Phrase, I WILL *now demonstrate,* is genuine English: it means, I now PURPOSE, I now DESIRE, I now INTEND to demonstrate."[76] It is a pity that Withers overlooked so excellent an illustration as Lowth's own normal variation from his own rule, given

---

[73]*English Grammar,* 1807 ed., pp. 165-6. But Baker says "by then" if not false English is a "terribly low expression." (*Remarks,* 1779, p. 63).
[74]Charles C. Fries, "The Periphrastic Future with *Shall* and *Will* in Modern English," *Publications of the Modern Language Association of America,* XL, No. 4, pp. 963-1024.
G. P. Krapp, *The English Language in America,* II, 266.
[75]*Short Introduction,* 1762. p. x.
[76]*Aristarchus,* p. 173.

above. John Fell, in his *Essay Towards an English Grammar*, 1784, apparently came closer than anybody in either the eighteenth or nineteenth centuries to describing the true status of *shall* and *will*: "*Will*, as an auxiliary term, is a mere sign of futurity, set before the infinitive mode . . . . *shall*, even as an auxiliary sign, always denotes something more than mere futurity, and constantly implies either obligation, possibility, contingency, or something conditional, and very often several of these together."[77]

Other problems of differentiation discussed by the grammarians were the distinction in use between the nominative and objective or accusative cases of pronouns and between the indicative and the subjunctive, and the proper forms for the genitive; but the discussion of these was carried on from so many different approaches, and all possible appeals of logic, esthetics, and usage were so confusingly invoked that discussion of these problems has been reserved to a separate chapter (Chapter XI), where all phases of the attack are illustrated. For the present purpose the discussion has been arbitrarily simplified by selection of only one line of approach in each chapter.[77]

16. *Differentiation—the dual number*. We have noted that Campbell, by some not very clear application of his principle of analogy, was led to prefer the comparative degree for two objects;[78] at another place he expresses the matter more dogmatically: ". . . the comparative degree implies commonly a comparison of one thing with one other thing; the superlative, on the contrary, always implies a comparison of one thing with many others." It would seem to accord more reasonably with the facts of usage if the words *commonly* and *always* were interchanged in Campbell's sentence. From Greenwood's free use of both forms in "When *This* and *That* are used in Relation to two foregoing Words, *This* has Respect to the last and nearer word of the two . . . ,"[79] to Noah Webster's

[77]*Op. cit.*, pp. 163-4.
[78]Above, § 4; *Philosophy* I, 435-6.
[79]*Essay*, 1711, p. 107.

"most definite" of two tenses and "most correct expression" of two,[80] examples of the reputable use of the superlative in this fashion could be collected sufficient, in all probability, to show it about equally current with the comparative. Webster, in speaking of "strongest of two" as "not so correct as stronger" close to the place where he himself uses a superlative in this fashion, is probably to be understood as satisfying only the decent claims of reason and analogy. Certainly nobody in the eighteenth century, so far as it was here explored, took this matter as a serious and irrefragable rule.

The possibility that this preference for the comparative was based in a sense of the need of a dual number, as in Greek and Anglo-Saxon, seems strengthened by a remark of Lindley Murray's upon *whether* as an interrogative pronoun referring to two: "Some grammarians think that the use of it should be revived, as, like *either* and *neither,* it points to the dual number; and would contribute to render our expressions clear and definite."[81]   I have not located any of these grammarians. Murray says further,[82] probably with the same idea in mind, that *either* "relates to two persons or things taken separately, and signifies, the one or the other.   To say 'either of the three,' is therefore improper."   The same reason led grammarians and critics to the limitation of meaning of *alternately,*[83] and the insistence that *each other* be confined to two, while "the word *another* when only two objects are mentioned, seems to be an impropriety.   It is better to say the other."[84]   The hardening of this principle into a rule was also attempted in the nineteenth century.

17. *Summary.* This chapter has illustrated two of the methods by which grammarians of the eighteenth century handled problems of usage: They either ruled in favor of an ex-

---

[80]*Dissertations,* 1789, p. 227; *Grammatical Institute,* 1790 ed., pp. 86-7 and 52, cited by Dr. Bryan "Notes," *Manly Studies,* pp. 390-1 n.; 1784 ed., pp. 48 and 65.
[81]*English Grammar,* York, 1807 ed., pp. 95-6.
[82]*Ibid.,* p. 98.
[83]Though Goold Brown writes that he was "alternately instructing youth in four different languages." Preface, *Grammar of English Grammars,* 1851.
[84]Baker, *Remarks,* 1779 ed., p. 88.

pression because of its analogy with some other in the language more or less resembling it at some point; or they discarded one and accepted another on the ground that any difference in structure means added exactness in discrimination and expression. Usually, whichever choice was made, it was immediately stated as a rule incapable of exceptions. It should be noted also that the claims for the study of language made at this period were entangled with the idea of formal discipline; hence the obvious educational value of pursuing rather subtle analogies or of mastering abstract differentiae in the resolution of false syntax. The multiplication of formal niceties, also, was not without relation to the perpetuation of class differences, as we shall observe later (Chapter X).

It is curious to note that the applications of the principle of analogy, frequently and expressly invoked, are few in comparison to the constant but not expressly attributed search for grammatical differentiation. Regardless of the fact that relations are expressed in English sentences largely by word-order and particles, grammarians have always insisted upon differentiations of form, as in more inflected languages. Their ideal of elaboration has clearly stood in the way of the normal process of simplification in English grammar, particularly in relation to the principal parts of verbs. Unfortunately, the analogy with the tremendously preponderant number of two-form verbs did not prevail in the minds of grammarians and dictionary-makers over the logical notion of the need for differentiated forms for the preterite and past participle. Throughout the eighteenth century we have found the grammarians noting the clear tendency of many strong verbs—*speak, write, drive,* and numerous others—to settle into two forms only. These grammarians might by the principle of analogy have stimulated this process, or at least caused less confusion by giving up their efforts to check it. The same principle of differentiation was in part responsible for adding and fixing the apostrophe in the genitive plural.[85]

[85]See Chapter XI, §§ 10-12.

In short, there are recorded in this chapter another set of mostly futile and wholly confused attempts to rebuild English according to contradictory notions of logic. Where, as in the vast majority of cases, these efforts were unsuccessful, they produced merely a clutter of prescriptions. Where, as in relation to the principal parts of some strong verbs, they either helped unnecessary forms to prevail in the language, or at least failed to assist the movement toward simplification, it seems clear they did a positive disservice to the development of English as a simple, widely useful medium of communication.

CHAPTER VI

VARIOUS LOGICAL CONSIDERATIONS

I. SENTENCE STRUCTURE AND WORD ORDER

It is inelegant to vary the construction of Members of the same Period.

Buchanan, *Regular English Syntax.*

CHAPTER VI

VARIOUS LOGICAL CONSIDERATIONS
I. SENTENCE STRUCTURE AND WORD ORDER

1. A great many observations as to sentence structure and word order, some of them useful and practicable in the development of clarity in English writing, a great many only meticulous and obstructive, were made by grammarians and rhetoricians in the eighteenth century. Practically all the rules were dictated by a purely logical analysis of constructions. The question of the actual effect of any form of words in real social situations—whether ready comprehension, doubt and confusion, or downright misunderstanding—was rarely asked; the sole test was agreement with the abstract reasoning of the critic. For example, Priestley has the following comment on the frequent use of *you* as an indefinite pronoun as in Addison's "Your men of more refined parts, . . . "[1] "The pronouns *you,* and *your* are sometimes used with little regard to their proper meaning; for the speaker has just as much interest in the case as those he addresses."[2]

2. *Parallel construction.* The grammarians went to an extreme in advocating some forms of parallelism. A sentence, used by Lowth without objection as an example of the superlative degree: "Socrates and Plato were wise; they were the *most eminent* philosophers in Greece," is roundly criticized by Buchanan, for "it is inelegant to vary the Construction of the Members of the same Period." Evidently Buchanan would have us keep to but one degree of comparison within any sentence.[3] Campbell is almost as extreme. Of "The Court of

[1] *On Medals.*
[2] *Rudiments,* 1769, p. 82.
[3] *Regular English Syntax,* 1767, pp. xi-xii.

Chancery frequently mitigates, and breaks the teeth of the common law," from *Spectator No. 564*, he asks, "What is the regimen of the active verb *mitigates?* Regularly it ought to be, *the teeth of the common law*, as these words make the regimen of the other active verb *breaks*, with which the former is coupled. But as this manner of construing the sentence would render the expression highly improper, if not nonsensical, it is evidently the author's view, that the verb *mitigates* should be construed with these words *the common law*, which, being in construction with the possessive *of* (or, as some would call it, in the genitive) cannot serve grammatically as the regimen of an active verb."[4]

That a reasonable attention to parallelism often adds to the ease and clarity of construction, and as well that a skillful variation from it may sometimes lend force to expression, is sufficiently evident. The extreme nicety of parallelism in phrases like "both by sea and by land" seems not to have been discovered by the eighteenth-century grammarians, and their own use is perfectly unfettered in this matter. We find for example "to read not only English, but to pronounce the most difficult Words of other Languages," in Greenwood's *Essay*, 1711 (p. 31); "used indifferently both of persons and things," in Lowth, 1762 (p. 104); "in consequence, either of ignorance or inattention," Webster, *Dissertations*, 1789 (p. 249).

Instances of non-parallelism criticized by the grammarians were various constructions joined by coordinate or correlative conjunctions. Baker writes, *"Not only, Neither,* and *Either*, by being out of their Places, makes Nonsense."[5] Of "He was not only an Eye-witness of those Affairs, but had a great share" and "He was neither learned in the Languages, nor Philosophy," both from the *Biographical Dictionary*, his comment is, "I own it astonishes me that our Writers should go on from Age to Age expressing themselves in this slovenly Manner." But he adds, "Sometimes indeed there is no avoiding the Impropriety without a Stiffness or Heaviness of

[4]*Philosophy* I, 448-9.
[5]*Reflections*, 1770, p. 124.

Expression. In either of these Cases it is to be suffered."[6] We have an example of one writer's attention to such matters in the correction sheets with which books in the eighteenth century were frequently provided. Baker, in the "Address to the King" which introduces his 1770 edition, had written "whatever is either innocently diverting, or whatever is instructive, and at the same Time so amusing as to fix the Attention . . . . ," but deleted *either* in his *Errata*.[7] Lowth, Bayly, and Mennye have a choice collection, from standard authors, of various non-parallel structures joined by *and* and *but* chiefly.[8]

One type of clause-parallelism is particularly demanded by Priestley: "Whatever relative be used, in one of a series of clauses, relating to the same antecedent, the same ought to be used in them all. . . . *Holland, against* which *the war was undertaken, and that . . . was reduced.*"[9] But the critics themselves freely employ the *and which* and the *and who* construction without attention to parallelism[10] and it seems to have encountered no censure in the eighteenth century.

Likewise the form of definition, "A compound sentence is when" (Greenwood), "An explicative sentence is, when a thing is said . . ." (Lowth), is freely utilized from the beginning to the end of the century. The only objection is Robert Baker's, based apparently on the principle of necessary concord of predicate nominative with subject. Of "The reason is because . . ." and "The subject was on . . ." he remarks, "This expression does not make sense . . . because you can't put 'by reason of' in place of *because*. But . . . there are scarce any, even of our greatest Authors, that avoid this way of speaking." His sensitiveness repudiated also the construction, ". . . made no other answer than by a low bow."[11]

[6]*Reflections*, 1770, p. 126; Remarks, 1779, pp. 105-6 and 109.
[7]*Reflections*, 1770, "Address to the King," p. ix, and errata page following title page.
[8]*Short Introduction*, 1762 ed., pp. 117-20.
Plain and Complete Grammar, p. 90.
Mennye's *Grammar*, pp. 88-9.
[9]*Rudiments*, 1769, p. 102.
[10]". . . a subject . . . of no small importance; and in which the want . . . seems to be . . ." Lowth, 1762, p. xv. ". . . . such as stand . . . and who therefore . . ." Blair, *Lectures*, I, p. 430.
[11]*Reflections*, 1770, pp. 80 and 82.

Some letters of Charles James Fox to Dr. Parr,[12] apparently in answer to the latter's editorial criticism of the speeches of Fox, contain a number of interesting remarks on usage. Of the arrangement of correlatives of which Woodrow Wilson was fond, as in the phrase "in his friendship not only etc.; but in him": this, says Fox, "may be an irregularity, if you refer to general and abstracted grammar; but I think it a true English idiom; and where our ancestors have fairly gained a conquest over the natural enemy of writers, which I consider strict grammar to be, I do not see why we should give it up . . . much less, if the acquisition has been so cultivated, as to render it valuable."[13]

3. *Redundancy.* That Robert Baker was not always sensitive to redundancy of expression is shown by numerous instances such as "the expression of *one of their Houses is fallen,*" "the expression of A Dog in a Dancing-School";[14] but he criticizes the "Adverb's being twice repeated" in "I expected that, when I told him the news, that he would . . .,"[15] and also this superlative instance of cautious pleonasm: "If I mistake not, I think . . ."[16] One other construction in which redundancy was detected and censured in the eighteenth century appears to have been *from hence, from thence,* which Dr. Johnson reprobated, but which Withers defended warmly and discovered Johnson himself using.[17]

4. *"Concealed grammatical errors."* The construction in which a verb or other word needing to be supplied appears elsewhere in an "incorrect form," as "He has never gone and never will," seems to have been first seriously questioned by Campbell. The phrases "to take the same measures . . . that I have," from *Guardian No. 1,* and "any book that has, is or shall be published," he censures as impossible to complete with

[12]*Works of Dr. Parr,* II, 613-16.
[13]*Loc. cit.,* p. 615. See, below, Chapter XIII, § 5, *note* 14.
[14]*Reflections,* 1770, pp. 123, 129.
[15]*Ibid.,* p. 70.
[16]*Reflections,* 1770, p. 28.
[17]In the *Life of Savage. Aristarchus,* p. 407. See, below, Appendix I, Glossary § 8.

the verb form already supplied in the sentence.[18] In previous writers precisely this sort of error is passed over without question in the hunt for other varieties of logical difficulty. Lowth notes specifically that the repetition of the verb in "He loves not plays, as thou dost," is unnecessary. Such phrases as "our best writers always have and still do use," (Webster), "If we neglect these few rules as we have already" (Robert Baker) were common and apparently caused no difficulty in the eighteenth century. Baker seems to have discovered but one such error: "Neither has he, nor any others . . ."[19]

Charles James Fox makes the following sensible defence of the "concealed grammatical error" in "can or ought to conciliate," and "compassionate and condole with his friends": ". . . no doubt liable to some objection, but whether it be, strictly speaking, ungrammatical, may be doubted . . . if one were to make it a rule to avoid [this type of expression] the circumlocutions would be infinite."[20]

5. *Reference of a pronoun to a "preceding sentence."*
Baker was the first to point out a difficulty with the reference of a pronoun to a sentence or phrase; but nobody else in the eighteenth century apparently regarded this as much of a discovery. His examples are:

"I should be glad to be introduced to him,"
"That I undertake very frankly to do." (Fordyce)
and
"All that can now be decently urged is . . . And this I shall do." (Warburton)

On the contrary, Ussher says in analyzing a sentence, ". . . *it* refers to the phrase *you have been ill;* which on this occasion is its antecedent."[21] So Murray writes, perhaps not very "elegantly," "This rule is often violated; some instances of which are annexed," and directs that a "pronoun is also used to represent an adjective, a sentence, a part of a sentence and sometimes even a series of propositions."[22]

[18]*Philosophy of Rhetoric*, 1776, I, 446.
[19]*Remarks*, 1779, p. 69.
[20]*Works of Dr. Parr*, I, 614.
[21]*Elements*, 1796 ed., p. 19.
[22]*English Grammar*, 1809 ed., pp. 210 and 90, *note*.

6. *Dangling verbals.* Lowth notes that the infinitive may be used absolutely or independently; but Baker alone in the eighteenth century seems to have found possibilities of incoherence in the construction. Baker notes that in the phrase "Mr. ———, left off trade" the verbal "has no substantive with which . . . connected."[23] Bayly supplies the ellipsis in "the voice of the Lord walking in the garden" with "as he was walking,"[24] noting that "here the participle agrees with the noun in the oblique case," but registers no censure.

7. *Construction with the gerund.* The problem of possessive or objective case with the gerund is treated later (Chapter XI) from various angles of theory. A gerund construction which troubled many of the grammarians, together with a complete freedom from inhibiting ideas about parallelism, contractions, and the like, is illustrated in this sentence from Greenwood:

> And indeed the acquainting Lads with the Reasons of Things, and to let nothing pass, before they have attained a tolerably sure and just Notion of it, would be of more service to 'em towards the exercise of their Reasons than . . . .
>
> *Essay,* 1711, p. 223.

Robert Baker, perhaps on the advice of critics, deliberately introduced in his *Errata* pages a verbal phrase similar to Greenwood's, by supplying *the* before *employing* in "spoken of employing a verb" and in several like places. But Lowth declared that this sort of construction offended by treating the "participles . . . as if they were of an amphibious species, partly Nouns, and partly Verbs . . . This Rule arises from the nature and idiom of our Language, and from as plain a principle as any on which it is founded: namely, that a word which has the Article before it, and a Noun, with the Possessive Preposition *of*, after it, must be a Noun; and if a Noun, it ought to follow the Construction of a Noun, and not have the Regimen of a Verb."[25] Webster, who quoted some fourteen pages of Lowth's notes (and eight of "Priestly's") in the appendix of his later

[23]*Reflections,* 1770, p. 53.
[24]*Plain and Complete Grammar,* 1772, p. 93.
[25]*Short Introduction,* 1762, pp. 111-12, *note.*

editions of the *Grammatical Institute,* does not repeat this one, but says, "Either *the* before the participle and *of* after it, ought both to be used, or both to be omitted.

"But our best writers always have used the article before the participle, without the preposition after it, and in some instances it is avoided without difficulty." This is making use of the appeal to superior custom, but without much enthusiasm.[26]

8. *"Improper" omissions.* On the subject of improper ellipsis of particles there was much discussion. The first mention of any aspect of this seems to be Lowth's remark that "in general, the omission of the Relative seems to be too much indulged in the familiar style; it is ungraceful in the serious . . . hazardous, and hardly justifiable, even in poetry."[27] He notes as particularly hazardous the omission of "both the relative and the preposition" in Addison's "in the temper of mind he was then" and Swift's "In the posture I lay." The following from the anonymous answer to Swift's *Proposal* would perhaps have offended Lowth still more: "from a quarter it never yet came."[28] Baker, though he ignorantly insisted upon the preposition before the pronoun in phrases like "write me," conceded the omission of the accusative relative; but his critics of the *Monthly Review* fell foul of him, for his own use rather than for his permission of this license. " ' 'Tis an egregious mistake many pretended judges of painting lie under . . .' " they quote him, and continue, "The word *which* is wanting between *mistake* and *many*."[29]

Blair expresses himself with positiveness on this matter, but even he is not wholly dogmatic. Of "the man I loved" and "the dominions we possessed"—the latter from Swift—he says, "But though this elliptical style be intelligible, and is allowable in conversation and epistolary writing, yet, in all writing of a serious or dignified kind, it is ungraceful. There, the relative should always be inserted in its proper

[26]On the genitive case with "participles," see below, Chapter XI, § 15. *Institute,* 1804 ed., p. 47.
[27]*Short Introduction,* 1769, p. 107; 1762 ed., p. 137, *note.*
[28]*Reflections on Dr. Swift's Letter,* p. 34.
[29]*Monthly Review,* XLV (August, 1771), 95.

place, and the construction filled up."[30]   Blair's use of indicative and subjunctive modes in the first clause, possibly to indicate a subtle shade of difference, and the redundancy of his last phrase, "and the construction filled up," are interesting examples of the grammatical-logical style. Bayly is even more positive: "But to omit the relative, a liberty which is continually assumed by Swift, seems highly improper; as 'a period of time (*which*) I intend to treat *on*,' . . . 'evil (*which*) I complained *of*.' "[34] Campbell not only defends the omission where it occasions no obscurity, but himself uses a type of ellipsis fairly common in the eighteenth century, that of the antecedent of the relative: "There are, indeed, who seem disposed to . . ."[32] So also does Monboddo—"There are, I know, who will think," and he defends Milton's use of "So fail not thou, who thee implores."[33]

9. Withers demolished Blair's position. He remarks that the omission of *which is, who are,* etc., as "A man (who is) devoted to sensual appetites," is "very elegant on many occasions";[34] and then follows: "Dr. Blair is of Opinion that the Omission of—WHICH—is inelegant, and accordingly he censures this Passage—The *Dominions we possessed and the Conquests we made,* &c. . . . They [the sentence with and without *which*] are equally clear and intelligible; but, in point of Strength and Elegance, the censured Passage is greatly superior.

"In this Essay, I have often used a languid Identity of expression, and countenanced many Phrases which in Judgment I condemn, that Metaphysical Grammarians may not suppose me ignorant of imaginary Excellencies.[35]   But were I at a Loss for high Authority to defend the omission of—WHICH —I would resort to *Dr. Blair himself,* for our learned Lawgiver is subject to the common fate of metaphysical Critics; in the same Page, in the very Sentence, in which he prescribes

[30]*Lectures*, I, 211-12 and 453. See Jespersen's "Notes on Relative Clauses," *S. P. E. Tract No. XXIV*, Oxford Press, 1926, pp. 103-17.
[31]*Plain and Complete Grammar*, 1772, pp. 84-5.
[32]*Philosophy* I, 403.
[33]*Origin and Progress* IV, 7 and V, 246 *note*.
[34]*Aristarchus*, 405.
[35]I have found nowhere in the eighteenth century a more lively appreciation of the tendency to stiff and "languid identity" of stereotype to which the grammatical school and the proponents of purity and propriety were tending to reduce their followers. See Webster on the users of the present subjunctive, in Chapter XI, § 19, below.

a Rule, he violated it.[36] *'It appears from the authentic Docu-*
ments (   ) he produces, that . . .' Again, *'The pleasure*
(   ) we receive from Imitations.' To this Point have tended
all the Rules (   ) I have given.''[37]

Murray specifically censures the omissions "those [who are]
intrusted with . . ." and "satisfaction and consistency [which
are] to be found," which Withers approved as "very elegant
on many occasions," and also "systems I have met with,"
though he usually permits leaving out the relative in the accusative. His stricture on the omission of a preposition in
"nothing men are more deficient in, than knowing their own
minds," which he revises to "nothing in which men are more
deficient than in knowing . . .," is possibly due to a feeling
for parallelism.[38] Elsewhere he himself writes, "sentences,
which none of those rules can be brought to bear upon."[39]

10. Two curious sentences criticized by Campbell are:
". . . looked upon as dull as talking on the weather,"[40] and "the
fatal mistake the world had so long been, in using silkworms."[41]
For the first, admitting that another *as,* which the sentence
"absolutely requires," would "render the expression very inelegant," he proposes "equally dull with." In the second he
says that another *in,* "necessary to complete the construction,"
"would have sounded harshly," and recommends giving the
sentence "another turn"; but he does not attempt this turn.[42]

J. Johnson has a curious rule of syntax, apparently founded
in odd logic with no relation to actual usage: "Where a relative is to follow and the subject has not been mentioned im-

---

[36]"Remarkably so, in one Instance." [Withers' note.] Most unfortunately, the usually meticulous Withers has cited no examples of this concur-
rence of inconsistency, but the phenomenon is by no means rare.
[37]"Dr. Blair, vol. I, 114, 21, 245." *Aristarchus,* 423-4. These citations are
probably from Blair's 1783 edition. For that of 1793 the pages are 107,
23, and 227.
[38]*English Grammar,* 1800 ed., p. 177.
[39]*Ibid.,* p. 178.
[40]*Spectator No. 321.*
[41]From *Voyage to Laputa.*
[42]*Philosophy,* I, 450-1.

mediately before, *those* is required."[43]   His example is:
"*Those* conquests which Alexander made . . ." What he may
possibly have meant is that when *those* is used without an antecedent clearly indicated, a relative clause or some other explanatory circumstance seems to be required.

11. Baker noted first the problem of repeating or not repeating the article, in censuring as incomplete such phrases as
"the ends of a divine and human lawgiver."[44] James Harris
makes a most interesting point, that the distinction between the
restrictive and the non-restrictive modifier was to be shown by
means of the article, since the eighteenth-century punctuation
of both was the same. His illustration is: "Ptolemy, having
presided over the Games, was honored," and "The Ptolemy,
who presided over the Games, was honored."[45]

Withers quotes a censure of omitted articles from the *Oxford Magazine,* 1768: "The Article—THE—before Superlatives, is frequently omitted by the SCOTS (who have not contributed a little to corrupt our Language by the Multiplicity of
their Works) and before Substantives, even when they are
used in an eminent or emphatical Sense, and require a Definitive the most."[46] Withers replies with spirit: "The Charge of
corrupting our Language by the Omission of the 'Article'—
THE—is groundless.

"In Fact, the Omission of '*Articles*' and '*Definitives*' of every
Sort, affords Strength and Elegance to Composition.   But the
frequent Recurrence of WHAT and THAT and WHICH, &c.
is inelegant and to be avoided. Excepting on certain Occasions,
. . . it is not more necessary to use them, than it is to hold a
Person by the Coat with one Hand and to point in his Face with
the other, in Order to inform him that he is the Object of your
Address, or the Subject of your Discourse." Withers gives an
amusing illustration of such pleonasm from a speech in Parliament, and adds, "In the Dictionary, I purpose to give Directions

[43]*Royal and Universal Dictionary,* 1762, p. 19, *note.*
[44]*Remarks,* 1779, p. 79.
[45]*Hermes,* 1771 ed., p. 231.
[46]*Oxford Magazine* I, 216.

when to insert, and when to omit—WHICH—THAT—and all
the 'PARTICLES' in our Language."[47]

Mennye gives instances of "wrong" omission or inclusion of
articles from the Bible, Pope, Hobbes, and the like, but attempts
no formulation of principles.[48]   Murray alone states a specific
distinction; he favors the ellipsis, as in "a house and garden,"
"a man, woman, and child" save "when some peculiar emphasis requires a repetition; as in the following sentence: 'Not
only the year, but the day and the hour,' "—here "the ellipsis of
the article would be improper,"—or "when a different form of
the article is requisite . . . as, 'a house and *an* orchard.' "[49]

12. *Different from, to, than.* We learn from Baker what we
find repeated in countless handbooks for the next century and
a half, that a "a *different Manner than* is not English. We say
different to and *different from,*" with a preference expressed
for "the last,"[50] and "I would banish the expression of *different
to.*"[51] This, it is to be noted, is given in part the form of a
statement of custom, but it all has the marks of logicizing and
appeal to authority. This is the only eighteenth-century reference I happened on; but there must have been a feeling against
different than, as Willich writes awkardly, "The English write
differently from what they speak."[52]

13. George Harris remarks that "such a portrait as," "such
men as" are constructions "as ungrammatical as '*men as*' . . .
should be w*ho* or *which.* [This] may at first appear stiff and
formal, but by being constantly practiced, will soon appear as
easy, as it is regular."[53] Oddly, a similar construction by Dr.
Johnson, "by the same principle as they received it," is reprobated by Fitzedward Hall more than a century later.[54]

[47]*Aristarchus*, p. 422. Unfortunately, the completion of his dictionary,
for which he gives enlivening particulars and some quite sensible suggestions in the Proposals appended to *Aristarchus*, was prevented by his
troubles with authority over an accusation of libeling Mrs. Fitzherbert,
and by his death in Newgate of a "putrid fever."
[48]Mennye, 1785, p. 75.
[49]*English Grammar*, 1800 ed., p. 174.
[50]*Reflections*, 1770, p. 100 and pp. 7-8.
[51]*Remarks*, 1779, p. 4.
[52]*Philological Essays*, 1798, pp. xcii and xciv.
[53]*Observations*, 1752, p. 23.
[54]*Modern English*, 1873, p. 199 *note*. But probably because of the adverbial use of *as* or the omitted preposition.

14. *The expression of the negative.* Greenwood begins the battle on the double negative, a struggle prolonged even today on logical principles and in ignorance of the "genius of the language." Having derived *never* from *ne ever*, Greenwood adds: "I cannot here omit an Observation . . . relating to this Expression, *Never so much*, E. G. *A man gives so much as he never gave before.* By inadvertency this Phrase has been used for a Kind of Superlative: Nay, some have blundered on *ever so much*."[55]

The next reference to the question was discovered in Zachary Grey's *Free and Familiar Epistle to W. W.* Noting Mr. Upton's "sneering you upon using two *Negatives,* which he observes make one affirmative,"[56] Grey quotes authority for "two *Negatives* don't always make an affirmative, but deny more strongly, as is well known from the *Greek* and *French* languages."[57] The tone of the rest of Grey's letter might suggest that he was rather "sneering" Warburton's scholarship than seriously proposing the foreign analogy.

Lowth has an elaborate note on misuses of *either, neither, nor,* and the like. He follows Johnson in accusing *Charm he never so wisely* of "Solecism." "It should be ever so wisely; that is, *how* wisely *soever.*[58] This seems to reverse Greenwood's principle quoted above. Baker[59] says much the same about *neither, nor,* and *no.*

Priestley notes two curiosities of the logic of English speech: "It is observable, that an answer to a question, in English, is rather a contraction of a sentence, expressing an affirmative or negative proposition, and that it does not at all depend on the manner in which the question is asked. Whether my friend say, Are you *disposed to take a walk;* or, Are you not *disposed to take a walk;* if I be disposed to walk, I say, *yes;* if not, I say,

[55]*Essay towards a Practical English Grammar,* 1711, p. 158.
[56]Warburton had written "he never asks but to abuse me, nor never talks but to misrepresent me." See Upton's "Critical Observations on Shakespeare," 1st ed. 1746, p. 316.
[57]Gray's *Epistle,* 1750, pp. 28-9.
[58]*Short Introduction,* 1769, p. 183-4, *note.*
[59]*Reflections,* 1770, pp. 112-13.

no." Again, "The particles *or,* and *nor,* may either of them, be
used with nearly equal propriety. '. . . *character not sufficiently vigorous, nor decisive'* (Hume) . . . *Or* would perhaps
have been better, but *nor* seems to repeat the negation in the
former part of the sentence, and therefore gives more emphasis
to the expression." Here logic is met by a consideration, rarely
to be found in the grammarians we are studying, of the real
effect of a construction.[60] Of *never so* Priestley merely states,
"*Never so* was formerly used where we now say *ever so,"*
instancing Addison and "our translation of the Bible."[61]

Campbell writes, "I subscribe to the judgment of Dr. Johnson" in regard to *never so*.[62] Curiously enough, an unobserving
or unconvinced reader of the copy now in the Columbia University library, on Campbell's writing "though his life were ever so
blameless," queried in pencil in the margin "never ?"[63]

Further examples show how puzzling to logicians and classi-
cists are the natural expressions of the negative in English. On
"In his nature there was nothing harsh, much less cruel,"
Baker observed, "much less nothing," treating the phrase to a
substitution of the omitted substantive—another case of "concealed error" ferreted out.[64]

The usual rule is dogmatically worded by Mennye, "Two
negatives may make an affirmative but cannot express a denial,"[65] and by Clarke, who says they "absolutely prove
what you mean to deny."[66] Withers says the same in effect;
but in concrete cases Withers' logic trips him badly: "NOR
follows NEITHER and any *other* Negatives. E. G. *He is*
NEITHER dead, NOR *indisposed. He is* NOT *dead,* NOR
indisposed. He is UNwell, NOR *have we any hopes of his*
Recovery."[67] He says emphatically that *neither* and *nor* are
both negatives; yet he fails to note, as logical grammarians

[60]*Rudiments,* 1769, pp. 137-8.
[61]*Ibid.,* p. 201.
[62]*Philosophy,* I, 380.
[63]*Ibid.,* p. 245.
[64]*Remarks,* 1779, p. 99.
[65]*Grammar,* 1785, p. 18.
[66]*Rational Spelling Book,* 1796, p. 83.
[67]*Aristarchus,* p. 416.

appear always to have done, that not alone his examples, but the conventionally required *neither* plus *nor,* contravene their principle of the effect of two negatives.

15. *Mixed comparisons.* Of Addison's "more beloved, but not so much admired," Priestley says, *"More* requires *than* after it, which is no where found in this sentence," and subjoins illustrations of like sort from Hume and the *Tatler.*[68] Campbell collects a dozen instances, chiefly from writers "of no small merit for harmony and elegance," of false expressions of comparison, including Milton's "the fairest of her daughters, Eve," and concludes by defending his revision of a mixed comparison to *"as old as tradition,* and even *older":* "The comparative, in this case, is not construed with the preceding words, but with words which, being ascertained by the preceding, are properly enough understood."[69] Thus must the grammatical logician buckler himself against every probable or improbable logical attack.

16. *Order of words in sentences.* Priestley discovered quite a number of constructions which should not be "split," but most of them he condemned on other grounds than logic— usually awkwardness. Two of his objections relating to the "split verb," however, he seems to make for logical reasons, though no grounds are assigned; and as these types of arrangement are still condemned by purists, their first proscription is worth noting: "Though the negative particles follow the auxiliary verb in an interrogative sentence, no other adverbs should be placed there along with them. *Would not then this art have been* . . . Harris's *Three Treatises";* and "When there are more auxiliaries than one, the adverb should be placed after them, immediately before the participle. *Dissertations on the prophecies which have remarkedly been fulfilled* . . . Title page to Dr. Newton's treatise . . . This combination appears very irregular and harsh . . ." The "irregular" apparently implies a grammatical or logical objection. Some common adverbs he allows between

---

[68] *Rudiments,* p. 200.
[69] *Philosophy,* I, 447-8. Proper comparison greatly interested Campbell. Other references are I, 435-7, 441, 481.

the auxiliaries, as "He has always been reckoned . . ."[70] Webster had obviously no scruples about this kind of separation, as he wrote, " 'I *never* will be seen there,' seems not so elegant; as 'I will *never* be seen there,' "[71] and he cites with approbation, "nor can a selfish heart easily conceive . . . ."[72]

17. Baker discovered, if he did not invent, what he stigmatized as improper separation of the participle from the adverb modifying it: "So well a bred man, so poorly a painted picture." These might probably have been queried as effectively for awkwardness, without resort to grammatical logic.[72a] We apparently owe to Blair the nice distinction about "what is called splitting of particles, or separating a preposition from the noun which it governs—always to be avoided."[73] His instance is, "Though virtue borrows no assistance from, yet it may often be accompanied by, the advantages of fortune"; and he remarks, "In such instances, we feel a sort of pain, from the revulsion, or violent separation of two things, which by their nature, should be closely united. We are put to a stand in thought; being obliged to rest for a little on the preposition by itself, which, at the same time, carries no significancy, till it is joined to its proper substantive noun."[74]

18. But the most striking circumstance in this array of censured constructions is that no mention whatever of the "split infinitive" was discoverable, nor was the construction itself observed save once or twice in the authors read.[75] Apparently, it was both a discovery and an aversion of nineteenth century grammarians.

19. *Other examples of logical order.* Robert Baker marked as a very exceptionable departure from logic the

[70]*Rudimnets,* pp. 180 and 182.
[71]*Grammatical Institute,* 1784, p. 85.
[72]*Ibid.,* 1804, p. 97.
[72a]*Reflections,* 1770, pp. 19-20.
[73]Withers, concurring, attributes to the Bishop of London (Lowth) the counsel that "to split prepositions" is vulgar and inelegant, but I have not located either the phrase or the counsel in Lowth. See *Aristarchus,* pp. 290-2.
[74]*Lectures,* 1793 ed., I, 211. Here we have again "particles without meaning" and "nature" appealed to.
[75]See below, Chapter IX, § 11 and XI, 2.

phrase "could neither read nor write";[76] it is "much more
proper to say 'He can neither write nor read,' " since "if he
cannot read, it follows of course that he cannot write."[77]
Withers has the same comment, in substance, in quotations, but
not in Baker's words and without citation, and expresses a
preference for "born and bred" over "bred and born."[78] Webster is similarly meticulous about Addison's "rushing torrents
and descending rains," since "the consequence is placed before
the cause."[79]

20.   No objections apparently were made in the eighteenth
century to an arrangement commonly reprobated by purists
later—illustrated by Swift's "Four last years of the queen,"
Zachary Grey's "your three last Productions . . .,"[80] a title of
Trusler's, "Four first rules of arithmetic," and, from Campbell
himself, "the four first canons" of usage.[81]

21.   *Placing adverbs, particularly* only.   The rules for placing modifiers were of course dictated by a general purpose of
securing greater clarity; but when grammarians came to look
about for actual instances, they rarely confined themselves to
sentences which might actually cause difficulty or misunderstanding in their context, since such sentences are not really
common in experienced writers.   Instead, critics took the usual
short-cut of pitching upon sentences of a fixed type, regardless
of their clarity or lack of clarity.   Sentences containing ab-
verbs like *only* came in handy.   It would take no extensive examination to show that *only* has, in the majority of cases
throughout the Modern English period, in writing as in speech,
occupied the "preverbal position" that it prevailingly occupies
today.[82]   But the following sentences, all criticized in the eighteenth century, are typical of this sort of purism:

[76]*Reflections*, 1770, p. 51.
[77]*Remarks*, 1779, p. 26.
[78]*Aristarchus*, pp. 152-3.
[79]*Dissertations*, 1789, p. 65.
[80]*Free and Familiar Epistle*, 1750, p. 30.
[81]*Philosophy of Rhetoric*, I, 403.
[82]See Harold Palmer, *Grammar of Spoken English*, § 386, p. 184.

The Pretenders to polish have chiefly multiplied abuses.

In Swift's *Proposal,* analyzed in minute detail for almost two pages by Blair (*Lectures,* I, 445-6) and revised.

. . . parted only by a channel 800 Yards wide.

Gulliver—amended to "of 800 Yards only," by Kames, *Elements* II, 58, and Buchanan, *Regular Syntax,* 169.

But "these only devour the Dead, those the Living," in another sentence which Buchanan carries through most vigorously parsing (pp. 202-3), is neither questioned nor amended.

I only spake three words . . . revised to "I spake only . . ."
Lowth, 1763 ed., p. 139 n.

Narrate.—A word only used in Scotland.
Johnson's *Dictionary.*

Not only Jesuits can equivocate. Dryden.

Campbell writes, "A very small alteration in the order gives a proper and unequivocal, though, a prosaic expression of this sense: Jesuits can not only equivocate." *Philosophy* II, 35. [But is this the meaning?]

From Campbell himself:

I shall only add an instance or two . . .
Ibid., I, 452.

. . . the degree of grammatical demerit . . . can only be ascertained by . . .
Ibid., I, 430-1.

Of similar non-parallel structure:

The speaker or writer doth not purpose to display his knowledge in the language, but only to employ . . .
Ibid., I, 431.

That the so-called misplaced *only* may sometimes be misinterpreted can be illustrated in a sentence cited by Withers from Dr. Johnson himself, and in one by Lord Monboddo and one in the Brightland grammar which nobody discovered and corrected:

. . . miseries which the Idler can only conceive.
Withers remarks, "I dare to say he FEELS them."
Aristarchus, 406.

I will only mention another instance.

Origin and Progress, II, 403—followed by a long paragraph, and but one other instance.

The text is what is only [alone] meant to be taught in the schools . . . the notes . . . more difficult enquiries . . .
Grammar of the English Tongue, 1721 ed., Preface, p. vii.

About placing *not,* the eighteenth century was quite free of formula:

Every just Observation does not occur to any one Mind.
Reflections, 1770, Preface, p. iv.

All subjects do not equally require precision.
Blair, *Lectures,* I, 176. See also Chapter IX, §5, below.

All opinions are not received into the language.
Michaelis, p. 2.

These forms were not objected to, and seem perfectly clear.

22. *Placing prepositions at the end.* Of "the preposition . . . separated from the relative which it governs, and joined to the verb at the end of the Sentence, or of some member of it," which Lowth mildly reprehends, he says, "This is an idiom which our language is strongly inclined to," an illustrative stating of the principle. He continues, ". . . the placing of the Preposition before the Relative is more graceful; and agrees much better with the solemn and elevated style."[83] Bayly and Blair treat the problem wholly as a matter of securing forceful effect or pleasing structure; nobody in the eighteenth century appears to have tried hardening this sentence-order into a rule.

23. *Logical resolution.* The procedure for a grammarian who wanted to understand a difficult construction was to turn it about some other way, much as Dryden turned suspected phrases into Latin. This of course has its dangers as a procedure for explanation, and particularly for determination of usage, as illustrated in Baker's analysis of "previously to" and

[83] *Short Introduction,* 1762 ed., pp. 127-8; 1769 ed., p. 162. A marginal comment in the Harvard copy notes the conciseness of the construction in permitting elision of the relative—an advantage Lowth did not note or utilize.

Lowth's of "the rule's being observed,"[84] and the incessant blundering with "concealed grammatical errors."[85] A most remarkable instance of such logical resolution is the following specimen of William Ward's table for "resolving the tenses . . . of any simple verb . . . by the tenses of the Verb 'to be.' " Whether this author was explaining the meaning of the tenses or proposing new forms which he considered more perspicuous is left to the imagination of the reader:

The first person of the tenses themselves		The tense resolved
Second preterit	I have had	I am having had
Pluperfect	I had had	I was having had
Second future	I shall have had	I shall be having had

He also resolves these in a more usual fashion as "I have, had, and shall have been having . . . by considering the state 'having had' as an object of mere memory, i. e., as past and over, and by referring this state to time present by 'I am,' etc.; or by considering the state 'having' as in continuance, and referring it to time ended at present by 'I have been.' "[86] This is offered as an extreme example of the logical treatment of structure in language.

Withers gives a "plain, unerring Rule resolving for [evidently 'for resolving'] verbs and Participles PASSIVE. Prefix IN to the 'present Tense of the Verb' if the present Tense be in Use as a Noun; if not, prefix IN to a synonymous noun. E. G.

You hopED—You were IN Hope
You are DeludED—You are IN Delusion."[87]

He uses this procedure to prove Lowth wrong in his analysis of "I am mistaken."

24. *Tense sequence.* A battle against the defenders of classical analogies who preferred "consistent tenses" was fought by the proponents of tenses that indicate the actual time expressed. Webster censures Priestley for a false consistency

---

[84]See Chapter V, § 14, and Chapter XI, § 15.
[85]See above §§ 4 and 14 of this chapter.
[86]*Essay on Grammar*, 1765, p. 196.
[87]*Aristarchus*, p. 357-8.

here.[88]   Some genuine clarifications of ideas was effected, as of the difference between "made a discovery that there *was*" and "that there is no God,"[89] and of the logical muddle of this sentence from Villiers: "The girl said, if her master would but have let her had money, to have sent . . . she might have been well long ago"—which at any rate gives a very vivid idea of what she actually said.[90]   Priestley did not succeed in formulating the principle for the tense of infinitives after past or perfect verbs, but Campbell is both clear and definite here.[91]   In the meantime there had been a busy citing of the scriptures and the poets, in favor of one or another theory, and as usual a considerable derangement of meter and sentence-movement, by the grammarians.

James Harris uses *says* as a historical present: "The Philosopher thus accosted them—'Enter (says he) boldly . . .' "[92] Withers likewise allows that license to the historian; though he notes that the word is most often unnecessary in well managed narrative, he turns immediately to the more interesting problem of establishing the distinction between *reply* and *rejoin*.[93]

25. *Summary*.   Most of the matters of syntax discussed in this chapter are constructions in which intelligent criticism can be of real value in pointing out more clear, concise, and forceful ways of expressing ideas.   Where the grammarians and rhetoricians failed to be useful here, it was because they believed that good criticism proceeds by minute logical examination of words and phrases taken apart from their context.   It is of course impossible to criticize fruitfully without keeping constantly in view the fact that ideas are usually expressed for genuine purpose of communication, and that the essential first step for the critic is a common-sense attempt to understand what the writer meant.   Aristotle's *Rhetoric* considers in the first two books the gathering and digestion of materials and their adapta-

[88]*Dissertations*, 270-4. See Baker, *Remarks*, 1779, pp. 75-6, 107.
[89]*Campbell*, I, 445-6.
[90]*Priestley*, 1769, p. 127.
[91]*Philosophy* I, 504 ff.
[92]*Hermes*, 1771 ed., p. 8.
[93]*Aristarchus*, 1788, pp. 44-6.

tion to real situations and real audiences. Only on this foundation does it take up the usual problems of structure, choice of words, sentence composition, and the like.[94] "The speech itself, the final utterance, which is the subject of Book III, has thus been approached as the art of adjusting the subject-matter of a given case through the intelligence and emotion of the speaker to the intelligence and emotion of the audience. This is the only book of very specific technique; and it comes last psychologically."[95] Eighteenth-century grammar and rhetoric, on the contrary, like most essays at the subjects since, considered words and sentences apart from actual uses—as it were in a vacuum under the microscope. Thus, what they had to say about syntax—and they of course stated some useful principles—has to be retested in relation to living uses of language—genuine problems of speaking or writing and of understanding. And above all no principles of sentence structure—whether parallelism or order of modifiers or what not—is of much value when stated as an inflexible rule, in the fashion which the eighteenth century developed and handed down to later makers of handbooks. The fruitful use of principles of syntax is likely to be as general counsels for revision, but not as dogmas of "correct and incorrect" use.

---

[94] See Baldwin's *Ancient Rhetoric and Poetic*, Macmillan, 1924, Chapter II, pp. 6-36.
[95] *Ibid.*, p. 12.

CHAPTER VII

VARIOUS LOGICAL CONSIDERATIONS
II. DISCRIMINATIONS IN CHOICE OF WORDS

Let Standard-Authors, thus, like Trophies borne,
Appear more glorious as more hack'd and torn.
And you, my Critics, in the checquer'd Shade,
Admire new Lights thro' Holes yourselves have made.

Duncaid IV, 123-6.

These seeming Minuties are by no Means to be despised, since they contribute to the Intelligibleness of Language.

Robert Baker, *Reflections,* 1770.

CHAPTER VII

VARIOUS LOGICAL CONSIDERATIONS
II. DISCRIMINATIONS IN CHOICE OF WORDS

1. Quite apart from problems of grammar, an industrious criticism and revision of language was concerned with questions of logic in the choice of words. We have seen that the considerations of analogy and differentiation for English grammar were largely a discovery of the eighteenth century itself, and did not have much attention till the last third of the century, following Lowth's first edition in 1762. But verbal criticism was an old and honored occupation, which had risen early in the century into what Johnson described as a "rage for emendation"[1] including incessant subtle distinctions of synonyms and quibbling niceties of diction. The purpose of this is best expressed by Robert Baker: "These seeming Minuties are by no Means to be despised, since they contribute to the Intelligibleness of Language."[2] To what extent they contributed may be judged from the following illustrations.

2. There were, of course, passages of keen and intelligent criticism. Occasional gleams of genuine discernment lightened the blackness even of Bentley's revisions of Milton.[3] His whole performance, indeed, aroused a strong protest. Yet, though Mackail states in a general way that they were inadmissible, he does not quote examples, but is inclined to cloak the erring scholar with faint blame.[4] It is true that Bentley left the lines as they were, only italicizing words he would change and relegating his corrigenda to the margin or

[1]Preface to Shakespeare, p. ix. This orgy is well described in Chapters II and III of Richard Jones' *Lewis Theobald*, New York, Columbia Press, 1919.
[2]*Reflections*, 1770, p. 115.
[3]As of the mixed passage in VI, 391 ff.
[4]"Bentley's Milton." *Proceedings of the British Academy, XI*, Oxford (no date).

the foot of the page. But the remarkable character of his changes, illustrated already by the "absolute construction" which Lowth could not accept, and which even Bentley himself reversed when the poet had written according to the formula he prescribed,[5] makes it seem worth while to give a few samplings of these amendments:[6]

Book II, Line 274 [reduced to the style of a passage from Parliamentary Debates] : "Then, *as was well observ'd,* our Torments may . . . " because "This Argument Mammon steals from Belial's Speech above . . . . to keep just Decorum, he should ascribe it to its true Author. . . . ."

Book II, lines 937f. Bentley wrote, "He had said, that in the *Vacuum Satan* had sunk *Ten thousand Fathom deep,* and now he was hurried aloft *As many Miles.* That's too much, ten thousand Miles to answer to as many *Fathoms* only ; and One Cloud to make such an Explosion. And besides, *Hurried Him,* where the Accent falls upon *Him,* is a poor Close of a Verse. Had he not better have given it thus?

HURL'D *him* BACK *As many* FATHOMS HIGH.

So that his Ascent by the *Cloud* exactly recompens'd his Descent by the *Vacuum.* That was truly an *ill Chance.*"

Book IV, 24-5. "the bitter memorie
Of what he was, what is, and what must be."
Bentley: "What rare Expression have we got here? The Memory of Future? . . . But no doubt, instead of *Memory,* the Author gave it, *The bitter* THEORY.
Theory, Contemplation, Meditation, Consideration."

Book IV, 555. [On "gliding through the Eeven."] "I never heard but here, that the Evening was a Place or Space to *glide* through . . . But it's the Printer's Language: the Author gave it, . . . *through the HEAV'N.*"

Book V, 198. [*"Ye Birds, That* singing *up to* Heaven Gate *ascend.*] The Sky Lark sings as she ascends; perhaps no other Bird. But *to ascend to Heaven Gate,* which *Milton* always places above the Sphere of Fix'd Stars, is outstretch'd beyond Possibility. He gave it thus: *That* SOARING *up to* HEAVENWARD *ascend.*"

[5]Above, Chapter IV, § 5.
[6]These are mainly from Mackail's citations in a footnote, *op. cit.,* p. 9.

These illustrate Bentley's theory of an editor and printer deranging the poem, and his cool assumption of what Milton "gave."

The revision of the last two lines of the poem is no doubt familiar, but it crowns the work. A very long note concludes, "And how can the Expression be justified, *with wand'ring Steps and slow?* Why wand'ring? Erratic Steps? Very improper; when in the Line before, they were *guided by Providence.* And why *Slow?* when even *Eve* profess'd her Readiness and Alacrity for the Journey . . . And why *their solitary Way?* All Words to represent a sorrowful Parting? When even their former Walks in Paradise were as solitary as their Way now: there being no Body besides Them Two, both here and there. Shall I therefore, after so many prior Presumptions, presume at last to offer a Distich, as close as may be to the Author's Words, and entirely agreeable to his Scheme?

> THEN *hand in hand with* SOCIAL *steps their way*
> *Through* EDEN *took,* WITH   HEAV'NLY   COMFORT
> CHEER'D."

Bentley represents so well the spirit of emending that it will be unnecessary to illustrate elaborately its further variations. Goold Brown, more than a century later, wrote, "to CORRECT an erroneous passage, usually demands or implies a knowledge of the author's thought."[6a] But the demand is too often unenforced, both in the eighteenth century and now.

3. By the time of Blair and Campbell the zeal of critics had been diverted from the publication of "corrected editions." The censure against these had been severe; and it was easier and more profitable to compile lists of errors for the instruction of others. Blair in particular felt that great progress in language would result from heed to nice distinctions in meaning. He spent four lectures, spread upon 85 pages of his first volume, in minute criticism of the style of certain numbers of the *Spectator* and of Swift's *Proposal.*

There were two special collections, Robert Baker's *Reflec-*

[6a]*Grammar of English Grammars,* 1851, preface p. 1.

tions on the English Language in the Nature of Vaugelas's Reflections on the French, 1770, and the Reverend John Trusler's *Distinction between Words Esteemed Synonymous in the English Language,* 1783, which acknowledges indebtedness to the *Synonymes François* of the Abbé Girard and draws liberally from him, without quotation marks, in the preface.[7] Trusler was the diligent compiler of such varied treatises as *The Way to be Rich and Respectable, Principles of Politeness, The Four First Rules of Arithmetic,* and a *Compendium of Sacred Writings,* used by Baker and others as a quarry of exceptionable expressions. In his second edition of the synonyms book, "with additions and amendments" including the expunging of some distinctions he had concluded were trifling. Trusler makes carefully minute distinctions among such words as *abandon, forsake, leave, relinquish, desert,* and *quit* (reminding one of Touchstone and William) ; *people* ("very general") and *persons; ill* ("health little impaired") and *sick* ("greatly diseased")—by no means the modern British usage or that reported by Webster;[8] *choose* and *make choice of* (the latter for persons only). He does not deal with such stock examples of later hand-books as *may* and *can, mutual,* and—as might be inferred from his title—*between* and *among.*[8a]

4. Examples of this sort of verbal nicety could be multiplied without limit, but to no purpose. A few may be instructive as showing the roots in those times of strictures still common. John Clarke censures the grammarian Fenning for objecting to the contraction in "I'll light my pipe"; but he adds, "we light the tobacco, not the pipe. Such kind of expressions are

---

[7]Campbell had cited some of the Abbé Girard's observations, and Blair noted the need of a similar book in English.

[8]If Trusler was right in this statement, the shift in meaning must have occurred very quickly indeed. In Johnson's *Dictionary,* meaning (2) is "ill in the stomach." Webster, in 1789, notes the distinction now restricting the word in England: "The modern English . . . say a man is *ill;* and confine *sick* to express the idea of a nausea in the stomach. The English are wrong. . . . *Ill* is a contraction of evil; and denotes a moral disorder." (*Dissertations,* p. 389). But the probability is that Trusler was romancing about *sick* as Webster clearly was about *ill.*

[8a]Mrs. Piozzi produced in 1794 *The British Synonymy,* which opens with the same distinctions of *abandon, forsake,* etc., as Trusler's.

so familiar . . . to object . . . bordering on the pedantic."[9]   A similar ellipsis is rated, among a great many others no whit more obscure, by Campbell: "He talks all the way upstairs to a visit," from *Spectator No. 2,* must be "as he walks upstairs to make a visit."[10]   Of Addison's "pure limpid stream, when foul with stains," Campbell writes, "A stream may doubtless be at one time limpid and at another foul, which is all that the author meant; but we cannot properly call it a *pure limpid* stream, when it is *foul with stains.* So much for those improprieties which involve in them some absurdity."[11]   Of "I cannot remember that I ever spoke three sentences together in my whole life," from *Spectator No. 1,* he notes solemnly that the author means of course *successively,* and that "If such a use of the word be improper in one case, it is so in every case."[12]   The insistence upon such generalization was extreme through all this period.

5.   Campbell indeed remarks of precision, which was the aim of both the grammarians and the word-choice logicians, that "though the want [of it] exposes the writer to much censure, the possession hardly entitles him to any praise."[13]   He did not, however, question the worth of any such censure passed by the most meticulous of his predecessors, but as we have seen, was as extreme as the worst in this.   In 1807, we find Webster remarking upon No. 50 of the *Rambler* that the learned author had used *obstructed* falsely for *deterred,* "for danger operates on the mind by *moral influence;* not by *physical powers*";[14] also that "discernible taste or smell is used by mistake," decause *"Discern* is applied to the *eye* and to the *mind,* but never to the sense of *feeling, taste,* or *smell."*   Yet he gives two quotations in which it is actually so used, and himself speaks, on the following pages, of "palpable nonsense," and of errors at which "the ears

Rational Spelling Book, 1796, pp. 80-1.
[10]*Philosophy* II, 10-11.
[11]*Philosophy,* I, 484.   Webster's similar comments on lines of Addison's are equally interesting.   Above Chapter VI, § 19.
[12]*Ibid.,* 463.
[13]*Philosophy,* I, 408-9.
[14]*Letter to Dr. Ramsay,* 1807, p. 15.

of a correct scholar cannot but revolt."[15]   That the
avowed champions of usage, Campbell and Webster, should go
to these extremes of logical purism illustrates clearly how little
adherence the oft-quoted usage doctrine of Horace and Quintilian really secured in the eighteenth century.

The sole grammarian to protest against these futile refinements appears to have been Horne Tooke. *"Relative* has indeed, within my memory, by a ridiculous affectation of false
and unfounded accuracy crept forward into improper use, to
the exclusion of *Relation.* Certain precise gentlemen will no
longer permit us to call our kindred our Relations: No, but
—our *Relatives.* . . . [16] But, I believe, they will be as little able
to justify their innovation, as Sir Thomas More would have
been to explain the foundation of his ridiculous distinction between NAY and NO, and between YEA and YES."[17] But
Tooke's remonstrance seems to have been moved partly by his
attempted etymology of *-ive,* with which this usage did not
accord.

   6. *Distinctions between verbs.*   The usual distinction of
may and *can* was first observed in Johnson's Dictionary,
1755;[18] *may* means "right, lawfulness, or possibility" and
can physical "sufficiency of power or strength."

   The distinction between *hung* and *hanged* was first formulated and, typically, formulated in various ways, during this
period.   The early grammars give only *hung* in the preterite
and past participle.   Priestley first states the rule that "different participles of the same verb are sometimes used in different
senses," as "the coat is *hung* up, the man is *hanged.*"[19] But
oddly enough, Priestley's catalog of irregular verbs gives the
"asterism," indicating regular formation also, to the preterite
of *hang* only, not to the participle.[20] Lowth has a different suggestion: "This verb, [hang] when Active, may perhaps be

[15]*Ibid.,* pp. 16-7.
[16]Johnson defined *relations* as *kindred,* without censure.
[17]*Diversions of Purley,* II, p. 495-6. The note gives a long quotation from
the *Confutacion of Tyndale.*
[18]But Johnson defined *may* "to have power" and "to be possible."
[19]*Rudiments,* 1769, p. 125.
[20]*Ibid.,* p. 25.

most properly used in the Regular Form, when Neuter, in the Irregular . . . But in the Active sense of furnishing a room with draperies the Irregular Form prevails. The Vulgar Translation of the Bible uses only the Regular Form."[21]

Hornsey has a distinction sometimes heard today among people of somewhat rustic gentility—that between *want* and *wish*.[22] Most of his examples are credited to Blair, including the distinction between *weary* and *fatigue,* noted in Johnson's *Dictionary.*

7. Baker, like Johnson, noted that "flee is a Word too much neglected," since even "our best Authors do not scruple to employ [*flew*]"; yet it seems "a Deformity in the Language." When it means to *flee,* he insists "the preterperfect Tense [apparently preterite and past participle] is *fled,* but the Participle present is *flying.*"[23] Withers has a quite different theory: "In the Opinion of Dr. Johnson, a Distinction was formerly observed by restricting Motion with Wings to—FLY—and motion with Feet to—FLEE. But, in Fact this Distinction never prevailed." He then, from three passages of Scripture, deduces his own distinction. Both words imply MOTION, but the Modes of Motion differ as an *Attack* from a *Retreat* . . . . This Distinction ought always to be observed in FLEW and FLED. As to FLEE it will not be noticed if you use—FLY— for both Purposes."[24] In this last he agrees with Baker.

The usual distinctions of *lie* and *lay, sit* and *set* were commonly given where these words were considered, but without attention to anomalous forms like *setting forth, laying in wait,* and the rest, where the easy differentiae do not apply. Baker's curious discussion of misuses of *lay* and *set,* in which he suspects French influence, extends to the forms *overlay* and "laid about him lustily." It is a pity that the laying and the setting hen did not come under his observation.[25] Dr. Johnson,

[21]*Short Introduction,* 1769, pp. 101-2, *note.* The note is not in the 1762 edition, but appears on p. 85 of that of 1763.
[22]*Short Grammar,* 1793, pp. 98-9.
[23]*Reflections,* 1770 ed., pp. 29-30; *Remarks,* 1779, pp. 15-6.
[24]*Aristarchus,* pp. 210-11.
[25]*Reflections,* 1770, pp. 32-3, 36, and 44.

on the other hand, admits *to lay for* without censure in the *Dictionary*. It was reserved for the purism of the nineteenth century to brand "the sun sets" as "quite indefensible."[26]

8. *Distinctions between prepositions.* An extraordinary elaboration is devoted to rules on uses of prepositions. Some two pages in the small type of the notes of Lowth's *Short Introduction*[27] are devoted to various misuses of these particles, from Bacon to Bolingbroke; Swift fares particularly hard at his hands and at Blair's for this sort of logical error,[28] in phrases like "reduce to their power" and "fell into their cognizance." And the panels of violators continue to grow, till in the eclectic Murray there are more than five pages illustrating mischoice of prepositions alone, from practically every famous English writer.[29]

The utmost precision was reached in the distinction of prepositions expressing place and those used only for motion. Baker gives the common rule for *in* and *into*,[30] and adds *up* and *down* for use with verbs of motion and *above, below* for place.[31] "I get, go, or come *up* or *down* stairs; I am *above* or *below* stairs." Baker allows *be* for motion in the phrase "was down stairs in a moment." He says, "These Distinctions have Nothing finical or affected in them. Most People make them mechanically: and such as confound the Words in Question . . . cannot be said to talk good English."[32]

9. The currently taught distinction between *beside* and *besides* does not seem to have been remarked in the period here considered, and Lowth clearly uses *beside* for *in addition*

[26]Richard Grant White, cited by Fitzedward Hall in *Recent Exemplifications of False Philology*, 1872, p. 109 *note* 2.
[27]1762 ed., pp. 163-6.
[28]Blair's *Lectures*, I, 449-56, analysis of Swift's *Proposal for Correcting.*
[29]*English Grammar*, 1809 ed., pp. 279-84.
[30]Johnson defines *in* "(4) noting immediate entrance," "(5) into any place." It is curious that in a quite elaborate diagram of the meanings of prepositions of place given in Bishop Wilkins' *Essay on a Real Character* (1668), *into* is given for motion, *within* for place; *in* does not appear. The diagram is repeated in Tooke's *Diversions of Purley*, I, 368-9.
[31]Dr. Johnson defines "*above*, (1) to a higher place; in a higher place," —1785 ed.
[32]*Reflections*, 1770, pp. 15 and 38-40; *Remarks*, 1779, pp. 20-1.

to :[32a] "Beside the foregoing, there are several others." Johnson's *Dictionary* says, "*Between* is properly used of two and *among* of more; but perhaps this accuracy is not always preserved."[33] It certainly was not in the title to Trusler's work, *Distinctions between Words Esteemed Synonymous,* for he distinguishes meticulously between all the members of groups of as many as nine words. The actual usage, as recorded in dictionaries today, is not that of either Johnson or the handbooks. Baker insists upon another familiar distinction, and adds to it: "Some very incorrect speakers would say 'a statue between every pillar.' . . . To be quite clear we must say 'between every two *proximate* pillars.' "

10. Lowth notes, "*Lesser,* says Mr. Johnson, is a barbarous corruption of *less,* formed by the vulgar from the habit of terminating comparisons in *er.* He cites Addison's vulgar error in using it, and adds, "*Worser* sounds much more barbarous, only because it has not been so frequently used," giving examamples, however, from Shakespeare and Dryden.[34] Baker brings up another point which has become familiar by repetition. "Less," says Baker, is "most commonly used in speaking of a Number; where I should think *Fewer* would do better . . . not only more elegant . . . but more strictly proper."[35]

11. The comparison of supposedly incomparable adjectives like *chief, extreme, round, perfect,* "already superlative in signification," was seriously debated. Of the double comparative and superlative, Lowth admits that "poetry is in possession of these two improper superlatives, and may be indulged in the use of them," and even approves strongly of "the Double Superlative *most highest* . . . a phrase peculiar to the Old Vulgar Translation of the Psalms; where it acquires a singular propriety from the Subject to which it is applied, the Supreme Being, who is *higher than the highest.*"[36] But even thus divagation from strict logic was the subject of serious concern.

[32a]*Short Introduction,* 1767, p. 51.
[33]*Dictionary,* 1755.
[34]*Short Introduction,* 1762, p. 42, *note.*
[35]*Reflections,* 1770, p. 55; *Remarks,* 1779, p. 28.
[36]*Short Introduction,* 1762, p. 42, *note.*

Mennye, after failing to discover a beauty in it by the route of classifying it as Catachresis, Oxymoron, or any of "'the classes of the flowers" of rhetoric—he has ten pages of such classes—concludes that both grammar and rhetoric have cast it out; it "therefore ought to be rejected." Finally *"maxime altissimus* would be rediculous," which clinches the point.[37]

12. Robert Baker objects to *propose* for *purpose,* remarking, "I don't see that the Substantive should have better Quarter than the Verb,"[38] and tells us that "to understand her meaning" means "to know the meaning of her meaning," which would be absurd.

But, as in his authoritarianism, so in his logic, Baker's strictures were promptly capped by those of his reviewers. They did not object to his corrections of other authors, but with the same logical thoroughness they riddled his own expressions. "He speaks of reading a Latin author with any *sort* of pleasure, and thus confounds kind with degree;[39] . . . he uses absolute terms relatively, 'however difficult or *impossible,* says he, it might be.' The impropriety of using the word *impossible* with *however* in this sentence is the more gross, as the word *difficult* fixes it in its absolute meaning."[40]   Similarly, Campbell remarks of a sentence of Shaftesbury's, containing "if peradventure he can . . .": "The adverb *peradventure,* expressing a degree of evidence or credibility, cannot regularly be construed with the hypothetical conjunction *if,"* and likewise for "if thou certainly return," from the Bible translation.[41]

13. It should not be supposed from the selection of illustrations in this chapter that merely purposeless revision was intended by any of the critics discussed.   Each one doubtless

[37]*English Grammar,* 1785, pp. 78-9.
[38]*Ibid.,* p. 43.   So does Withers, explaining that "PURPOSE is not dependent on external Will," and ridiculing Dr. Blair for two "errors" in this use.
[39]This distinction Priestley gives: ". . *Sort* seems to refer to a number of things, and . . *Kind* seems to be more proper when the quality of one single thing is spoken of" (*Rudiments,* 193).
[40]*Monthly Review XLV* o. s. (August, 1771), p. 95.
[41]*Philosophy,* I, 452-3.

felt that, through urging precision of expression in words, he was waging a campaign for greater clarity. They all speak constantly of the usefulness of exact meanings: "Different Meanings ought undoubtedly to be expressed in different Words; without which, the Intention of Language is not answered."[42] This intention of language it was their earnest purpose to help fulfill. But their logic was based upon the supposition that clarity of meaning is to be attained, and that understanding is in fact secured, by detailed logical classification and definition of the words, one by one, which compose discourse. Their endeavors were of a piece with the usual beginning at teaching the vernacular with letters and syllables, and the continuing preoccuption with single words and detailed structures. This false method still retards the pace of reading in our schools until an understanding of only slightly difficult matter is impossible to most high-school students. A totally new conception of language, based upon the psychology of reading and comprehension, was necessary before such conceptions could be succcessfully attacked; we now have the materials for such attack, and are making a beginning at better procedures in our schools. But the distinctions of words in most handbooks and the definition-chasing in many literature classes still reflect the eighteenth-century view, and are frequently as meaningless and obstructive as the examples cited here.

14. *The reaction.* Of course the logical emenders do not represent all the criticism of the century. As has been stated, there was a strong reaction against them in the century itself. The absurdity of much of Warburton's Shakespearian criticism has never been more sharply appreciated than in its own period by Thomas Edwards, who supplied the "Canons of Criticism and Glossary" which Warburton had promised but failed to provide.[43]

The clarity of this contemporary view may be judged from

---

[42]Baker, *Reflections*, 1779, p. 60.
[43]*A Supplement to Mr. Warburton's Edition of Shakespear* . . . anonymously published in 1748, and repeatedly later with the author's name and much supplementary material.

the following speciments of Edwards' Canons, which he fully illustrated from Warburton's emendations:

> Canon I. A Professed Critic has a right to declare, that his Author wrote whatever he thinks he should have written.[44]
> Canon II. He has a right to alter any passage which he does not understand. [There are nearly eight pages of illustrations for this, including the revision of "such small deer."]
> Canon IV. Where he does not like an expression, and yet cannot mend it, he may abuse his author for it.
> Canon VI. As every author is to be corrected into all possible perfection, and of that perfection the profess'd critic is the sole judge; he may alter any word or phrase which does not want amendment, or which *will do,* provided he can think of any thing, which he imagines *will do better.*
> Canon IX. He may interpret his author so as to make him mean directly contrary to what he says.
> Canon XI. He may make foolish amendments or explanations, and refute them, only to enhance the value of his critical skill.[45]

Later editions added further Canons and illustrations—such as that the critic, since his sole purpose is to show his critical skill, may change any passage whatever, whether or not his amendments make any sense. Severe as all this is, it seems well supported by the examples given. As Cibber remarked of *meaning,* in his *Familiar Epistle* to Warburton (1752), "The Critic seems to have but little of *his own,* and never gets into another Man's—yet He keeps going on, and blunders round about a Subject, as benighted."

Another piece of acute criticism is Archibald Campbell's *Lexiphanes,* in which Dr. Johnson, the "word-shiner," is relieved of polysyllabic verbosity by a device employed by Lucian, Rabelais, and Jonson, and is given very plain and wholesome advice about writing. The parody of his style at its worst is excellent, and the author develops sensible principles of organization, choice of words, and revision. Best of all are the passages in which he gives advice to Dr. Johnson:

> Though I am sensible that herein I differ from some writers, for whose authority I have the highest veneration, yet I cannot help

[44]Recalling Bentley's fictitious "editor" of Milton.
[45]*Op. cit.,* 4-44 *passim.*

thinking a living language stands in small need either of a grammar or dictionary. The existence of either is plainly impossible before people have begun both to speak well and to write well. While they continue to do so, they are needless; and after a bad taste is once introduced, they will rather do hurt than service, at least if we are to judge from your [Johnson's] writings. The Syntax and choice of words are best left to be learned from good authors and polite company. . . . Above all things, sacrifice to the graces and perspicuity, both of which you have hitherto neglected, especially the former.

Lexiphanes, pp. 141-3.

. . . the main excellence of a style consists in the choice of the words; the next in their order or arrangement; and what ought to be considered in the last place, is the grammatical construction, for none but a Pedant will be offended with a trivial slip of that sort, unless it be attended with obscurity.

How it has happened I know not, but this order is now quite reversed. You especially are faultless with respect to grammar, even to a degree of pedantry; you have not omitted a single *who, that, what,* or *which* . . . whereas you bring [personification "of every vice and virtue, of every passion and affection"] in, at every turn, a most eminent proof of the utter corruption of your taste.

Ibid., pp. 136-7.

We know, from the story of Dr. Johnson talking with a street boy, that he was capable of perfectly simple colloquial and idiomatic expression;[46] that he did not make more use of it was apparently the result of the extreme neo-classic theory of style which runs through the grammars and rhetorics of this period. Against this, Archibald Campbell's satire is an excellent diatribe. Another writer who made clear and useful observations, as well as some very stupid ones, was Lawrence Temple, author of the *Sketches,* 1758. Even the worst of the grammarians and rhetoricians have shrewd and useful comments scattered among their multitudes of pseudo-logical observations, if one has the patience to look them out. But for the most part the eighteenth century built up an elaborate critical apparatus for inhibiting expression, upon false theories of the nature of thought and of communication.

[46]Boswell's *Life,* Birkbeck Hill ed., Oxford, 1887, IV, 184-5. A different idea of Johnson resolving always to talk his best is given in Volume II, p. 323.

CHAPTER VIII

EIGHTEENTH-CENTURY OPINIONS OF THE HISTORICAL STUDY OF LANGUAGE

. . . though he is for justifying this, and the like phrases, by having recourse to the Saxon; which I should apprehend there is not occasion to do any more than to the Hebrew . . . or to the Latin.

Anselm Bayly, *Plain and Complete Grammar*, 1772.

CHAPTER VIII

EIGHTEENTH-CENTURY OPINIONS OF THE HISTORICAL STUDY OF LANGUAGE

1. The very shadowy and inexact nature of eighteenth-century knowledge of the history of English was equaled by the contempt commonly expressed for such study in that period. Bayly, whom we have noted as having some conception of the nature and extent of changes in language, had nevertheless no idea of the value of studying such changes. He agrees with Lowth in accepting *wo is me* as English, but adds "though he is for justifying this, and the like phrases, by having recourse to the Saxon; which I should apprehend there is not occasion to do any more than to the Hebrew, of which 'well is thee' is a strict translation; or the Latin, *bene est tibi.*"[1]

Similarly, Michaelis[2] writes concerning the proposal for an Academy that ordering the language is "a task for classical scholars alone," and calls for the services also of "original geniuses" if it is to be respected in proposing "standards of purity and elegance." He has an excellent passage also on the dangers and abuses of etymology, to be noted later; but it is clear that he did not imagine any contribution toward solving such problems could be got from the history of the English language itself and of its Germanic ancestors.

Murray, noting the respect felt by some critics for "the Saxon tongue," observes that "if their opinions were adopted and reduced to practice, our language would be disorganized, and many of its rules and principles involved in obscurity." Etymological deductions, he is sure, may certainly be pushed

---

[1]*Plain and Complete Grammar*, 1772, p. 71. See Walpole's opinion of the Saxon tongue, above, Chapter IV, § 3.
[2]*Dissertations*, 1769, p. 5.

too far, and valued too much, "though within proper limits they may be highly conducive to perspicuous and accurate language. . . . We . . . must be allowed the privilege of forming our own laws, and adapting them to our wants and convenience."[3] This is very sensible observation; it overlooks only one major consideration: In thus forming and adapting laws, particularly in a period of reverence for false and misleading analogies from more remotely related languages, a knowledge of the history and development of English itself out of its Germanic ancestry would have been highly valuable in preventing baseless, dogmatic conclusions.

2.   As we have noted, the materials for such study were already at hand, in Hickes' and the Elstobs' grammars and collections of Germanic texts, and in more popularly available form in the reprints of a considerable body of English texts from 700 A. D. to Spenser, in Greenwood's *Essay,* 1711, and from Alfred's *Boethius* onward in Johnson's *Dictionary,* 1755. The method of study, as Henshall notes in his collections,[4] had been to translate the Saxon documents into Latin and comment on them roundabout through the classical languages. Henshall himself believed in such wild etymologies as the appropriate derivation of *ladies* from *love-dys;* and like Webster and others he overvalued the guerilla forays into the histories of words which Horne Tooke prosecuted with zeal.

Tooke's *Winged Words,* or *The Diversion of Purley*[5] is a discursive study in two volumes, backed by copious exhibits of material in various stages of the development of English, but with no sort of critical method for dealing with the materials. The documents were ready for the scientific researches which were to place the Germanic languages in their proper relations and establish the science of comparative philology; but during the eighteenth century, no adequate scientific procedure of criticism and comparative study was even well begun.

[3]Murray, 1809 ed., pp. 190-1, *passim.*
[4]*The Saxon and English Languages Reciprocally Illustrative of Each Other,* 1798.
[5]The editions of 1786 and 1806 were consulted.

A typical example of Horne Tooke's mixture of penetration and ignorance is given quite clearly in the following quotation, sound in its view of the late coming and the huge difficulties of scientific grammar, wholly in accord with the ideas of the time in its assumption that forms not readily parsed are anomalies to be rooted out by grammarians, not phenomena to be observed, accounted for, and for the most part let alone:

> But thus it is, that when grammar comes at length (for its application is always late) to be applied to a language; some long preceding corruption causes a difficulty; ignorance of the corruption gives rise to some ingenious system, to account for these words, which are considered as original and not corrupted. Succeeding ingenuity and heaps of misplaced learning increase the difficulty, and make the error more obstinate, if not incurable.[6]

3. *Lord Monboddo as a historian of language.* Lord Monboddo's *Origin and Progress of Language,* 1774, is an attempt at systematic treatment of the entire subject, in six large volumes. The work was regarded highly; the author of the article on "Grammar" in the Philadelphia (Dobson's, 1795) edition of the *Encyclopaedia* speaks of its "exquisitely learned author," and brackets him with James Harris, author of *Hermes.* Withers and Horne Tooke, on the contrary, attack him sharply; the latter constructed the word "monboddizes" to signify "conveys nothing in an ingenius manner," and recommended reasoning directly contrary to Monboddo as a way to be "right . . . in almost everything . . . he has advanced."[7]

Some account of the *Origin and Progress* may sufficiently determine its value so far as it touches the problem of correctness. Monboddo has a passage, quoting Aristotle, on the significations of words as determined "only by institution . . . that is, convention or agreement,"[8] and he attempts to follow the reasoning of Locke. Evidently he had read several accounts of primitive languages in the *Jesuit Relations* and other accounts of travel. He then goes on to describe the

[6]*Diversions of Purley,* 1806 ed., I, 248.
[7]*Ibid.,* I, 72 and II, 543.
[8]*Origin and Progress,* 1774, II, 194-221.

nature of primitive languages: There was no art or regularity, no standard, or anything fixed or established; they were differently spoken by different families or tribes—he credits reports of separate languages of Carib men and women—and constantly changing; their words were long and "full of vowels and quantity";[9] there were different words for great bear and strong bear, for your hut and my hut and little hut, for tenses, plurals, comparatives, where these were expressed, etc.; primitive languages had no connectives or "substantive verbs."[10] In this, and particularly the last two points, will be recognized several true particulars probably never presented in English previously. As to the kinship of languages, Monboddo imagined a world family, including not only the Indo-Germanic group as we now conceive it, but the languages of both the Caribs and the Eskimos, related to the Celtic; the Hebrew and Egyptian he considered akin to the Latin, "a dialect of Greek."

4. Even so little scientific method as Monboddo and Tooke possessed, and a little study of the documents available, might have saved eighteenth-century and later grammarians many foolish statements. J. Johnson censures Greenwood for explaining the irregular comparisons of adjectives by borrowing from other languages, since these likewise have irregular forms.[11] But he himself considers the plural children "an imitation of the Dutch plural."[12] Wallis' contention that *least* ought to be written *lest,* as a contraction of *lessest,* runs through several of the grammars; Lowth even proposes writing the conjunction *lest* with an *a,* for distinction.[13] Lowth also notes the irregular plurals "antiently *sowen, cowen,* now always pro-

---

[9]This point particularly excited Withers' rage, as it contradicted the neat scheme for primitive languages previously assumed, of regular monosyllables as in Hebrew; Withers writes of one of Monboddo's examples, "If this be a PRIMITIVE Word, let us be thankful that our Language is grown Old." (*Aristarchus,* 221).

[10]Monboddo, Vol. I, Book Three, Chapter V, pp. 510-20.

[11]*Royal and Universal Standard Dictionary,* 1762, p. 14.

[12]*Ibid.,* p. 20. He follows Wallis and Greenwood here.

[13]*Short Introduction,* 1763, p. 61, *note;* not in the 1762 edition.

nounced and written *swine, kine.*"[14]   George Harris laments
that "the antient regular Words *knowed, falled, rised,*" etc.,
"can . . . never be again introduced."[15]

5. Dr. Johnson, followed by Lowth, Campbell, and the
rest, correctly derived the constructions *methinks,* "wo is me,"
and "wo worth the day" from the "Saxon," and Lowth reprehends the Translator who tried an amendment to "well is he,"
and Addison for *methoughts.*[16]   Says Campbell, "It would not
be easy to conjecture what hath misled some writers so far as
to make them adopt the uncouth term *methoughts,* in contempt alike of usage and of analogy, and even without any
colourable pretext that I can think of, for *thoughts* is no part
of the verb at all."[17]   Baker, who was off the main stream of
this criticism, having seen Dr. Johnson's *Dictionary* only short-
ly before his first edition was printed in 1770, and Lowth's
grammar not until 1779, considered "write me often," "write
each other every week" "very barbarous . . .   The preposition is absolutely necessary."[18]   He adds the sting of low-caste
imputation, "often used, especially by people in trade."

6.   Other attempts to regulate the language in ignorance of
its history were: the proposals to restrict *that* as a relative to
things, and even to discredit it altogether as a relative pronoun,[19]
and to hold *whose* as the genitive of *who* only; the objection
to the illogical misagreement of *it* in "it was these," and "'twas
two or three . . . ," and even to "a few men," "many a man";
the attempts to regulate the expression of the negative by Latin
rule; the discussions of number in nouns like *pains* and *means,*
and of forms like "he *need* not and *dare* not"; most of the

---

[14]*Short Introduction,* 1762, p. 23-4, *note* 2.   Yet in the note immediately
following he describes the German umlaut ("change into diphthongs with
e") of *o, a,* and *u,* and succeeding that cites *mys, lys, teth, fet, ges,* as
Saxon plurals.

[15]*Observations on the English Language,* 1752, p. 24.

[16]*Short Introduction,* 1762, pp. 131-2 and *note.*   See Temple's comment,
below, Chapter IX, § 10.

[17]*Philosophy* I, 496.

[18]*Reflections,* 1770 ed., pp. 2-3; *Remarks,* 1779, p. 1.

[19]"The Humble Petition of Who and Which," *Spectator No. 78,* May 30,
1711.   This idea appears as late as 1752 in the *Observations on the English
Language,* which seems to have furnished Lowth and others with a number
of their ideas.

tinkering with regularization, by analogy or differentiation, of irregular verbs; and the attempts to distinguish fully between adverbs and adjectives and other parts of speech. All these have been discusssed in previous chapters or will be considered at large in Chapters XI and XII.

7. The question of possessive derivation, however, forms so good an illustration of general ignorance of the simplest facts of the history of English that it may be told at this place. Addison sometimes used the Middle-English invention of a variant possessive form, "Ulysses his bow," and he specifically stated that the "single letter (s) on many occasions does the office of the whole word, and represents the *his* and *her* of our forefathers."[20] George Harris, accepting this explanation, wrote, "I need not tell you this *s* displeases me . . . when wrote at length it is ungrammatical, and can not be translated. . . . A Petition to the Gracious Majesty of the King would in a little time sound as easy as . . . to the King's Most Gracious Majesty." Moreover, in *world's sense, queen's birthday,* and *men's actions* the substitution of *his* makes nonsense, as in *ours, theirs, yours;* but here it "cannot easily be avoided." Yet *"this's being done* would mark a man of no education. . . . In short, *of* ought always to be exprest, for it is the only true sign of the genitive case in English words."[21]

Robert Baker likewise commented severely on the illogical absurdity of writing "that woman's estate" and "these men's properties," since these were in his view contractions of "woman his," "men his"; yet he himself wrote *it's* commonly for the possessive without, apparently, considering that this must mean "it his." Just before the publication of his first edition, he got through a circulating library the abridgement of Johnson's *Dictionary.* He was shaken, but not dislodged from his position, by Johnson's argument and his reference to the Saxon; Baker quotes the relevant passages, leaving blanks for the words in Old English character, which he admits he does not understand. He continues, concerning Dr.

[20]*Spectator, No. 135.*
[21]*Observations on the English Language,* 1752, p. 22.

Johnson's statement that *"his* cannot be understood."   "Here I am afraid Mr. Johnson pays the world an undeserved compliment.   I apprehend that, on the contrary, nothing of this sort can be too preposterous for men to be guilty of."[22]   He gives five pages of the preface of his 1779 edition to this question, ending with a note: that he is inclined to alter his opinion "after seeing what the *Short Introduction* says."   But his argument and "Reflection No. 104" on this subject nevertheless stand.[23]

8. *The Golden Age of the language.*   Already in the eighteenth century, writers were come to lamenting the decline of English from a better estate in the past.   It would be most significant and interesting if we had the comments on this same subjected by cultivated Anglo-Saxon scholars of the tenth and succeeding centuries.   During the sixteenth and seventeenth, glances were cast forward toward a better language in the process of becoming.   But we find Bayly in 1772 noting that "nothing can exceed the beauty of periods in our old writers Askam and Hooker."   This coincides with Swift's opinion, that "the period, wherein the English tongue received most improvement, I take to commence with the beginning of Queen Elizabeth's reign, and to conclude with the great rebellion in forty-two."   The Restoration period he considered altogether bad—debasing the language through "ignorance and caprice," and the Court influence was in his view the root of worse evil.[24]

That this was not the consensus of writers is indicated by the fact that Buchanan, Sheridan, Monboddo,[25] and Webster[26] place the *Augustan* period of English in the Restoration or the Queen Anne period.   Priestley specifically calls this the "classical period" of the language.[27]   This begins to sound very familiar.

---

[22]*Reflections,* 1770, pp. 104-5 and preface pp. v-xii.
[23]Baker, *Remarks,* 1779, preface pp. vii-xii, *passim.*
[24]*Proposal for Correcting,* 1712, pp. 17-18.
[25]Preface to *Dictionary,* 1785 ed., p. 6; *Origin and Progress* V, 242-53.
[26]*Letter on the Errors of English Grammar,* 1798, p. 16,
[27]*Rudiments,* 1769 ed. preface, p. xi,

Probably the first use of *classical* as applied to English was in Leonard Welsted's "Dissertation concerning the State of Poetry" (1724).[28] Strangely enough, its reference is prospective:

> It is not, unless I mistake, much more than a Century, since *England* first recover'd out of something like Barbarism, with respect to its State of Letters and Politeness: The great rude Writers of our Nation, in early Times, did indeed promise what the *English* Genius would one Day be capable of, when the Refinement of our Language, and other Improvements, might afford favourable Opportunities for the exerting of it; and at the Restoration it was, that Poetry and the polite Arts began to spring up: In the reign of *William* the Third, the Founder of *English* Liberty, they acquir'd a great Strength and Vigour, and have continued to thrive, gradually, down almost to our Times . . . May it not . . . be reasonably hop'd, that the Peace, the Happiness, the universal Quiet and Tranquillity . . . may, in Time, and under just Encouragements, bring them to that *Standard* of Perfection, which denominates a Classical Age?[29]

Likewise Godwin, near the end of the century, wrote his "Essay on English Style" "to shew that the English language was never in so high a state of purity and perfection as in the present reign. . . ."[30]

But the conviction that the Golden Age was irrevocably past and the language suffering constant degradation, was the most common and positive idea in the eighteenth century. William Ward remarks, "Mr. Addison says, that the English language sunk under Milton. [He gives no citation.] So would the Greek language have sunk under Homer, if he had made an epic poem on Milton's subject."[31] Monboddo likewise remarks that "Milton's English Attick is now reckoned uncouth and pedantic."[32] But Milton's "Attick" is of course a little aside from the main current of development. More to the point is Monboddo's sure proof that the language has grown

---

[28]Reprinted in W. H. Durham's *Critical Essays of the XVIIIth Century* (Yale Press, 1915), pp. 355-95.

[29]*Ibid*, pp. 357-8.

[30]In *The Enquirer*, 1797, pp. 369-70. Cited by Fitzedward Hall in *Modern English*, 1873, p. 291 *note*.

[31]*Essay on Grammar*, 1765, p. 291.

[32]*Origin and Progress*, V, 253.

corrupt since the Restoration period, in the fact that Lowth gives no examples of false English from Wilkins, Shaftesbury, and Harris. This, incidentally, leaves Monboddo little standing room for a position he has just previously assumed: "Our best authors are guilty of barbarisms and solecisms through hurry and inattention; but such frequent and repeated blunders as Lowth has cited could not have proceeded but from absolute ignorance of the grammatical art."[33] It was noted that the earlier great writers had Latin grammar to direct them.

Buchanan notes that "the prose writings of Swift and Addison are the best Models for forming the Style of Youth, by writing Exercises from them. . . . No one equals Swift in adjusting his language to his Subject."[34] He quotes praise to the same effect from Lord Kames. All this accords somewhat awkwardly with the use Buchanan and the rest make of these same writers as examples of the breach of all their grammatical rules.

9. *Restoration of past forms.* These opinions are sufficient to account for the very earnest way in which the grammarians and rhetoricians, including Campbell in despite of his doctrine of "present use," hold hard to dying forms of speech, as the late glories of a receding golden age. Especially notable is the care with which Lowth and Baker[35] and Murray insist on the *-st* forms of verbs agreeing with *thou,* and censure most of the poets for their immemorial and constant neg· lect of this shibboleth and for mixing *thou* and *you.* Pope is censured as "not a little faulty in this particular," apparently from a predilection for the sound of verses. But, as Horne Tooke remarks, "the muses (as I have heard Mrs. Peachum

---

[33] *Ibid.*, II, 495-6. Dryden himself, where he had anything good to say of the English language, placed the Golden Age very near his own day, noting that "Shakespeare's language is likewise a little obsolete," and that the writers of the former age "can produce nothing so courtly writ, or which expresses so much the conversation of a gentleman, as Sir John Suckling; nothing so even, sweet and glowing, as Mr. Waller," etc. (Wyld, *Hist. Mod. Colloq. Eng.*, p. 152).

[34] *Regular English Syntax*, 1767, Cf., above, Chapter I, § 3.

[35] *Reflections*, 1770, p. 96.

say of her own sex in cases of murder) are bitter bad judges in matters of philosophy."[36]   Murray likewise held hard to the rule for agreement with *thou*.   But Priestley, instancing the harshness of the termination—generally with him an indication that a form was not frequently heard—observes without comment that the *"est* is generally dropped in common conversation, and sometimes by the poets, in writing."[37]   The same attempt by the logical grammarians to preserve a distinction between *ye* and *you* met with no better success.   As might be expected, Lowth stands firm for ancient and obsolete—even wholly chimerical—forms, remarking with satisfaction that "Dr. Middleton hath with great propriety restored the true Participle:—'To have sitten . . .' Works. Vol. II, p. 30."[38]

10.   Baker cites Congreve's objection to *Humour* as meaning "what is Comical or Facetious," rather than "what is *Characteristic of a Certain Temper"*—an excellent illustration of the common attempt to holds words to historic meanings.   But Baker comments, " . . . it is no sort of Prejudice [to the current meaning] that [the word] also bears another Signification, there being many Words that have different Senses."[39]   Priestley writes, "Derivation is no certain rule to judge the sense of words.   The word *humourist* does not signify *a man of humour."*[40]

11.   Campbell is particularly divided in his sentiments on this matter of holding to ancient usages.   As we shall observe (Chapter IX), by his basic principle of "present use" he might be expected to stand against tendencies to revival of dead or obviously dying forms, and indeed he remarks of Lowth's attempts in this direction, "If you will replace what hath been long since expunged from the language, and extirpate what is firmly rooted, you yourself become an innovator."[41]   But he

[36]*Diversions of Purley*, I, 43.

[37]*Rudiments*, 1769, 115.

[38]*Short Introduction*, 1762, p. 75, *note*.

[39]*Reflections*, 1770, p. 19.

[40]*Rudiments*, p. 145.   But Dr. Johnson had defined humour in one sense as "grotesque imagery" and a *humorist* as "one who has odd conceits."

[41]*Philosophy*, I, 362.   For explanation and discussion of his canons of usage, see the following chapter, §§ 6-16.

uses always *hath* and *doth,* save once or so to avoid unpleasantly recurrent sounds, and even *conduceth* and the like, though
the *Britannica* article on "Language," first—1775—edition, observes that these forms had been displaced; and he writes *slidden,* which appears quite parallel to the *sitten* he condemns in
Dr. Middleton and Lowth. In fact, his fifth canon, which he
makes no serious attempt to reconcile with the principle of
"present use," is that in cases of divided usage, "where neither
perspicuity nor analogy, neither sound nor simplicity [the "four
first canons"] assists us in fixing our choice, it is safest to prefer that manner which is most conformable to ancient usage."[42]
This affords "another reason [besides a useful distinction in
meaning] for preferring . . . *ye* as the nominative plural of
thou, for it may be remarked that this distinction is very regularly observed in our translation of the Bible, as well as in all
our best ancient authors." He particularly commends Milton
as attentive to this, a remark that ill agrees with the findings
of the grammarians who have a choice collection of examples
of the "manifest Solecism" of employing *ye* as the accusative,
especially by Shakespeare and Milton.[43]

12. Webster is quite clear in theory here, and apparently
fairly consistent in his own usage. He writes, "When a particular form or use of words ceases to be *current* in practice,
. . . it ought to stand in grammars as *obsolete* . . . authors
have struggled to preserve the *old* rules of practice; . . . instead of assisting to preserve an agreement between books and
practice, they have contributed very much to create and perpetuate differences between the written and spoken language."[44]
But Webster is sometimes too charitable in his view of ancient
and honorable forms which by his time had come to be rated as
vulgar. "The New England people preserve the ancient use of
there and *here* after a word or sentence, designating the *place
where;* as *this here, that there.* It is called vulgar in English;
and indeed the addition of *here* or *there* is generally tautologi-

[42]*Philosophy* I, 385-6.
[43]*Short Introduction,* 1763 ed., p. 33 *note*; 1769 ed., pp. 48-9 *note, etc.*
[44]*Errors of English Grammars,* 1798, p. 20.

cal. It is however an ancient practice, and the French retain it in the pure elegant language of their country; *ce pays la, celui la, cet homme ici;* where we observe this difference only between the French and English idioms, that in French, the adverb follows the noun. [He does not observe that *ce* has in itself no such differentiation as between *this* and *that*] . . . This form of speech seems to have been coeval with the primitive Saxon, otherwise it would not have prevailed so generally among the common people."[45] He notes the appearance of *ax* for *ask* "even in the royal assent to acts of parliament, down to the reign of Henry VI . . . and still frequent in New England,"[46] and says of the "old Saxon *uren* . . . *Ourn* and *yourn* are obsolete in books, but are not a corruption. *Ours* and *yours* are the most modern words."[47]

13. *Appeals to etymology.* Monboddo stated an opinion popular with the students of language in the eighteenth century: Noting the sad deterioration of the Greek and Latin languages in their later days, he says the best way to preserve English is to keep to the etymologies of words from the Latin; i.e., *"ingeniousness* should be held distinct from *ingenuity* [derived] from *ingenuous."*[48] He does not mention *ingenuousness,* though Dr. Johnson has it, as also two meanings for *ingenuity.* Baker suggests *ingeniety.*[49]

Campbell had a clear theoretical notion of the inevitable result of such attempts: "And with regard to etymology, about which grammarians make such useless bustle; if every one hath a privilege of altering words, according to his own opinion of their origin, the opinions of the learned being on this subject so various, nothing but a general chaos can ensue."[50] Michaelis realizes a related danger. Language he describes as "a treasure of sense, knowledge, and wisdom . . . an accumulation of the wisdom and genius of nations . . . and preserver of truths." The danger of using language for the proof of propo-

[45]*Loc. cit.*
[46]*Dissertations,* 1789, pp. 364 *note* and 385-6.
[47]*Grammatical Institute,* 1804 ed., p. 12, *note.*
[48]*Origin and Progress,* 1774, IV, 168 ff.
[49]*Reflections,* p. 9.
[50]*Philosophy,* I, 363. See, below, § 16.

sitions, however, he sees clearly, though he gives no indication of knowing Locke's listing of specific perils and their remedies. He instances the word *Bergmehl* to show the peril of literal etymologizing; having been called "mountain meal" because it resembled meal, it was actually supposed to be fit for food.[51]

14. But the regulation of language, and in many cases of thought, by etymology, went merrily on. Bayly agreed with Milton in preferring *accedence* to *accidence* as derived from *accedo* rather than *accido,* though he takes this somewhat inapposite occasion to describe Milton "as monstrous in literal as in political freedom."[52] Lowth and Johnson, on the score of etymology, insisted upon *averse from* rather than *to.*[53] Campbell notes that this form occurs only once in the Bible translation, and comments: "The argument from etymology is here of no value, being taken from the use of another language. If by the same rule we were to regulate all nouns and verbs of Latin original, our present syntax would be overturned";[54] He proposes that strict logic would require us to say "either *aversion a change* or *version from a change.*"[55] Withers has the further suggestion that a strict consistency would lead these grammarians to *"submission under* and *predilection before."*[56]

15. Dr. Johnson gives only the sense of *reciprocal* to *mutual;* but one of his two quotations—Shakespeare's "make a mutual stand"—hardly bears this out. Baker is positive in restricting *mutual* to places where interchange is meant; he condemns "our mutual benefactor" and praises Locke for using "our common friend."[57] But *common* had in Johnson as one sense "vulgar, mean." It was even then suffering a degrada-

---

[51]*Dissertation on the Influence of Opinions on Language, and of Language on Opinions,* (originally in German, translated apparently by the author), 1769, p. 13.

[52]*Plain and Complete Grammar,* 1772, title page and preface, p. xiii. But he had published an *English Accidence* in 1771.

[53]*Short Introduction,* 1762 ed., p. 131 *note.*

[54]*Philosophy of Rhetoric,* 1776, I, 374, *note.*

[55]*Ibid.,* pp. 426-7, *note.*

[56]*Aristarchus,* p. 398.

[57]*Reflections,* 1770, pp. 52-3.

tion similar to that of *elegant* in New York City today,[58] and
so this prescription has had a hard life. Baker proposed also
to substitute "pre-sensation" for *presentiment* because of a
theory as to what etymologically the latter ought to mean, and
soberly insisted, as have generations of schoolmasters since,
that "a *verse* in poetry is only one line," in spite of "great
numbers of persons of good education" who have used it otherwise.[59]

16. A few writers, as we have observed, stood firmly for
the current meanings of words in defiance of their etymologies.
But the tide was strong against custom in the books of theory
we are here considering. In addition to his position on ancient
meanings, already noted, and in spite of his warning of the
dangers involved, Campbell observed that cases of divided
usage are to be settled among other considerations by "a regard
to simplicity (in which I include etymology when manifest)"
—certainly a remarkable combination.[60] And even where usage
is agreed, Campbell presents as *Canon the seventh:* "When
etymology plainly points to a signification different from that
which the word commonly bears, propriety and simplicity both
require its dismission. I use the word *plainly,* because, when
the etymology is from an ancient or foreign language, no regard should be had to it. The case is different, when the roots
either are, or strongly appear to be, English, are in present use,
and clearly suggest another meaning." He instances the un-
warranted use of *beholden* for indebted; for, though he admits
the term is not equivocal, since "it hath been long since dis-
used," as a participle of *behold,* yet "the formation of the word
is so analogical, as to make it have at least the appearance of
impropriety, when used in a sense that seems naturally so foreign to it."[61] To such lengths did etymological prepossession
go in the eighteenth century.

[58]It describes apartments just above the slum level, "with hot water and
janitor service."
[59]*Remarks,* 1779, pp. 30 and 74.
[60]*Philosophy* I, 383-4, *Canon the fourth.*
[61]*Philosophy,* I, 397-8. "*Beholding,* to express the same thing, is still
more exceptionable than the other, and includes a real impropriety, being
an active form with a passive signification."

CHAPTER IX

THE APPEAL TO USAGE AND ITS PRACTICAL REPUDIATION

No custom can prevail against right reason and the law of nature . . . The will of the people is the foundation of custom. But if it be not grounded upon reason but error, it is not the will of the people.

Taylor, *Elements of Civil Law*, quoted by Horne Tooke

CHAPTER IX

THE APPEAL TO USAGE AND ITS PRACTICAL REPUDIATION

1. *Custom the sole arbiter.* The appeal to custom as the norm and arbiter of language was professed from the beginning to the end of the eighteenth century. Practically every writer whose works were examined noted some point at least of actual domination by usage, even where this sway was unwillingly acknowledged, as by Johnson and Lowth; and most of the critics specifically stated that custom is the proper basis of appeal in theory also. In this connection Horace was frequently quoted to the effect that "use is the sole arbiter and norm of speech." Reference to Quintilian's *consensum eruditorum*[1] also occurs, but none to Cicero's comment, that the best Latin in purity of usage is that of cultivated matrons. He recommended "a Roman and urban tone" fleeing "not only country roughness, but foreign bravado."[2] Cicero seems to have been a source of Vaugelas' treatment.[3]

It is significant that Locke is apparently not cited in this mat-

[1] *Institutes,* I, vi, 45.
[2] *De Oratore,* Book III, Ch. I, 44. See C. S. Baldwin's *Ancient Rhetoric and Poetic,* (Macmillan, 1924), p. 54.
[3] C. de Vaugelas, *Remarques sur la Langue Françoise:* Vaugelas' theory is definite: that usage is not law, but the record of observations; that we must follow usage blindly, "sometimes without, sometimes against reason"; that usage includes all the language of "honest men," and all the style of good writers; but that it is not enough that it is French (not "of the people")—rather the custom of the soundest part ("la plus saine partie des auteurs de tems"). The best writers offend occasionally against usage; because nature moves more to evil than to good they insist on going against the torrent of common opinion. Languages are living and change constantly; French, out of barbarism, has achieved a peak of perfection; for utility, and for the honor of our language, we should conserve it there. Careful provincials write best because they are conscious of the need of attention to proper usage. (Preface, 94 pp. *passim,* to the 1738 edition). But Vaugelas' application of these theories was so bad that he was pilloried by Moliere in the *Femmes Savantes.*

ter in the eighteenth century. Withers refers to him on the point that ideas are not innate, and quotes his exposition of the importance of definition; but Withers fails to base squarely on Locke, and in this resembles most writers of the period.

The Art of Speaking, 1708 edition, a translation "from the French of MM. du Port Royal," contains a definitive statement of the sway of custom, with specific reference to the treatment of the problem by Vaugelas. As there were English editions by 1676, the following quotation is of special interest as anticipating Locke's *Essay,* "Sounds . . . though of themselves they have nothing resembling those Ideas, do notwithstanding represent them."[4] And as to usage itself, "Reason permits that we give way to Custom, though contrary to Reason . . . Analogie is not the Mistress of Language . . . she prescribes only the Laws of Custom."[5] The authors comment on the distinction between "pure" and "clear" expression, and consider that no great pains are required to avoid censure; they obviously wrote before the heyday of amending in the eighteenth century. As we shall see in discussing levels or élites, however, they are sharply against "the depraved language of common People," and so open the gates to as copious objections and exceptions as Vaugelas himself.

Greenwood, like Jonson, quotes Quintilian, calling "the Custom of Speech, the Agreement of the Learned, as that of Life, the Agreement, or Practice of the Good."[6] But he gives no details of application.

We come next to James Harris, whose metaphysical ideas and principles of universal grammar have been already described.[7] In precise contradiction to these notions, and with no attempt at reconciliation of the two contrary schemes, appears the statement that *"there never was a Language, nor indeed can possibly be framed one, to express the Properties*

---

[4] *The Art of Speaking, rendered into English from the French of Messieurs du Port Royal,* 2d ed., London, 1708, p. 4. An earlier edition, of 1668, is apparently referred to in Pepys' *Diary,* under December 12 of that year.
[5] *Ibid.,* p. 44.
[6] *Essay,* 1711, p. 37.
[7] Chapters II, §§ 1, 2, and IV.

and real Essence of things, as a Mirrour exhibits their Figures
and their Colours,"[8] but, "ALL LANGUAGE IS FOUNDED
IN COMPACT, and not in Nature, for so are all Symbols,
of which Words are a certain Species."[9]

A shrewd observation on the habituating effect of custom is
given by John Ward: " . . . our English version of the *Bible*
has, I think, always expressed the article [in "the death"
and the like.] Though the other way would be doubtless more
accurate, were we but accustomed to the sound by general
use."[10]

2. Johnson and Lowth are but unwilling witnesses to the
force of custom. Of *flee* the *Dictionary* remarks: "This
word is now almost universally written *fly,* although properly
to *fly* . . . is to move with *wings* and *flee* . . . *to run away.*
They are now confounded." Of lesser: ". . . adopted by
the poets, and then by writers of prose, till it has all the authority which a mode originally erroneous can derive from
custom."[11] He nevertheless brands it a "barbarous corruption," and is followed in this opinion by Lowth. To a similar
comment on "nowadays" in the *Dictionary,* Campbell takes exception strongly: "I have always understood a barbarism in
speech to be a term or expression totally unsupported by the
present usage of good writers in the language. A meaning
very different is suggested here, but what that meaning is, it
will not be easy to conjecture. Nor has this celebrated writer
given us, on the word *barbarous,* any definition of the term
which will throw light on his application of it in the passage
quoted."[12]

Like Johnson in his unwilling acceptance, Lowth remarks of
the defective verbs and the irregular comparison of adjectives
like *good* and *bad:* "They are in general words of most frequent and vulgar use, in which the caprice of Custom is apt to

[8]James Harris, *Hermes,* 1751, (1771 ed., pp. 336-7).
[9]*Ibid.,* p. 337.
[10]*Four Essays,* 1758 ed., p. 75.
[11]Quotations are from the sixth edition of the *Dictionary,* 1785.
[12]*Philosophy* I, 361-2. See his comment upon Johnson's position on singular nouns in *s—Ibid.,* p. 373.

get the better of analogy."[13]   The remark is repeated, without acknowledgment, by Murray.[14]

3.   Priestley is undoubtedly the first writer in English, and apparently the only one in the eighteenth century, to take a clear and reasonably consistent view of usage.   His grammar alone makes a beginning at carrying out in a sensible and practical way the philosophy of Locke and, better than Vaugelas himself, the theory of usage formulated in the preface to the *Remarques,* though he nowhere cites this aspect of Locke's *Essay,* nor Vaugelas at all.   His position can be most clearly shown by the following quotations from the preface and text of Priestley's *Rudiments,* of which the first edition was issued about a month before Lowth's *Short Introduction;* comparison may well be made of the urbane and tentative tone of his specific recommendations with those of the other grammarians, and of Campbell, arch-defender in theory of the omnipotence of custom.[15]

"It must be allowed, that the custom of speaking is the original, and only just standard of any language.   We see, in all grammars, that this is sufficient to establish a rule, even contrary to the strongest analogies of the language with itself. Must not this custom, therefore, be allowed to have some weight, in favour of those forms of speech, to which our best writers and speakers seem evidently prone; forms which are contrary to no analogy of the language with itself, and which have been disapproved by grammarians, only from certain abstract and arbitrary considerations, and when their decisions were not prompted by the genius of the language; which discovers itself in nothing more than in the general propensity of those who use it to certain modes of construction?   I think, however, that I have not, in any case, seemed to favour what our grammarians will call an irregularity, but where the genius of the language, and not only single examples, but the general practice of those who write it, and the almost universal custom

---

[13]*Short Introduction,* 1769 ed., pp. 59 and 104.
[14]*English Grammar,* 1808 Am. ed., p. 87.
[15]See in this chapter §§ 6-16.

of all who speak it, have obliged me to do so. I also think I have seemed to favour those irregularities, no more than the degree of the propensity I have first mentioned, when unchecked by a regard to arbitrary rules, in those who use the forms of speech I refer to, will authorize me."[16]

For the "exceeding great simplicity of structure" of English, Priestley supposes, "we are, perhaps, in some measure indebted to the long-continuing barbarism of the people from whom we received it. The words we afterwards borrowed from foreign languages, though they now make more than one half of the substance of ours, were like more plentiful nourishment to a meager body, that was grown to its full stature, and become too rigid to admit of any new modification of its parts. They have added considerably to the bulk and gracefulness of our language; but have made no alteration in the simplicity of its original form."[17] Consistently with this last, we have observed[18] that Priestley objected to any regulation of the grammatical structure of English by French or Latin analogies, but that, quite inconsistently, he favored all possible differentiations in form. As to vocabulary, he notes later in his text that "custom prescribes how far we may take advantage of . . . the rules for the composition and derivation of words . . . . Latin prefixes and terminations do not well suit with Saxon words, and *vice versa*. *Dislikeness* (Locke). For this reason, *disquietness* is not so good a word as *disquietude*, or *inquietude*. There are, however, several exceptions to this observation; as the word *genuineness*.

"I wish we had more liberty to introduce new words, by a derivation analogous to others already in use, when they are evidently wanted. We have, for instance, no term to express a person who understands mechanics. A *mechanic* is a mere workman. And yet I am afraid that *mechanist*, which Mr. Johnson has introduced in this sense, will not be generally adopted."[19] As further examples of new compounds he finds

[16]*Rudiments*, 1769 ed., pp. ix-x.

[17]*Ibid.*, pp. xvii-xviii.

[18]In Chapter IV, § 6 and V, § 6.

[19]*Rudiments*, pp. 142-4, *passim*. The word *mechanist* he cites from *Rasselas*. It is not in Johnson's *Dictionary*.

disagreeable, he gives, among some really curious specimens, *naturalness* (Addison), and *informalities* (Hume), very "easy" today. Of the superfluous prepositions in *from thence* and *from whence,* he remarks, in accord with his principle of allegiance, "the origin of these words is so little attended to, and the preposition *from* so often used in construction with them, that the omission of it in many cases would seem, stiff and disagreeable."[20]   These two last adjectives, and even oftener "harsh," are frequent with Priestley to describe the effect of constructions not customary.

To complete our view of Priestley's position, the following quotation, again from the preface to the *Rudiments,* will serve: "Our grammarians appear to me to have acted precipitately in this business of writing a grammar of the language. This will never be effected by the arbitrary rules of any man, or body of men whatever."—Priestley is clear that the "decisions of *Time*" are better than those of *Synods* or *Academies*[21] because the latter plan supposes the "language actually fixed already, contrary to the real state of it; whereas a language can never be properly fixed, till all the varieties with which it is used, have been held forth to public view, and the general preference of certain forms have been declared, by the general practice afterwards.   Whenever I have mentioned any variety in the grammatical forms that are used to express the same thing, I have seldom scrupled to say which of them I prefer; but this is to be understood as nothing more than a conjecture, which time must confirm or refute."[22]

Priestley was wrong in supposing that the other grammarians thought the language already fixed; they thought it their business to reform and then fix it, without too much trouble in really observing it.   And he apparently did not realize that such a consummation as the final decisions he anticipated must follow only upon its death.   But he will no doubt be counted right in his view as to what the intelligent student of language

[20]*Ibid.,* p. 134.
[21]*Ibid.,* pp. xix-xx.
[22]*Ibid.,* pp. xvi-xvii.

should do in the meantime. Priestley's scientific training stood him in good stead here, and an examination of his
judgments in detail confirms the belief that he for the most
part actually carried out his promise of proposing conjectures
on the trend of the data he examined, rather than uttering dogmatic rules.

4. It has been observed that statements of the authority of
usage were common in this period, even by fairly consistent
practitioners of the authority of *ipse dixit*. Thus Robert
Baker remarks, "Now it is to be considered that Words are
Nothing at all in themselves. They signify that, and that only,
which by common Consent is understood by them."[23] In his
comment on the meaning of the word *humour,* questioned by
Congreve, he actually followed his theory; for nearly a century had sufficiently proved Congreve wrong. And Baker even
remarks on the "unaccountable pleasingness that irregular expressions sometimes have," and writes of the word *anguishing,*
in Molyneux, "perhaps a word of his own coining": "I think
it very expressive," and would be "pleased to see it adopted."[24]
But these are largely authoritarian pronouncements. Nearer to
indicating an acceptance of usage is this: *"It is very true what
he says* [Warburton's *Divine Legation*], is certainly very ungrammatical. Yet . . . frequently used by the learned,[25] and
having a certain air of ease, it cannot be condemned as bad
English."[26] Here again, more than frequent use by the
learned, the quality of pleasingness—to Baker—is a requisite.
Thus he makes a typical double appeal, such as are to be found
in plenty in the critics of the eighteenth century and later.[27]

William Kenrick, in the "rhetorical Grammar" prefixed to
his *Dictionary,* shows some notion of custom: "Words are supposed to follow each other in some natural order; but on due
examination perhaps we ought to say habitual, instead of

[23]*Reflections*, 1770, p. 19.
[24]*Remarks*, 1779, p. 45; 1770 ed., p. 86.
[25]Reminiscent of Quintilian's *consensum eruditorum.*
[26]*Remarks,* p. 102.
[27]See Chapters XI and XII, below.

natural."[28]   But Webster quotes Kenrick to a directly contrary effect.

> "Nothing," says Kenrick, "has contributed more to the adulteration of living languages, than the too extensive acceptation of Horace's rule in favor of custom. Custom is undoubtedly the rule of present practice; but there would be no end in following the variations daily introduced by caprice.—Rhet. Gram. page 6.

John Fell's *Essay towards an English Grammar* makes a similar profession in its preface, but the author in most cases conspicuously avoids all reference to instances of usage differing from his announced rules and so he, like most of this fellows, merely utters a fine sentiment. He does, however, evidence observation of usage in the matter of *shall* and *will*. Monboddo also remarks that custom rules, and as usual quotes Horace and Aristotle.[29]

5.   Blair's *Lectures* (1783) I think nowhere refer to the arbitrament of use, but follow Lowth as to grammar, and remark: "All the rules of Latin syntax, it is true, cannot be applied to our language. . . . But . . . it is to be always remembered, that the chief and fundamental rules of syntax are common" to these languages.[30]   He divides "all the qualities of a good style . . . under two heads, perspicuity and ornament,"[31] remarking that Swift "is esteemed one of our most correct writers, . . . but we are not to look for much ornament and grace in" his style.[32]

Perspicuity, "the fundamental quality of style," Blair divides into the famous "purity, propriety, and precision," which are readily fitted into equivalent divisions of the schemes we have been considering.[33]

Blair's direct source here appears to have been John Hughes' essay "Of Style, written at the Request of a Friend in the Year MDCXCVIII." It was not apparently published before

[28] *New Dictionary*, 1773, p. 17. Webster, *Dissertations*, 1789, III, 164.
[29] *Origin and Progress*, II, 500.
[30] *Lectures*, 1793 ed., I, 166-7.
[31] *Ibid.*, p. 170.
[32] *Ibid.*, p. 439. Blair then proceeds to eighteen pages of minute analysis of the *Proposal for Correcting*, listing all its sins against purity, propriety, and precision (pp. 439-58).
[33] *Ibid.*, pp. 170 and 174.

1735. It is included in W. H. Durham's *Critical Essays of the XVIIIth Century*.[34] Hughes writes: "All the Qualifications of a good Style I think may be reduced under these four heads, *Propriety, Perspicuity, Elegance,* and *Cadence;* and each of these, except the last, has some relation to the Thoughts, as well as to the Words . . . There is another Particular which I shall mention here, because I think it differs but little from *Propriety* and that is *Purity,* which I take more particularly to respect the Language as it is now spoken and written. The Rule of this is *modern Use,* according to that of Horace . . . By this Rule all obsolete Words are to be avoided. But to a Man of long Practice and Reputation in the Language, the Privilege may be allowed sometimes of reviving old, or bringing in new Words, where the common ones are deficient . . . A good Instance, in my Opinion, of a new Word is the Verb *falsify,* which Mr. *Dryden* borrowed from the *Italian* . . ."[35] Hughes was not fortunate enough to devise an alliterative triptych, and so has remained quite unknown to fame.

Blair is particularly narrow and logical about precision. He quotes, and translates in a footnote, but without citation, Quintilian's "not only that every hearer may understand us, but that it shall be impossible for him not to understand us,"[36] and applies this principle with devastating effect to standard authors. Offence against precision comprehends using words which either "do not express that idea which the writer intends, but some other which only resembles, or is akin to it"; or which "express that idea, but not quite fully and completely"; or "express it, together with something more than he intended. Precision stands opposed to all these faults; but chiefly to the last."[37] It will be observed that the assumption here is contrary to Locke's clear statement that "no one hath the power to make others have the same ideas . . . . in their minds, when they use the same words that he does," but that "the idea, which each word stands for, must be learned by those who would ex-

[34]Yale Press, 1915, pp. 80-85.
[35]*Op. cit.,* pp. 80-81.
[36]*Lectures,* 1793, I, 171.
[37]*Ibid.,* p. 174.

change thought," which "should teach us moderation, in imposing our own sense" upon authors.[38]   The neglect of this plain principle is possibly the first and fundamental vice in criticism.   If Blair could have known and comprehended the idea Locke expressed, and thereby come to a sense of proportion in criticism, he might have done valuable service; he has, for instance, an excellent passage on the "loose style," overloaded with a superfluity of words and ideas.   But he offends in precisely the manner against which he warns us, by so covering his chief idea with meticulous objections to words and turns of expression, that it is soon lost to sight.

6.   *Campbell's usage theories*: We may next consider George Campbell, author of *The Philosophy of Rhetoric*, 1776, and inventor, out of materials provided by the classical rhetoricians and by Vaugelas, of the famous criteria of "national, reputable, and present use."   His source, in addition to Cicero, Horace, and Quintilian, and possibly John Hughes, appears to have been chiefly Vaugelas, to whom he makes reference.   But Vaugelas' main insistence is on reputable use, for which he had the advantage of a court usage lacking in England, and to some extent on present as opposed to obsolete and over-new forms and words.   He specifically remarks that it is not enough that an expression be French; it must not, that is, be of the people; we must go against *"le torrent de l'opinion commune."*[39] Campbell likewise considers that "the colloquial dialect, as Johnson calls it," in which he places "there's the books" and "you was," though "ten times oftener heard," decides nothing as to *"good Use."*[40]

Campbell is explicit in stating that usage alone determines, and commends Priestley's remarks, quoted above.[41]   He illustrates the force of use in anomalies like "a great many men," which grammarians from Jonson onwards had commented

---

[38]See Chapter II, §§ 4 and 5, of this study.

[39]*Remarques*, 1737 ed., preface.

[40]Since this study was completed, Dr. Bryan's analysis of Campbell's theory has appeared: W. F. Bryan, "A Late Eighteenth Century Purist," *Studies in Philology*, XXIV, (Jan. 1927), pp. 358-70.

[41]*Philosophy of Rhetoric*, 1776, (2 vol.); I, 339 ff. and 362.

upon. And he ridicules Swift, and Lowth his follower, for thinking that a language could "offend against every part of grammar": ". . . what could the Doctor's notion of grammar be, when he expressed himself in this manner? Some notion, possibly, he had of grammar in the abstract, an universal archetype by which the particular grammars of all different tongues ought to be regulated . . . I acknowledge myself to be entirely ignorant of this universal grammar; nor can I form a conjecture where its laws are to be learnt . . . One thing, indeed, every smatterer in philosophy will tell us, that there can be no natural connexion between the sounds of any language, and the things signified, or between the modes of inflection and combination, and the relations they are intended to express. . . . If he meant the English grammar, I would ask, whence has that grammar derived its laws? If from general use (and I cannot conceive another origin), then it must be owned, that there is a general use in that language as well as in others; and it were absurd to accuse the language, which is purely what is conformable to general use in speaking and writing, as offending against general use. But if he meant to say, that there is no fixed, established, or general use in the language, that it is quite irregular, . . . he ought to have said, that it is not susceptible of grammar; which, by the way, would not have been true of English, or indeed of any the most uncultivated language on the earth."[42]

We have quite obviously come a long way from the ideas of "language as entity" and of "universal grammar."

7.   Campbell goes on to define custom much as Priestley did: Expressions are rendered good English by custom; "that is, in other words, our ears are familiarized to them by frequent use."[43] Again "No absolute monarch hath it more in his power to nobilitate a person of obscure birth, than it is in the power of good use to ennoble words of low or dubious extraction; such, for instance, as have either arisen, nobody knows how, like *fib*,

---

[42] *Philosophy*, I, 342-3.
[43] *Ibid.*, 337. But see the discussion of Campbell's Third Canon, below, § 12.

banter, bigot, fop, flippant, among the rabble, or like *flimsy,*
sprung from the cant of the manufacturers.[44] . . . *use* . . . is the
sole mistress of the language. In truth grammar and criticism
are but her ministers; and though, like other ministers, they
would sometimes impose the dictates of their own humour upon
the people, as the commands of their sovereign, they are not so
often successful in their attempts, as to encourage the frequent
repetition of them . . . In these matters it is foolish to attempt
to struggle against the stream. . . . To the tribunal of use, as to
the supreme authority, we are entitled to appeal from the laws
and decisions of grammarians; and . . . this order of subordina-
tion ought never . . . to be reversed."[45]

8. Campbell then proceeds, ". . . if use be here a matter of
such consequence, it will be necessary before advancing any
farther, to ascertain precisely what it is. We shall otherwise
be in danger, though we agree about the name, of differing
widely in the notion that we assign to it."[46] His definition, as
we have seen, is that good use is "reputable, national, and present." Reputable use, in default of a court or its equivalent,
rests upon the practice of "authors of reputation"—rather than
good authors, about choosing whom opinion will naturally be
less uniform.[47] The attempts of grammarians and other critics

[44]*Ibid.,* I, pp. 404-5.

Campbell ridicules Dr. Johnson for calling *"punch"* a mix'd liquor," a
"cant word" because its origin is obscure, while accepting *sherbet* "because
it is Arabic; though, for aught we know, its origin among the Arabs, hath
been equally ignoble or uncertain." Yet Campbell expressly denies the cre-
dentials of words from "professional dialects, or the cant that is sometimes
observed to prevail among those of the same profession or way of life,"
which, though not local like provincial dialects, "is not on that account
more extensive or reputable." His three examples are from our point of
time humorously inapposite: *"Advice,* in the commercial idiom, means information or intelligence; *nervous,* in open defiance of analogy, doth in
the medical cant, as Johnson expresseth it, denote, having weak nerves;
and the word *turtle,* though pre-occupied time immemorial by a species
of doves, is, as we learn from the same authority, employed by sailors and
gluttons, to signify a tortoise.*

"See those words in the English Dictionary." [Campbell's note.]

[46]*Ibid.,* pp. 336, 381, and 344. But see §§ 11-16, below.

[46]*Ibid.,* pp. 344-5.

[47]*Philosophy,* I, 351-2.

to fix the standard of what was reputable will be discussed in Chapter X of this study; it is of course crucial in any theory of usage.

9. *National use* Campbell considers "in a twofold view, as it stands opposed both to *provincial* and to *foreign use.*"[48]

We have observed in the battle over universal grammar and foreign analogies (Chapter IV) that the current of opinion in the eighteenth century turned against admitting foreign grammatical constructions as determining the English. In Priestley, for example, we find, among other like suspicions already treated, that "a protestation where they repeated" (Hume) and "the same course where he was already" are in imitation of the French idiom and should be discarded. And Campbell, though he classes *idiotisms and latinisms* with improprieties rather than barbarisms, objects to the use of French and Latin terms and turns of expression, such as *impracticable*, for impassable roads, *affection* "when applied to things inanimate and signifying the state of being affected by any cause," and *"integrity* when used for entireness." These last, *latinisms*, may be permitted to philosophical disquisitions, but "the less, even here, this liberty is used, it is the better."[49] The structure of this last sentence of Campbell's might be called an idiotism or cant form of the grammarian. Tooke felt that on the whole the borrowing from foreign languages which altered the Anglo-Saxon had been a great advantage toward briefer expression.[50]

The discussion of national usage as applied to "provincial words," taking the form chiefly of baiting the usage of Scotch and Irish writers, and including in Campbell's view "cant terms,"[51] will be discussed in Chapter X.

10. Fixing the boundaries of *Present use* naturally created a still more serious difficulty. "As use . . . implies duration, and as even a few years are not sufficient for ascertaining the

[48]*Ibid.*, p. 353.
[49]*Philosophy*, I, 469.
[50]*Diversions*, II, 506-7.
[51]See above, § 7, *note* 44.

characters of authors, I have, for the most part, in the following sheets, taken my prose examples, neither from living authors, nor from those who wrote before the Revolution; not from the first, because an author's fame is not so firmly established in his lifetime; not from the last, that there may be no suspicion that the style is superannuated." Campbell, however, excepted from the latter restriction the "vulgar translation of the Bible," and gave the poets a wider range, including "Milton and Waller," but thinking it not "prudent often to introduce words or phrases, of which no example could be produced since the days of Spenser and of Shakespeare."[52]

Some other eighteenth-century comments on the problem of present use may be of interest: In the *Art of Speaking*, we find, " 'Tis the same thing with us in respect of Language, as in respect of Habit. Some people push on the Modes to the highest extremity. Others with as much eagerness and vanity oppose themselves against them. Some people affect such terms and expressions as are modern or new; Others digging into the Dialects of their Great Grand-fathers, will not speak a word now, that was not in use two hundred years since. Both of them are to blame. When Custom affords not terms proper to express what we have to say, it is lawful to use such words as are almost antiquated and lost: Nay, a Man is excusable, if to make himself understood, he coins a new word . . . with this proviso, . . . that the word be a-la-mode, not dress'd up in a sound quite differing from the usual words."[53]

Temple, in his *Sketches,* proposes degrading many old words and committing them "to the Care of the Paviours": His aversions are *enroach, inculcate,* "for all its Latinity," *purport, betwixt,* "except you have first repeated *between* till we are quite tired of it," *froward, vouchsafe.* In his view *"methinks* strongly resembles the broken Language of a German in his first Attempts to speak *English; methought* lies under the same Objection, but it sounds better.

[52]Philosophy I. 366 and 359.
[53]*Op. cit.,* 1708, p. 40.

"From what rugged Road, I wonder, did *swerve deviate* into the *English* Language? . . . But this *Subject Matter!* . . . in the Name of every thing that's disgusting and detestable, what is it? Is it one or two ugly Words? What's the Meaning of it? Confound me if I ever could guess! Yet one dares hardly ever peep into a Preface, for fear of being stared in the Face with this nasty *Subject Matter.*

"*Wittol* is an old-fashioned, ill-sounding Word; but as there is frequent occasion for it, and no other Word so perfectly expresses its Meaning, we cannot afford to part with it."[54]

11.   It is pretty plain that "good use" as Campbell defined it is not likely to result in an overwhelming number of unequivocal decisions on such matters as we have seen eighteenth-century grammarians and critics disputing about. The margin of time left by Campbell's allocation of *present use* is not wide; incidentally, it corresponds almost precisely with the Augustan or Golden Age of English discussed in the preceding chapter of this study. Moreover, though the tale of reputable writers that can be agreed upon in this period is small, especially when those suspected of provincialism are barred on the count of national use, nevertheless there would be very few points upon which we could expect an agreement by the writings of *"a great number if not the majority, of celebrated authors."*[55] "I acknowledge," Campbell tells us, "that in every case there is not a perfect uniformity in the determinations even of such use as may justly be determined good."[56]   And in point of fact, save for the expressly manufactured barbarisms *shallest* and *calt* (for *called*), and the "provincial dialect forms" *goot, gude, and gued* for good, positively the sole decisions reached by a "preponderance of usage" in all Campbell's lengthy discussion are the acceptance of Lowth's condemned *aversion from,* which we have al-

---

[54]Temple, *Sketches*, 1758, pp. 23-5. The objection to *Subject Matter,* among others, probably belongs to his comments on new, not obsolete words, but there he instances only *volupty.*
[55]*Philosophy* I, 352-3.
[56]*Ibid.,* p. 371.

ready found pretty well settled by logic, and of the word *news* as a singular.[57] That is as far as the "dictator usage" can carry us.

His discussion so far given is in fact only preliminary, in Campbell's scheme, to the main duty of the grammarian and the critic in interpreting usage: and that is "to compile a succinct, perspicuous, and faithful digest of the laws"—not, be it understood, to legislate—and "to vigilantly attend to every illegal practice that were beginning to prevail, and evince its danger, by exposing its contrariety to law." In this description Campbell uses the figure of a useful codifier and enforcer of the country's statutes.[58] Whereas Campbell's threefold definition of usage is familiarly known, it is rather remarkable that his "digest" of the law of usage, in nine canons, and his additional three canons of grammatical purity, should have been almost entirely overlooked. For this treatment is obviously the key to his entire structure; the nine canons occupy over thirty pages of the text, and are followed by almost three times as many on the additional canons of "grammatical purity."

12. *The canons of usage.* Since use is thus divided, that is "whenever a considerable number of authorities can be produced in support of two different, though resembling modes of expression for the same thing, . . . the authorities on the opposite sides" being "equal, or nearly so," Campbell says, "the following canons are humbly proposed, in order to assist us in deciding the preference. . . . Custom, when wavering, may be swayed, but when reluctant, will not be forced. And in this department a person never effects so little, as when he attempts too much."[59]

The canons proposed are

1. Preference for "the strictly univocal" expression; this principle, expressed by Quintilian in the advice to write so that no one could possibly misunderstand, we have seen driven to its ultra-logical conclusions of word-criticism in Chapter VII and of Syntax in Chapter VI, and pressed hard by Blair as quoted in § 5, above.

[57]*Ibid.*, pp. 339-366 and 373-4, *note; cf. means,* § 14, below.
[58]*Ibid.*, pp. 370-1.
[59]*Ibid.*, I, 374-86.

2. Analogy—discussed, with several of Campbell's illustrations, in Chapter V, above.

3. Euphony: That term or expression "ought to be preferred which is most agreeable to the ear." We have seen Baker and others settling points in part by this appeal; in a majority of cases it probably means, as with Priestley, preference for the more familiar or used form; Bayly remarks that "the ear abhors the hiatus of 'who art in heaven'" (*Plain Grammar*, p. 26.) But it probably covers also most of the license even Lowth and his followers allowed to the poets, and especially to "noble poetry," such as permission to retain *chiefest* and *extremest*. Bayly likewise defends placing prepositions at the end as "this, when done with judgment, makes variety and gives a peculiar harmony and freedom to the period." (See Chapter VI, § 22, above.)

But Campbell, despite his recognition cited earlier that custom is simply "familiarization by frequent use," repudiates that principle under this third canon: " . . . a regard to sound hath, in some instances, had an influence on the public choice, to the prejudice of both the former canons, which one would think ought to be regarded as of more importance. Thus the term *ingenuity* has obtained, in preference to *ingeniousness*, though the former cannot be deduced analogically . . . and . . . would be equivocal, being a regular derivative from the term *ingenuous*, if the newer acceptation had not before now supplanted the other altogether."

Campbell considers gross violations of harmony or euphony in *Canon Six* (§ 14, below).

Euphony seems rarely to have been appealed to for resolution of problems like the use of *slow* or *slowly*, *feel bad* or *badly*, and the like, which probably are actually settled to fit sentence cadence; it probably explains the acceptance of *lesser*. Johnson had recognized the principle in marking *godly* an adverb. "By analogy it should be *godlily*, but the repetition of the syllables is too harsh." So other grammarians felt. But Johnson formed *lowlily* or accepted it for the *Dictionary*, and approved *soonly* from More.

4. "A regard to simplicity (in which I include etymology when manifest.)" This is rather mixed; Campbell's instances are *was approved* rather than *approved of* and, on the double count, *subtract* rather than *substract*.

5. "Conformity to ancient usage," where none of the other four canons assist. This has been discussed in the preceding chapter.

13. *Further limitations.* ". . . though nothing in language can be good from which use withholds her approbation, there may be many things to which she gives it, that are not in all respects good, or such as are worthy to be retained and imitated. In some instances *custom* may very properly be checked by *criticism,* which hath a sort of negative, and though not the censorian power of instant degradation, the privilege of remonstrating, and by means of this, when used discreetly, of bringing what is bad into disrepute, and so cancelling it gradually; but which hath no positive right to establish any thing."[60] Campbell here specifically and avowedly parts company from Priestley, and also from what he himself has just been remarking about "struggling against the stream."[61]   Good use, in fact, appears now as no dictator, but a mere tribune, with power of nay, but none of yea: ". . . though we cannot say properly of any expression which has the sanction of good use, that it is barbarous, we must admit that in other respects, it may be faulty. . . . Now, in order to discard [such expressions], nothing more is necessary than to disuse them. And to bring us to disuse them, both the example and the arguments of the critic will have their weight. . . . It is by carefully filing off all roughnesses and inequalities, that languages, like metals, must be polished,[62] . . . the first rudiments of taste no sooner appear in any people, than the language begins, as it were of itself, to emerge out of that state of rudeness. . . . As they improve in arts and sciences. . . . it not only becomes richer and more comprehensive, but acquires greater precision, perspicuity, and harmony. This effect taste insensibly produces among the people long before language becomes the object of their attention. But when criticism hath called forth their attention to this object, there is a probability that the effort will be accelerated." But "though the critical art may retard a little, it will never be able to prevent degeneracy. I shall therefore [!] subjoin a few remarks under the form of canons, in relation to those words or expressions, which may be thought to merit degradation from the rank they have hitherto maintained, submitting these remarks entirely, as every thing of the kind must be sub-

[60]*Ibid.,* pp. 387-8.
[61]*Ibid.,* p. 381.
[62]Quintilian has a good passage on "false ideas of polishing" resulting in "filing quite away." *Institutes* II, x, iv, Watson tr., London, 1856, pp. 291-2.

mitted, to the final determination of the impartial public."[63]

14. The remaining canons, then, call for the degradation of:

6. All words "remarkably harsh and inharmonious, and not absolutely necessary." These are all difficulties of pronunciation. At the same time Campbell notes that even the most harmonious languages such as Greek have harsh words, notes the "greater risk of going too far in refining, than of not going far enough," and censures the "squeamishness" betrayed by Temple in his *Sketches,* which object to *encroach, purport, inculcate, methinks*—and some other words "of which we have no single equivalents."[64]

7. Words plainly different in meaning from their etymological sense. This topic has been covered in the preceding chapter, and touched by Canon 4.

8. Obsolete words; in this he includes only stereotyped popular phrases; "the introduction of words which never appear but with the same attendants, gives the style an air of vulgarity and cant," as *I had as lief go, by dint of argument, not a whit better, pro and con, a moot point.*

9. "All those phrases, which, when analyzed grammatically, include a solecism, and all those to which use hath affixed a particular sense, but which, when explained by the general and established rules of the language, are susceptible either of a different sense or of no sense." This is another *omnium gatherum.* Campbell begins with *had rather,* which he can see no inconvenience in dropping altogether, though it "hath come at length to establish itself, and to stand on its own foot." Of *a means* he is much in doubt, but concludes that no person "will venture so far to violate the present usage, and consequently to shock the ears of the generality of readers, as to say 'By this mean,' or 'By that mean!' ". This leaves him and other objectors with no phrase at all.[65]

The only example of phrases with a different meaning in logic and usage is "He sings a good song" for "he sings well."[66] Those "which can scarcely be considered as literally conveying any sense" are such "vile, but common phrases, sometimes to be found in good authors, as 'having a month's mind,' 'currying favour,' *hold* for *continue* in 'hold long in one mind,' and 'seven ladies, every one prettier than another.' " "Such trash is the disgrace of any tongue . . . As

[63]*Philosophy* I, 387-91, *passim.*

[64]*Ibid.,* pp. 391-6. See his remarks on ill-formed adverbs, above, Ch. V, § 13.

[65]*Ibid.,* pp. 401-2. This problem Campbell had supposedly settled by "good use" in the discussion of *news* and the like, pp. 373-4, *note.*

[66]For the same reason Baker rejects "the best part he plays"; it must be "the part he plays best." (*Remarks,* 1779, p. 64.)

such idioms, therefore, err alike against purity, simplicity, perspicuity, and elegance, they are entitled to no quarter from the critic." Obviously it is no stereotyped nature of these expressions that Campbell dislikes, but their sin against literalness. The picturesque expressiveness of some of them—particularly the last in its representation of the confusion of mind induced by so much prettiness—does not apparently strike him at all.[67]

15. *Canons of grammatical purity.* Campbell specifically affirms that "the first thing in elocution that claims our attention, is purity; all its other qualities have their foundation in this."[68] "Purity of expression hath but a small share of merit; it hath, however, some share. . . . on the account of purity, a considerable part of the merit discovered in the other virtues of elocution, to which it contributes, ought undoubtedly to be charged."[69] ". . . this is one of those qualities, of which, though the want exposes the writer to some censure, the possession hardly entitles him to any praise. . . . The more necessary each is, and the more blameable the transgression is, the less merit has the observance."[70] Hence Campbell adds, to the nearly seventy pages of discussion so far summarized, no less than eighty pages on grammatical purity, before proceeding (in his second volume) to discuss the positive virtues of style. Purity, including detections of misuse of words, he specifically assigns to the care of the grammarian.

At the same time, Campbell repeatedly notes that there is a real danger of carrying improvements too far in language. . . . "Our mother-tongue, by being too much impaired, may be impoverished, and so more injured in copiousness and nerves, than all our refinements will ever be able to compensate."[71] He considers that the French critics "have refined on their language to excess, and by needless repetitions have sometimes enervated the expression."[72] And he speaks repeatedly of

[67]*Ibid.*, pp. 400-406, *passim.*
[68]*Ibid.*, pp. 367, 101-2.
[69]*Ibid.*, 455.
[70]*Ibid.*, pp. 408-9 *passim.*
[71]*Ibid.*, p. 404.
[72]*Ibid.*, II, 9, *note.*

"recurring to circumlocution" as "an expedient which invariably tends to enervate" and "flatten the expression."[73]

In dealing with "grammatical purity, the first, and in some respects the most essential of all the virtues of elocution," the distribution is suggested, Campbell says, by Quintilian : Purity implies that words be English—the violation is called *barbarism;* the construction English—the violation is *solecism;* and both words and constructions "employed to express the precise meaning which custom hath affixed to them"—the violation is *impropriety.* In order not to go too far in revision, he undertakes to note only gross instances of these evils.[74]

1. The *barbarism* arises from the use of words entirely obsolete; of words entirely new, especially from the French; and of good words new-modeled. Campbell is particularly disturbed by combinations of the type *self-love,* by the attempt of logic to substitute *koran* for *alcoran,* and by unauthorized contractions; but he agrees with the Public, which "is rarely in the wrong," in accepting *mob.*

2. *Solecism.* Campbell has an interesting discussion here of the difference between the rhetorician's and the grammarian's measures of error. Since the latter "employs the language in order to the attainment of some further end,"—not, like the former, "to display his knowledge in the language—" an "offense is more or less heinous, precisely in proportion as it proves a greater or smaller obstruction to the speaker's or writer's aim. . . . Hence it happens, that when *solecisms* are not very glaring, when they do not darken the sense, or suggest some ridiculous idea, the rhetorician regards them as much more excusable' than *barbarisms.*"[74a]

Nevertheless, and in spite of the fact that he admits a considerable curtailment of his remarks on this head through being anticipated by Lowth and Priestley on many, Campbell has twenty-five pages of examples, including false comparison, tense, mode, and parallelism, and such instances of close logic as his objections to "cutting polysyllables into one (Swift)"[75] and "my christian and sirname (Addison)." Many of his examples have been included in Chapters IV and V or will appear in Chapter X.

3. Sufficient examples of *improprieties* censured by Campbell and other grammarians have probably been given in Chapters VI and VII. Under improper uses of single words, Campbell considers, rather gen-

[73]*Ibid.,* I, 508 and II, 40.
[74]*Ibid.,* I, 407-10, 487 and 457.
[74a]*Ibid.,* p. 431.
[75]Again censured under "impropriety."

erally, vulgarity, such as *on't* for *of it,* fustian and bombast, and barren insufficiency—rightly traced, with an acknowledgment to Abbé Girard's *Synonymes François,* to barrenness of ideas and their tedious repetition. Examples of Campbell's treatment of impropriety in words and in phrases are: failure to distinguish between *enough,* denoting sufficiency "in quantity or in degrees of quality," and *enow* for sufficiency "in number";[76] and "A view of *the* epic poem," which contains two improprieties—the use of *poem* in the French manner for poetry in general, and the similar use of *the,* never in English applied "to abstracts . . . unless with a view to appropriate them to some subject."[77]

16. Campbell's elaborate treatment of "good usage" has been shown thus in detail because it represents the entire process of appeal to "the best usage," as commonly practiced both then and now. It is clear that no questions of unanimous use ever come into discussion except as raised by ultra-purists; and only elaborate scientific investigation could determine whether one side or the other does or does not "greatly preponderate"—even granted we could get and observe sufficient authors of admitted reputation at precisely the right distance between the present day and undue antiquity. Thus, for practically every question at issue, as Campbell himself clearly demonstrated, one or another of his nine canons of use or three principles of purity must be appealed to; and so we come out at last by the same door where we went in, and run the gauntlet of the same criteria as before—of logic, etymology, and authority very thinly disguised—restated in Campbell's aggregate of twelve canons.

The service of the Scotch rhetoricians was distinctly less than that of Priestley; but it may be said in extenuation that, as Richard Grant White, in Dr. Wolff's apt phrase, "made up for having been accidentally born in New York by exhibiting all the linguistic . . . prejudices of Boston,"[78] so they seem to have felt that they had a considerable penance of their own, and a duty to their unfortunate fellow-countrymen, who had been cut off by political shifts from the collapse and merging

[76]First suggested by Priestley.
[77]*Ibid.,* I, 410-88, *passim.*
[78]*Cambridge History of American Literature,* III, 474.

into Midland of the Northern dialect across the Tweed. Lord Beattie specifically located standard English in the traditional region—London, Oxford, and Cambridge,[79] and with a similar belief Campbell and Blair spent their energies in propagating this standard, as they imagined it, in Scotland and the world.

Nevertheles, the re-emphasis of the theory that usage is the sole arbiter, even when the resulting practice was so complete a repudiation, possibly had some liberalizing effect in the following century, where it was sadly needed; and in any case, Campbell may be said to have given the death blow to the pale retreating forces of "universal grammar" and of "language as an entity." Though these are again and again reaffirmed, the statements are little regarded after Campbell's time.

17. Horne Tooke considers that "fashion can only help us in our commerce in the world to the rule (a necessary one I grant) of

Loquendum ut vulgus

But . . . unless we watch it well, it will mislead us widely from the other rule of

Sentiendum ut sapientes."

He does not consider Horace "any authority whatever upon this occasion,"[80] and obviously would have none of Campbell's "present use." He is for sticking to the established church, government, and language, "because they are established," and he trembles "at the very name of reform."[81] This is of course ironic reference to his unfortunate experience with radical ideas and authority; but it apparently does represent his real attitude toward language.

He does not tell us, however, how to ascertain what is established. His interest was in a freelance exploration in etymologies, but he did not bring out of it many specific principles or even examples of preferred usage. But if we may judge from his attitude toward Horace and the Muses[82] in general,

[79]*Theory of Language,* 1774, p. 92.
[80]*Diversions,* II, 97.
[81]*Ibid.,* p. 486.
[82]See the quotation in Chapter VIII, § 9.

he accepted complacently his own thesis that "reason is an arrant despot; who in his own dominions [Tooke evidently includes language here] admits of no authority but his own."[53] That he himself was swayed by the idea of "universal reason," like Harris and Monboddo, in spite of his scorn of their conclusions, and had no more reverence for custom than for fashion, is suggested by the following quotation from Dr. Taylor's *Elements of Civil Law,* (pp. 245-6), which indeed Tooke gives as relevant to his own ideas on civil disobedience:

> No *custom* can prevail against *right reason* and the *law* of nature . . . The will of the people is the foundation of *custom.* But if it be grounded not upon *reason,* but *error,* it is not the will of the people.[84]

Thus, in effect, did the maintainers of custom legalize and rationalize its overthrow, in language as in law.

18.   Philip Withers, as usual, is on both sides of this question. He has a number of really brilliant passages defending the sole potency of custom or compact. He notes that though our English words *persecute* and *prosecute* are an exact reversal of the Latin, with "no reason but Custom," nevertheless it is "absolutely necessary to conform to the established Distinction, as no Judge or Gentleman at the Bar ever talks of PERsecution" for offences against the Law.[85] Similarly, "Should have GONE is more *usual,* but not more *proper,*" than "should have WENT."[86]

But on the "appeal to the ear" Withers was devastatingly sarcastic: ". . . when the Propriety of either Mode of Expression is problematical, . . . an Appeal to the Ear . . . is just as extravagant as an auricular Solution of the Problems of Euclid. . . . It is the Duty of a Critic to gratify also the *Understanding.* . . . In Fact, there is no *Concord of sweet Sounds* half so melodious as STERLING SENSE."[87]   Oddly enough, this attack is delivered against Lowth, who had appealed to the

[82]*Diversions,* I, 43.
[84]Quoted in *Diversions* II, 16. The italics are probably Tooke's.
[85]*Aristarchus,* pp. 150-1.
[86]*Ibid.,* p. 209, *note.*
[87]*Ibid.,* pp. 363 and 408.

"shock to our ears" from *have knew, have saw, have gave*
as proof that *have wrote* and *have bore* are barbarous also.
This argument Withers turns neatly by suggesting the equal
shock of *knewen, founden, weren*. But he objected also to the
common-sense use of appeal to the ear as constantly employed
by Priestley to indicate preponderance of custom. Logic and
not good usage is indubitably first with Withers as with
Tooke.

19. We have seen what Noah Webster made of the "well-
nigh universal misuses of English" condoned by Dr. Johnson's
Dictionary.[88] Here, on the other hand, is his theory of custom: *"Grammar is built solely* on the *structure of language.*
That which is not found in the *practice of speaking a language*
can have *no place"* in grammars; their business is "to show
the student what a language is—not, how it *ought to be."*[89] But
teachers and the rules of English grammar as they now stand
"tend to introduce and confirm" differences between written
and spoken language.[90]

The difficulties of following custom Webster pictures as
"like fixing a light house on a floating island . . . so long as it
is supposed that a local practice has no standard but a *local
practice;* that is, no standard but *itself."* He has the same objection to make against the proposal to imitate the English
standard, which resolves itself into "the practice of a few men
in London," i. e., a shifting local standard again. "If the
most eminent speakers are not to direct our practice, where
shall we look for a guide? The answer is extremely easy; the
rules of the language itself, and the *general practice of the
nation,* constitute propriety in speaking."[91] "The business of a
grammarian is not to examine whether or not national practice
is founded on philosophical principles; but to *ascertain*[92] the
national practice, that the learner may be able to weed from

[88]See Chapter III, § 7, above.
[89]*Errors of Grammars*, 1798, p. 6.
[90]*Ibid.*, p. 24.
[91]*Dissertations*, pp. 25-7, *passim*.
[92]Here the current meaning, not the older and etymological one used by
Swift in his *Proposal*, is evidently intended.

his own, any local peculiarities or false idioms . . . Dr. Priestley is the only writer upon this subject, who seems to have been guided by just principles."[93] But Webster does not tell how to go to work to ascertain general or national practice—only that he himself has been at great pains to do so—nor what to do when divisions in practice are found. And so we, like him, are again thrown back upon "the rules of the language itself" or "the principle of analogy running through the whole," which gives every one a free hand at logical interpretation. These principles "become an authority superior to the arbitrary decisions of any man or any class of men. There is one exception only to this remark: When a deviation from analogy has become the universal practice of a nation, it then takes place of all rules and becomes the standard of propriety."[94]

The impracticable nature of this principle resides in the fact that when a standard is universal, there is no question about it, unless one is raised by the mousing grammarian and logician; it is only against such men that the barrier of custom is even supposedly effective, and it is a barrier they of all others have the least inclination to respect.

Webster earnestly tried, however, to follow usage, at least so far as grammatical form and syntax are concerned, as in his statement: *"a pair of bars,* a *pair of stairs,* in strictness of speech, are very absurd phrases; but perhaps it is better to admit such anomalies, than attempt to change universal and immemorial practice."[95] This attempt at a scientific attitude is shown again by the radical change in his ideas about the subjunctive mode and other topics which continued observation, under the impetus of Horne Tooke, effected in successive editions of the *Grammatical Institute.*[96]

20.   Murray, eclectic as usual, accepted even the principle of

[93]*Ibid.,* pp. 204-6.
[94]*Ibid.,* pp. 27-8.
[95]*Ibid.,* p. 214, *note.* The autographed copy of the first (1784) edition of his *Grammatical Institutes* in the New York Public Library gives further evidence of this in matters added and struck out. Not all these corrections appear in later editions.
[96]See Chapter XI, §§ 18-21, below.

custom and gave it perspicuous statement: "With respect to anomalies and variations of language thus established,[97]
it is the grammarian's business to submit, not to remonstrate.
. . . In pertinaciously opposing . . . he may, indeed, display
learning and sagacity, and, in some degree, obscure points that
are sufficiently clear and decided; but he cannot reasonably
hope, either to succeed in his aims, or to assist the learner in
discovering the true standard and principles of language. . . .
Cases which custom has left dubious are certainly within the
grammarian's province . . . but when authority [i. e. custom]
speaks out and decides the point, it were perpetually to unsettle
the language to admit of cavil and debate . . . Anomalies then,
under the limitation mentioned, become the law, as clearly as
the plainest analogies."[98] In one definite case Murray is to be
recorded as actually observing his principle of custom in opposition to the main stream of conservative followers of Lowth
in which he mainly belonged: the use of *whose* as genitive of
which he not only allowed, but defended as valuable for its
terseness.[99]

21. In summary, many of the writers on language in the
eighteenth century professed to follow custom or usage or acknowledged its determining influence in one or more particulars. But none save Priestley made the appeal to usage with
anything approaching consistency. As Campbell's *Philosophy
of Rhetoric* amazingly illustrates, the appeal to usage in the
eighteenth century resulted in a complete repudiation of usage.

---

[97]He cites *none are, you have,* etc.
[98]Murray's *English Grammar*, 1800 Am. ed., pp. 134-5.
[99]See the discussion of gender, above, Chapter V, § 9.

CHAPTER X

THE STRUGGLE OF ELITES

My Animadversions will extend to such Phrases only as People in decent Life inadvertently adopt . . . Purity and Politeness of Expression is . . . the only external Distinction which remains between a Gentleman and a Valet, a Lady and a Mantua-maker.

Withers, *Aristarchus*, 1788.

CHAPTER X

THE STRUGGLE OF ELITES

1. The language described by the grammarians and rhetoricians of the eighteenth century was of course that of gentlemen. In one or two cases, to be sure, it was forseen or even desired that the efforts to fix a standard for the speech would result in its being imitated by the lower classes. Farro's *Grammar* said, "This GRAMMAR contains a Method so easy, that every *Female Teacher* in the British Dominions may open an *English* Grammar School, and render themselves much more useful to the public."[1] Something like this appears to have happened. Buchanan announced that his book was fitted to advance the English of Tradesmen, that they "may not be stigmatized even by foreigners" for their barbarous speech,[2] and John Ash that grammar is valuable "for young Gentlemen designed merely for Trade."[3] Both Coote and Withers, publishing in 1788, argued among other points the advantages to persons in trade or manufactures, of command of the language.[3a]

But the majority of writers seem to have felt that they were writing for the edification and use of gentlemen, to warn them against inadvertent contamination with the language of the vulgar. The following quotations will illustrate the nature of these pronouncements:

> My Animadversions will extend to such Phrases only as People in decent Life inadvertently adopt. . . . Purity and Politness of Expression . . . is the only external Distinction which remains between a Gentleman and a Valet; a Lady and a Mantua-maker.
> Philip Withers, *Aristarchus*, pp. 160-1.

[1]*Royal Universal Grammar*, 1754, preface, p. vii.
[2]*Regular Syntax*, 1767, p. xviii.
[3]*Easiest Introduction*, 1766, preface.
[3a]Coote's *Grammar*, Preface iii, iv; *Aristarchus*, p. 31.

And Bayly writes:

> . . . though sometimes it may be difficult, if not impossible to reduce common speech to rule, and indeed it is beneath a grammarian's attempt.
>
> Bayly, *Plain and Complete Grammar*, 1772, p. 43.

2. The attack on vulgar usage begins with the *Art of Speaking*: Changes in language occur because "The best Expressions grow low and degenerate, when profan'd by the populace, and applied to mean things. The use they make of them, infecting them with a mean and abject Idea, causes that we cannot use them without sullying and defiling those things, which are signified by them."[4] "But it is no hard matter to discern between the depraved Language of common People, and the noble refin'd expressions of the Gentry, whose condition and merits have advanced them above the other."[5] The methods are "Experience [observation], Reason, and Analogie" and "Experience is the best of the three," though "Languages are never refined, 'till men begin to canvass and examine them; till such expressions as corrupt use has introduced . . . are exploded by learned and sagacious Men, and Men that have exact knowledge of this Art."[6]

3. *The war upon contractions.* Whether it was "no hard matter to discern" vulgar speech may be illustrated by examples of the attempt to ban contractions from the use of gentlemen. The words *till* (also spelled *'till* in the paragraph above) and *fix'd*, especially the latter, represent the sort of evil that Swift campaigned against, "most of all in the poets"; he referred apparently to the "false idea of spelling as we speak." He also spoke of "so jarring a sound" in *rebuk't, fledg'd,* and the like.[7] Did he invariably pronounce the final syllable himself?

Bayly's *Introduction to Languages* also has *'till;* it makes objection, however, to *has, leads, loves, does,* for *hath, leadeth,*

---

[4] *Art of Speaking*, 1708 ed., p. 50.
[5] *Ibid.*, p. 41.
[6] *Ibid.*, pp. 41-4.
[7] *Proposal for Correcting,* etc., 1712, p. 41.

loveth, doeth, dont for *do not, heard* for *heared*, which though "allowable enough in the Hurry of Conversation, ought undoubtedly to be avoided in correct Writing."[8]

George Harris, the author of the *Observations*, 1752, writes, "ADO is an Abbreviation of *to do,* and ought never to be used by any Man, who has the least Regard for the *English* Language or his own Credit." He cites specifically "with much ADO," "has much ADO."[9] He says again, "Sometimes even two words are unnaturally abbreviated into one—*tis* and *it's* are used for *it is . . . shant* for *shall not, . . . hant* for *have not, maynt* for *may not,* &c. And the greatest Part of these strange Words are now so familiarized, that the Apostrophe, which is a Kind of Apology for Omission, is already discarded, as unnecessary." He expects next to see *genr'l, natral.* Suggesting an authoritative Academy to supervise preparation of a grammar and a dictionary, he adds, "I mean only to force them [the populace] to spell with Uniformity and without Elisions."[10]

Buchanan remarks: *"It's* for *it is* is vulgar; *'tis* is used."[11] Campbell also writes—spelling oddly, since he elsewhere uses the possessive form *its*—of the mistake of using *"it's* the genitive of the pronoun *it,* for *'tis,* a contraction of *it is."*[12] Withers remarks that *"a'nt* ought to be avoided, even when the Construction admits a Verb in the plural Number," and adds, "Let it be remembered by those Economists, who desire to save Ink and Breath by a prudent Abbreviation of their Phrases, that *a'nt* is the plural Contraction; and *isn't* the singular."[13]

Withers is of the opinion that concise forms of Expression are "very proper in familiar intercourse"—in a note he particularly mentions "both Writing and Conversation"—"provided they neither cause OBSCURITY nor infringe any RULE of GRAMMAR." But, under the specific heading of vulgar expressions, he says of "house to let" that as *"House* is

[8]*Op. cit.,* 1758, I, 100.
[9]*Observations upon the English Language,* p. 21.
[10]*Ibid.,* pp. 12-13.
[11]*Regular Syntax,* p. 76.
[12]*Philosophy* I, 460.
[13]*Aristarchus,* pp. 51-2.

passive on this Occasion, BE—after—TO is indispensable," and even *"to be let* is improper, because it has the Verb active —LET—after the passive *Sign*—BE." It must stand "TO BE LETT."[14]

Blair himself does not escape censure on the principle set going by Swift, when he writes *penult,* objected to by Campbell. But Campbell admits *mob,* alone of the words stigmatized by Swift, and remarks that the "humor of abbreviating arose about the end of the last century."[15]

Hornsey gives the matter in the form which it was to take throughout the following century, and even to the present in utra-precise handbooks of correct English: speaking of *wont,* a contraction of *will not,* "But this and all such like contractions ought to be avoided as much as possible, especially in the writing of prose. In poetry and in familiar conversation contractions are allowable; as, *lov'd, prais'd,* for *loved, praised,* &c."[16] A stiffening and formalizing of schoolroom style, by this and the like arbitrary rules—omitting no relatives or connectives like *that,* always (or never) inserting the first *and* in a series of the form "red, white, and blue"—has resulted from taking seriously the baseless notions of eighteenth-century and later theorizers about elegance; the process can be traced clearly through the grammars, rhetorics, and handbooks from then to now.

4. *Other examples of vulgarity and elegance.* The *Royal English Grammar,* 1737, notes that *yes* "is more usual and modish than *yea,"* and of *ay,* "this method of affirmation is rude and ungenteel."[17] Buchanan repeats the comment; he also notes that *yea* is confined to the Quakers, and that *I* (ay) "is accounted rude, especially to our betters."[18]

Expressions "very common, but yet very disgustful" to George Harris are "chaulking out a way," "handleing a sub-

[14]*Aristarchus,* pp. 145-7.
[15]*Philosophy,* I, 428-9. Temple (1758) carefully wrote *Mobility.*
[16]*Short Grammar,* 1793, p. 37.
[17]*Greenwood,* 1737, p. 98.
[18]*Regular Syntax,* 1767, p. 179.

ject," "driving a bargain," and "bolstering up an argument."[19] The objection to metaphor, in a later period covered by lumping as slang all examples of it which one does not like, thus begins very early in the literal minds of critics. It accounts for numbers of Bentley's and Warburton's emendations, and for many strictures by Campbell already cited. Frequently the objection arises often from a sensitiveness to anything having to do with trade or labor.

A curious bit of elegance appears in "An Answer to Certain Passages in Mr. W———'s Preface to his Edition of Shakespeare."[20] It is an earnest exception to Warburton's emendation of a line in which apparently he had changed the word *female;* the writer comments on this as "the prettiest and most poetical Word in the sentence." A similar shift of fashions in elegance then and now is illustrated by the following phrase in Potter's *Art of Criticism,* a sharp attack upon the style of Dr. Johnson: "A tasty modern, the author of . . ."[21]

In J. Johnson's *Dictionary* is the remark that Greenwood says the plural *chickens* "seems a mistake founded on the errors of the vulgar."[22] I have been unable to find this quotation. In the *Essay,* 1711, Greenwood gives the singular *chick* and plural *chicken* with other plurals "imitated from the Dutch," and in the *Royal English Grammar,* evidently apprised of the error, he has without comment: singular *chicken,* plural *chickens.*[23]

Priestley is quite sensitive to vulgarisms: *"since when,"* *"worth their while"* he thinks "rather suit familiar and low style," as also "to do a thing anyhow, somehow," and "Somehow . . . they look upon . . ." from *Louisa Mildmay.*[24] *"For all that* is too low and vulgar," though "we want a conjunction adapted to the familiar style, equivalent to *notwithstanding."*[25] The phrase with the pronoun possessive, "my Lord Bedford"

[19]*Observations upon the English Language,* 1752, pp. 24-5.
[20]London, 1748, p. 18.
[21]*Op. cit.,* 1779, p. 11.
[22]*Royal and Universal Dictionary,* 1762, p. 20.
[23]*Essay,* 1711, p. 49; *Grammar,* 1737, p. 33.
[24]*Rudiments,* pp. 134-5.
[25]*Ibid.,* p. 139.

"seems to imply some degree of familiarity, and persons who pretend not to any sort of intimacy with the nobility, do not commonly use it." But the contraction of a sentence, "I beg of you, my Lord," is "not common, and low."[26]

Buchanan remarks "a sort of tautology often to be met with in low Writers. . . . Words inserted which have no Relation to the Sense." His example is from Pope.[27] On the other hand, "Words are elegantly left out by our best Writers, though otherwise necessary to make the Sentence full and grammatical."[28]

Dr. Salisbury in his onslaught upon *had rather* comments, "That the Learned do suffer themselves to be governed in the matter of Language by the ignorant, is too notorious to be denied, and abundance of instances might be given of it."[29]

5. This battle of élites, as Dr. Livingston has aptly termed it,[30] was naturally fought most hotly by persons who had had to earn and prove their gentility. Robert Baker says frankly that he had had only six years of schooling, no Greek, and only Latin enough to forget, though he apparently could read French and knew continental art appreciatively. He had "few more books than what an old church-going woman may . . . have upon her mantel-piece," and never saw a folio copy of Johnson's *Dictionary*—though he lived near London and did not publish his book till 1770—nor the abridged dictionary till, about a week before his book went to press. he got it from a circulating library to which he subscribed. He acknowledges with thanks that Garrick sent him a pass to his theater, adding that because of this courtesy he destroyed some strictures he had written on the acting of Garrick's company. This is a real loss, for the few specimens of these criticisms which he preserved and recorded are interesting and intelligent.[31]

[26]*Ibid.*, pp. 88 and 110.
[27]*Regular Syntax*, p. xxix.
[28]*Ibid.*, p. xxvii.
[29]*Two Grammatical Essays*, 1768, p. 12.
[30]Arthur Livingston, "The Myth of Good English," *Century Magazine* (110:398-405), August 1925.
[31]*Reflections*, 1770 ed., preface, pp. iv-v and xv-xxii.

Baker takes up the cudgels firmly for the language of Gentlemen:

> Of "themselves and Families," from the *Monthly Review,* he re-
> marks, "a very bad Expression, though very common.   It is mere
> Shopkeepers cant" like *Harris and Son,* etc. "and will always be
> found contemptible in the Ears of Persons of any Taste."
> *Reflections,* 1770, p. 118.

> Of *demean* as signifying debase or lessen, used often in *Pamela,*
> and in Swift, "if I mistake not," once or twice: "This must be an
> oversight because of *mean, meanness.* . . . If the "lower People
> . . . were once to get hold of" the substantive *Demeanor,* they
> would equally misapply it.
> *Ibid.,* pp. 10-11.

> On *most an end* for "most commonly, for the most part," Baker is
> bitter; it "is an expression that would almost disgrace the mouth of
> a hackney-coachman."
> *Remarks,* 1779, pp. 82-3.[32]

Of the "vile phrases" and "barbarous contractions" used by
Baker himself, according to the critics of the *Monthly Review,*
we have already seen an account.[33]   Baker also reports that a
friend had told him "the expression of 'a dog in a Dancing
School,'" quoted apparently from Congreve, was "too familiar
to use in the 'Address to the King'" concerning an Academy
and other matters, which Baker had prefixed to his first edition.
He refutes the imputation and retains the phrase in his first
edition,[34] but in that of 1779 omits address and all.

6.   Bayly uses a phrase apparently common and uncensured
then, but now regarded as "commercial and low": "Admits of
contractions . . . and . . . introduceth the same into writing.[35]
Blair notes that *vulgar* already in his day had come to mean,
when applied to language, "impure, or debased language, such
as is commonly spoken by the low people," and consequently

[32]Fitzedward Hall found the phrase in Warburton, Sanderson, and Milton
(bis).
[33]Chapter III, above, § 4.
[34]*Reflections,* 1770 ed., following page 128.   It is pleasant that Baker was
mentioned in the obituaries of the *Gentleman's Magazine* of June, 1781, as
"Robert Baker, esq."
[35]*Plain and Complete Grammar,* 1772, p. 44.

censures Swift for using it in the older meaning; it nevertheless kept this sense through the eighteenth century at least, as
shown by numerous references to "our vulgar translation of
the Bible." Blair censures Swift for "left to shift for themselves," as "too low for a grave treatise," and is in turn rent
by Withers for "pitched upon,"[36] which is "improper in a
serious and elaborate performance."

Withers treats the topic of vulgar use in full from page 136
to 213 of *Aristarchus,* including under this condemnation misuse of *shall* and *will, let* and *to be lett,* and many other distinctions. He is, apparently, the first to condemn the use of
got with *have* "when possession is implied,"[37] and so is the
progenitor of many pages of handbooks. He notes that "in
London well-bred People never use the word CATCH"—which
he equates with "none of your JAW"—though they use
caught; overtake is preferred for pursuit.[38]

Withers quotes Chesterfield as saying that "a vulgar Man
is perpetually using vulgar Proverbs" and describing the language of a gentleman as "neither deformed by SOLECISMS,
nor disgraced by low and vulgar WORDS, . . . characteristic of
low Company and bad Education." In this connection Withers
censures "cast about for" and "passion flags." He adds, *"To
leave in the Lurch*—and *to swallow contradictions*—are Ideas,
which may be elegantly expressed by a thousand Modes of
Circumlocution, and to Circumlocution I counsel the Student
to have Recourse on all similar Occasions. The Caution may
be thought unnecessary, but I assure my Reader that a Lady
of Name in the Republic of Letters has used the above Phrases,
in a serious and very important History."[39]

7. Campbell notes that impropriety in phrases arises often
from "affectation of an easy, familiar, and careless manner,"
as in Addison, "or from love of novelty or variety."[40] He in-

[36]Blair, *Lectures,* I, 448 and 457; *Aristarchus,* p. 205 f.
[37]*Aristarchus,* p. 143.
[38]*Ibid.,* pp. 149-50.
[39]*Aristarchus* (1788), pp. 163 and 136 ff. See Campbell on "circumlocution" above, Ch. IX, § 15.
[40]*Philosophy* I, 475-7.

stances a great many errors, most of which have been already considered under his doctrine of usage in general. The best illustrations are his opposition to the "cant" uses of *advice, turtle,* and *nervous.*[41]

Mennye seems to have been the first to insist specificially upon *so* after *not.*[42] He had a large number of followers in the nineteenth-century handbooks.

Webster, in the *Letter to Dr. Ramsay,* 1807, censures Johnson most severely for admitting "low, vulgar, cant words," with a total want of just discrimination; some of his examples are familiar in sound: *jackalent, parma-citty, jiggumbob,*[43] and the first quite fails to bear out his statement that Shakespeare wrote English rather acceptably until he attempted the learned style.

Various writers in this period glimpsed dimly the notion that different styles are appropriate to different occasions—even Dr. Johnson himself felt this.[44] But this notion did not become part of the theory of criticism in the eighteenth century, or in the nineteenth for that matter.

A plea for easy style in speech is given in the letters of Fox to Dr. Parr, already referred to. Admitting that "however heavy" is "an inaccuracy," Fox adds, "but . . . one of those *carelessnesses* which in anything that purports to be speech, is much to my taste."[45] This fits well with the statement that Fox used to plunge into the midst of a sentence and trust to God Almighty to get him out.[46] He appears, in spite of his complacency under many of Dr. Parr's strictures, to have felt definitely the value of informality and ease even in parliamentary debate.

8. *Provincialisms.* Campbell's assault upon both provincial dialect and professional cant, which he grouped with it, has been described. Practically all discussions of this problem took

---

[41]Above Chapter IX, § 7, *note* 44.
[42]*Grammar,* 1785, p. 19.
[43]*Letter to Dr. Ramsay,* 1807, p. 11.
[44]See above, Ch. VII, § 14, *note* 40. Cicero's treatment of levels of style was of course familiar from classical and medieval rhetoric.
[45]*Works of Dr. Parr,* I, 613.
[46]George Herbert Palmer, *Self-Cultivation in English,* p. 16.

the language of Scotchmen as the center of attack. J. Johnson's *Dictionary*, 1763, condemns as Scotch the plural *acquaintances*, for the proper form without *s*,[47] and has a list almost two pages long of Scotticisms from Hume's *Political Discourses* (1752), of which the following are samples:[48]

proven	furnish goods to him *for* furnish
maltreat *for* abuse	him with goods
in the long run *for* at long run	pled
question if *for* whether	tear to *for* in pieces
simply *for* absolutely impossible	denuded *for* divested
common soldiers *for* private men	learn *for* teach
terrible argument *for* good argument	compete *for* enter into competition
ment	butter and bread *for* bread and
a pretty enough girl *for* a pretty	butter
girl enough	on *for* of a sudden
paper, pen, and ink *for* pen, ink,	nothing else *for* no other thing
and paper	

These obviously range widely, from historic confusions as of *learn* for *teach,* probably as common in England as in Scotland, to personal predilections in order and choice of words probably peculiar to J. Johnson.

Priestley considers that the omission of *to* after dare, except in *dare say, dare go,* since "it does not seem natural . . . must be acccording to the Scotch idiom," which omits *to* after *help*— "to help carry on . . ." He will allow the Scotch no quarter for their errors: "It will be no objection to the . . . use of any of my remarks, . . . that many of them were suggested by the perusal of the writings of Scotchmen. It is sufficient for my purpose, that they write in the English language. Many of their readers will not know that they were Scotch. If they excel in other articles of good stile, their example is not the less dangerous." But he adds, "he must be prejudiced to a degree that deserves ridicule, who will not allow that several of the most correct writers of English are Scotchmen."[49]

No discussion of the *shall* and *will* matter in the latter part of

[47]He may have persuaded Burns to *acquaintance.*
[48]*Royal and Universal Dictionary*, 1762, pp. 19-20.
[49]*Rudiments*, pp. xii-xiii.

the eighteenth century, as later, could get under way without condemnation of the Scotch and Irish for their misuses. Withers is particularly harsh here. Kenrick speaks of their attempts to "set up schoolmaster": "There seems indeed a most ridiculous absurdity in the pretensions of a native of Aberdeen or Tipperary to teach the natives of London to speak and read."[50] Buchanan is especially bad; Sheridan is better. Kenrick's dedication is to the King, George III, "the most accomplished speaker of the English tongue."

Blair, in apology for "adventuring to criticize the sentences of so eminent an author as Mr. Addison," notes as justification that Blair was reading his lectures "in that part of the Kingdom . . . where the ordinary spoken language often differs much from what is used by good English authors." We have noted that Beattie specifically located the area of standard speech in the conventionally proper region of southern England; to approximate that standard and to assist other provincials to do so was the purpose of a large number of the students of language during the eighteenth century.[51]

9. Webster was, on the contrary, a strong advocate of English as used in America; "On examining the language, and comparing the practice of speaking among the yeomanry of this country, with the stile of Shakespeare and Addison, I am constrained to declare, that the people of America, in particular the English decendants, speak the most *pure English* now known in the world. . . . in a vast number of instances, they have adhered to the true phrases, where people, who despise their plain manners, have run into error. Thus they say, 'a man is going *by*' and not *going past,* which is nonsense. They say, 'I *purpose* to go,' and not *'propose* to go,' which is not good English. . . . They say 'a ship *lies* in harbor,' not *lays,*

[50]*Dictionary, . . to which is Prefixed a Rhetorical Grammar,* 1773, Introduction, p. 1.

[51]At least fourteen of the authors whose books were particularly examined for this study were either probably Scotchmen or Irishmen, or at least published first in Scotland or Ireland, and twelve Americans, as against some twenty-five probably English among those appearing after 1750. Others like Hornsey were northern men (York). Murray published first in York, though he was native to the colonies. This of course does not include translations from the French and German.

which is a modern corruption. They say, 'I have done,' and never 'I *am* done,' which is nonsense. They say, 'It was *on* Monday evening,' not 'of a Monday evening,' which is an error. They never use the absurd phrase *expect it was* . . . They never say 'he is home' but always, 'at home.' They use the old phrase, 'It is half after six o'clock,' which is more correct than *half past six.*"[52] Webster writes that he never heard "a wrong use of *shall* or *will* among them—his climactic statement. His determination to erect a national custom largely out of New England materials was laudable, but of a piece with his zeal in reforming pronunciations and word-choices.

10. *Summary.* In adjusting this matter of class and regional dialects, it is usually assumed that the eighteenth-century grammarians gave most help. Their effort appears in this chapter, however, to have been as confused a struggle as that over words or logical theories of correctness. Very few points here suggested were settled by the strictures of the theorists. In fact, most of their pet aversions have become part of standard and unquestioned speech. The likeness of their performance to that of the makers of handbooks and lists of misused words today is fairly clear from these examples.

In the discussion of class dialects, the eighteenth-century writers came nearest to a modern and scientific view upon usage. But none of them except possibly Priestley and Fox actually saw that an opinion on the "correctness" of an expression means neither more nor less than an estimate of its probable social effect: that is, its impression of formality, ease, rusticity, illiteracy, vulgarity, or the like. Even where this principle was in part recognized, its actual applications were of little value; the prepossessions of the language theorists hindered their observation, and they were too ready to accept authoritative pronouncements in place of objective data. The same difficulties affected most of the writing upon usage in the following century, and a valid description of levels of usage did not appear before Dr. Murray's preface to the *New English Dictionary* and Dr. Krapp's *Modern English.*

[52]*Dissertations,* pp. 288 and 388 f.

CHAPTER XI

VARIOUS SOLUTIONS OF PROBLEMS OF INFLECTION

Of the doubtful points [in grammar] . . . not half of them have been correctly settled by Lowth and his followers, and I have no hesitation in affirming, that the grammars now taught in our schools *introduce more errors than they correct.*

Noah Webster, *Letter to Dr. Ramsay.*

CHAPTER XI

VARIOUS SOLUTIONS OF PROBLEMS OF INFLECTION

1. The preceding chapters of this study have presented the subject with an arbitrary simplification. In order to discover precisely the nature of the various appeals used to solve problems of correctness, each has been for the most part isolated, and its application to a variety of such problems illustrated. But few difficulties were considered on a single principle. Not only did different authorities come to conclusions by different routes—and, naturally, not often to the same conclusion; but the same writer often tried varied theories on the same debated construction, and sometimes came to a settlement satisfactory to himself by a combination of two or more principles. Thus Bayly describes the censured words *whereof* and *whereby* as "proper, useful, and analogous," and accepted by "one of the best criticks of the age, Dr. Johnson," and is for retaining them on these counts.[1] Of "previous to" and "agreeable to" he remarks that the logic of a supplied noun, also invoked by Webster, "justifies the use of the adjective form rather than the adverbial, even though it should be urged that the adverbial form is usual and preferred by good writers . . . The phrase *suitably to* . . . would introduce into grammar an unknown construction, that of adverbs governing a dative and ablative case."[2] Baker admits that displacement of *only* and the correlative conjunctions, though "slovenly," "is to be suffered" wherever "there is no avoiding the Impropriety without a Stiffness or Heaviness of Expression,"[3] and that even omission of the relative in the nominative case is to be tolerated

[1] *Plain and Complete Grammar*, 1772, p. 26.
[2] *Ibid.*, p. 75.
[3] *Reflections*, 1770, p. 126; *Remarks*, 1779, p. 106.

"in *Shakespear* and other great Writers, . . . where the Omission adds to the Spirit of the Sentence, without causing any Obscurity."[4]

2. But the usual purpose of appealing to various principles was not to sanction by one of them a liberty the others restricted. Often such appeals led only to an unsolved confusion, as when Priestley wrote: "In all cases, *that* should have been used" after *greatest, same,* etc. *Whom* is here "very aukward . . . But if a preposition must precede the relative, there is a kind of necessity to replace *who* or *which;* because the pronoun *that* does not admit of such a construction." "The same indifference to which they saw him totally abandoned" is indeed a poor result of "right order" of the preposition.[5] This is like the crux created by the Latin rule that a gerund must be construed with a genitive, and the nineteenth-century discovery that a noun like *city* or *foundation,* and presumably therefore the pronoun *it* referring to such a noun, must never be construed in the genitive. Here, as in deciding the proper case of pronouns after "seems to be" and the concord of verbs after "I am he that . . .," logic meets problems of expression which it is not equipped to solve, and the writer of conventional grammars is baffled. Bayly had a neat way of disposing of such difficulties: "The construction of a sentence is figurative, when it departs from common forms and general rules."[6] But this kind of solution by no means satisfies your true logical grammarian.

An extreme instance of caution butressing itself with all possible principles and theories is given at the end of Volume I of Campbell's *Philosophy of Rhetoric.* After more than three pages of examination of Lowth's objection to "the rule's being observed," the conclusion is announced importantly in a separate paragraph: "I am of opinion, therefore, upon the whole, that as the idiom in question is analogical, supported by good

[4]*Reflections,* 1770, p. 4; *Remarks,* 1779, p. 2.
[5]*Rudiments,* 1769 ed., p. 100.
[6]*Plain and Complete Grammar,* p. 63.

use, and sometimes very expedient, it ought not to be entirely repudiated."[7]

3. As will be shown in the following pages, attempts were sometimes made in the eighteenth century to keep a practical command of two principles going strongly in opposite directions. We see this occurring with Withers' "Principles of Common Sense, and the Usage of our best Authors,"[8] or Webster's equivalent "well-nigh universal [or] national usage, and the analogy of the language." The following discussions of problems of case, in particular the varying fortunes of the genitives of nouns and pronouns, and of the subjunctive mood, will illustrate the dubious results of criticism which could not agree on its principles of attack, but applied any that seemed possibly applicable.

4. *Nominative and accusative case.* Murray reports that he "long doubted the propriety of assigning to English substantives an objective case," but came by a "renewed critical examination of the subject" to a "full persuasion, that the nouns of our language are entitled to this comprehensive case."[9] The actual problem of correctness here of course centers in the personal pronouns and *who*. Nevertheless, a curious question about the propriety of Pope's use of a noun in a "double capacity" (both nominative and objective) is seriously raised by Lowth:[10]

In him who *is,* and him who *finds,* a *friend.*

Similarly, Baker insists that *which* cannot be in the same sentence both nominative and accusative.[11] If he had said that this construction is usually clumsy and ambiguous, rather than that it cannot be used, he would have made a possibly useful observation, for he and other writers[12] give sufficient instances of its awkwardness. Here is a problem attempted by logic only, with no recourse to usage, per-

[7]*Op. cit.,* I, 511.
[8]*Aristarchus,* p. 101.
[9]*Grammar,* 1809 ed., p. 84.
[10]*Short Introduction,* 1769 ed., p. 125; not in previous editions.
[11]*Reflections,* 1770, pp. 77 ff. *Remarks,* 1779, pp. 40 f.
[12]See Lowth, 1762 ed., p. 137, *note,* and Baker, *loc. cit.*

spicuity, or euphony, any or all of which might have been appealed to. For the discussion over *ye* for accusative *you,* see Chapter VIII, § 11, above.

5. *"Oblique cases of pronouns."* The case of pronouns after linking or copulative verbs, on the contrary, was debated from various angles of Latin analogy, custom, euphony, and conflicting appeals of grammatical logic. Most of the writers examined held inflexibly to the Latin rule, and gave considerable lists of "improprieties," from Shakespeare to their contemporaries. Lowth, holding this position, incidentally states that the verb in the infinitive requires always the accusative case of the pronoun after it,[13] and thus opens the brisk controversy on this point which still continues. Most prescriptive grammars insist on "it seems to be ,he," but the contrary ruling is also to be found.

The side of the observers of custom is, as usual, best stated by Priestley: "All our grammarians say, that the nominative case of pronouns ought to follow the verb substantive [*is* and the like] as well as precede it; yet many familiar forms of speech, and the example of some of our best writers, would lead us to make a contrary rule; or, at least, would leave us at liberty to adopt which we liked best: *Are these the houses?* . . . *Yes, they are* them. *Who is there? It is* me. *It is* him. *It is not* me *you are in love with.* Addison. *It cannot be* me. Swift. *To that which once was* thee. Prior. *There is but one man that she can have, and that is* me. Clarissa.

"When the word *if* begins a sentence, it seems pretty clear. that no person, whose attention to artificial rules did not put a sensible [i.e. *noticeable*] restraint upon his language, would ever use the nominative case after the verb *to be.* Who would not say, *If it be* me, rather than *If it be* I?

" . . . I think no person, who reads the following sentence will question the propriety of the use of the oblique case. '. . . become in some measure *him* . . .' Smith's Moral Sentiments." But Dr. Bryan notes that Priestley himself wrote "It was *we.*"[14]

[13]*Short Introduction,* 1762, pp. 105-6; 1769, p. 132.
[14]*Rudiments,* pp. 104-5; p. 191. *Manly Studies,* p. 386 *note.*

Robert Baker, while praising Congreve as superior to most writers "in Elegance of Stile," contends that to Petulant's "You were the quarrel," Millamant should have been made to answer "I!" *"Me* is wrong. . . . Yet it must be owned there are some Places where the Nominative is required, and where the Word *I,* as having too thin and unsubstantial a Sound, would not do." For "another me" in the same play he proposes another "my-self." A pencil note in the Harvard copy (1770 ed.) comments, "Self alone would do, & be better than my-self." Though he admits that oblique cases are frequently used, "even by the better sort of people," Baker's condemnation is characteristically decided: "This is bad English."[15] Here appeals to euphony and to custom are overruled by grammatical logic built on the Latin analogy.

Baker speaks ironically of the "extraordinary correctness" of the use by "inferior Writers" of the forms "It was not *him* they attacked, *us* they slandered," where he erroneously supposed the government to be by the following rather than the preceding verb.[16] Campbell is hoist by precisely this false logic. He writes of this construction, citing one of Priestley's examples: "I shall observe in passing, that one of Priestley's quotations is defensible on a different principle, and therefore not to his purpose. 'It is not *me* you are in love with.' The *me* here is governed by the preposition *with.* 'It is not *with me* you are in love.' Such transpositions are frequent in our language."[17] One wishes Campbell had interpreted the construction of the "omitted relative" in this sentence. Lowth had already analyzed this construction with whatever logic applies, stating that the preposition governs the omitted relative, not the personal pronoun.[18]

A specific comment on "between you and I," in a footnote to Archibald Campbell's *Lexiphanes,* suggests that it was commonly censured: "In the first Edition of this work, I had used the phrase *between you and I,* which tho' it must be

---

[15]*Reflections,* 1770, pp. 48-50.
[16]*Loc. cit.*
[17]*Philosophy,* I, 438-9 and *note.*
[18]*Short Introduction,* 1762 ed., p. 146, *note.*

confessed to be ungrammatical, is yet almost universally used in familiar conversation, and sometimes by our best comick writers: see Wycherley's *Plain Dealer*. This very trivial slip, if it be one, has not escaped the diligence and sagacity of the learned and candid Reviewers. One of our worthy labourers in that periodical drudgery has declared this phrase, and a few others, which are only improper in his crazy imagination, to be more offensive to a judicious reader, than all the hard words I had attempted to expose. See Critical Review. His fellow drudge in the Monthly has used me with still less ceremony: 'The author of the Rambler, says he, is censured for writing ill by a person who cannot write at all.' To prove which, he instances this unlucky, *between you and I, old Veteran, I cannot for my heart.* Such are Reviewers, and such are their learned labors . . . I have observed in the Sale of Authors, and I repeat the observation, that our Reviewers, like Sir Roger de Coverly, who would suffer no body to sleep at church but himself, will not suffer an adventurer at the pen to be reprehended, tho' ever so justly, by any but themselves."[19]

In a letter written in 1774, Horace Walpole says, "You will be diverted to hear that a man who thought of nothing so much as the purity of his language, I mean Lord Chesterfield, says, 'you and *me* shall not be well together,' and this not once, but on every such occasion. A friend of mine says, it was certainly to avoid that female inaccuracy of *they don't mind you and I,* and yet the latter is the least bad of the two. He says too, Lord Chesterfield does, that for forty years of his life he never used a word without stopping a moment to think if he could not find a better. How agreeably he passed his time!"[19a]

6. *Interrogative who or whom.* Bayly, Priestley, and Webster dissent, in characteristic ways and with varying degrees of certainty, from the usual dictum that the interrogative *whom* must be used when it is governed by a following transitive verb or preposition—*whom is it for, did you see,* etc. Lowth is of course positive for the rule, citing in a footnote violations by

[19]A. Campbell, "*Lexiphanes,* Second Edition, corrected, 1767." p. 67 *note.*
[19a]Letter to Mason, April 17, 1774. Toynbee, *Letters of H. Walpole,* VIII: 448.
[20]*Short Introduction,* 1769 ed., pp. 121-2.

Shakespeare, Dryden, Swift, and Addison.[20]   Bayly writes
that "in these and the like phrases the ear is so accustomed to
who, that it will not be reconciled to *whom,* till forced by the
judgment" [that is, apparently, forced by Lowth's logic].[21]
This "ear is accustomed" is the appeal to usage, stated in fuller
form by Priestley: "When the pronoun precedes the verb, or
participle by which its case is determined [he does not mention
the preposition, though his first example is of that government],
it is very common, especially in conversation, to use the nominative case where the rules of grammar require the oblique.
As Who *is this* for? Who *should* I meet *the other day but my
old friend.* Spectator, No. 32. This form of speaking is so
familiar, that I question whether grammarians should not admit it as an exception to the general rule. Dr. Lowth says,
that grammar requires us to say, Whom *do you think me to be.*
But in conversation we always hear, Who *do you think me
to be.*"[22]

Buchanan has a remarkable passage amending Touchstone's
"who Time ambles withal" and so on.   He makes it "with
whom Time ambles withal," since *withal* should mean *likewise,*
and its use for *with* is an "impropriety."[23]

Webster says the nominative in this construction "must perhaps be admitted as an anomaly.   It is the invariable practice
to use *who,* except among people who are fettered by grammatical rules.   In spite of rules, *who is she married to?* is
more agreeable than *whom* is she married to?"[24]   We have
already noted that Webster tried also to solve this difficulty
by the Latin analogy.[25]   Dr. Bryan notes his progress from
arbitrary condemnation of this usage in the first edition of the
Institute (1784) through a statement that the "corruption"
would probably become established "in the undated fourth
Connecticut edition (preface dated 1787)," to the position already cited.[26]

[21]Bayly, *Grammar,* 1772, p. 85.
[22]*Rudiments,* 1769 ed., pp. 107-8.
[23]*Regular English Syntax,* 1767, pp. 138-9.
[24]*Institute,* 1804 ed., p. 67.
[25]Above, Chapter IV, § 4.
[26]W. F. Bryan, "Notes" p. 388 *note* in *Manly Studies,* 1923.

John Hornsey fell into a curious trap of logical construction in this matter. His rule, common to several grammars, is: "When a relative pronoun comes immediately before a verb, it is in the nominative case."[27] As a result he wrote[28] "Who did you ride with?" This was not corrected on the first *errata* page following page 103, the last of his text; but in a later correction printed on the back of the title page it is squared with Lowth's rule, the dangerous clause "whom I learned with"[29] is made into "with whom I learned," and "The binder is requested to paste page 104 to the end leaf." He failed to do so at least in the Columbia University copy.

The case of the interrogative with a regimen logically determined by a following word was thus debated by all possible principles, but there was a preponderance among the liberal grammarians of satisfaction with the decision of Custom in the matter. The very difficult case of pronouns with a doubtful government roused still more unsettling discussion.

7. *Pronouns of ambiguous regimen.* Priestley was thoroughly confused by the use of *whoever* in phrases like "have the head of whoever had advised it" and "recompense to whomsoever would help him . . . ," both from Hume. He calls the usage "a double construction" of the pronouns, "in imitation of the French idiom." He adds strangely, "The pronoun *whoever* seems, sometimes, to require two verbs; and if only one follow, there seems to be a defect in the sentence. *They frequently emit a poisonous juice, whereof* whoever *drinks, that person's brain flies out.* . . Swift's *Tale of a Tub,* p. 60." Since this is apparently a pleonasm, Priestley's remedy by our additional verb is odd.[30]

An entertaining discussion was waged over the quotation "Whom do men say that I am?" from the Authorized Translation of the Bible. As might be expected, most of the grammarians who mention it censure it strongly. Bayly, however makes an attempt to justify it:

[27]*Short English Grammar,* York, 1793, p. 49, *note.*
[28]*Ibid.,* p. 54, § 4, line 21.
[29]On p. 49, line 3.
[30]*Rudiments,* 1769 ed., pp. 103-4.

"The ear, in this place, requires *whom,* and misseth it in a familiar passage, John 9:19, where the translators having gone contrary to the original, the ear is not satisfied: 'Is this your son, *who,* ye say, was born blind?' for, 'is this your son, *whom* ye say, *that* he was born blind?' "[31]   Since, however, custom seems to Bayly an insufficient armor, there follows a defence of *whom* by the analogy of the Greek, and a rather confused attempt to call the verb "an infinitive after the nominative case."[32]

8. *Case of pronouns after* as *and* than.   This construction caused more uncertainty and controversy than any we have so far considered.   Bayly commends Lowth for the rule, common later, that *the same case is required after these conjunctions as before them.*[33]   This is repeated as late as Hornsey's grammar, with the examples "*he* writes better than *I; I* love *him* better than *her,* etc."[34]   But apparently Bayly had read Lowth carelessly; for, except in the *than whom* construction, Lowth states the rule usually accepted by grammarians today, that the case is governed by whatever words are to be supplied or understood.   With this Lowth confutes another of Bentley's emendations of *Paradise Lost*—"others to make such as I," which Bentley had altered to *me* "as the Syntax requires."[35]

Priestley attacked the problem with another theory: "Since it is allowed that the oblique case should follow prepositions; and since the comparative degree of an adjective, and the particle *than* have, certainly, between them, the force of a preposition, expressing the relation of one word to another, they ought to require the oblique case of the pronoun following; so that *greater than me,* will be more grammatical than *greater than I.*"   He supposes the objection to the former to be based on the analogy to Latin, which he repudiates.   He cites without objection three sentences from Smollett's *Voltaire,* one of

[31]*Plain and Complete Grammar,* 1772, p. 86.
[32]*Loc. cit.*
[33]*Plain and Complete Grammar,* pp. 19-20 and *note.*
[34]*Short Grammar,* p. 50, with reference to Harrison and Ash.
[35]*Short Introduction,* 1762, pp. 146-7, *note.*

which, "Tell the Cardinal that I understand poetry better than *him,*" is possibly ambiguous when taken out of context.[36]

William Ward, in a passage which gives a fair notion of his folio *Essay on Grammar,* presents both sides of the question and permits either construction:[37] "If the sentences [clauses] are supplied, the mode of expression is conceived to be of one kind; and if the oblique cases are used, the mode is conceived to be of another kind; and therefore the form of expression varies when the mode of estimation does so, although the result of either form amounts to the same thing." Buchanan seems to attempt explaining the same point Lowth has stated, but does not make it clear; he says that " 'You have given him more than *I*' is not good grammar because a Verb or Preposition understood comes between *than* or *as* and the pronoun."[38]

Campbell is mildly astonished at Priestley's position on the case after *than* and *as.* Specifically averring his loyalty to usage, he grants Dr. Priestley the "colloquial dialect, as Johnson calls it," but insists that this proves no more than the prevalent *you was* and "there's the books." He then proceeds in the usual way to explain the ellipsis, using the same quotations from Smollett which Priestley gave, and concludes, "But supposing good use were divided on the present question, I acknowledge that the first and second canons proposed on this subject,[39] would determine me to prefer the opinion of those who consider the aforesaid particles as conjunctions."[40] The ingenious Withers was the only grammarian logical and subtle enough to discover that this whole procedure of supplying a construction after *than* harbors a hideous error: " . . . the Instance adduced by Lowth to corroborate this Hypothesis unfortunately subverts it—*thou are wiser than I am WISER.*"[41]

---

[36]*Rudiments,* 1769, pp. 106-7.
[37]Wm. Ward, 1765, pp. 483-4. In his *Grammar,* 1767 ed., pp. 112-13, he lists *than* as sometimes a preposition governing the ablative.
[38]*Regular English Syntax,* p. 217. Cf. pp. 93-4 and 131, where he states that the nominative is always used "when the Verb is not repeated."
[39]See above, Chapter IX, § 12.
[40]*Philosophy of Rhetoric,* I, 437-9.
[41]*Aristarchus,* p. 408.

9.   Lowth states that *than whom* alone is correct, since the relative has "reference to no Verb or Preposition understood, but only to its Antecedent, when it follows *than*."[42]   Robert Baker, who did not see Lowth's grammar before his own first edition was issued, finds a difficulty in justifying the phrase even in verse: "to have written strictly good English [Pope] must have said, *Than who no sluice of Mud*, since the Word is in the same case with Sluice, which is a nominative."   He nevertheless admits a force in *whom* lacking in *who*.   "Using this last Word would have enfeebled the Sentence, and in great Measure have spoil'd two of the most beautiful Lines in English Poetry."[43]   Later, when he was invited to call by "Dr. Salter, Master of the Charter-House," and met with the traditional argument for *than whom*, Baker listened with due respect, but saw no reason to change his opinion.   And indeed he has on his side whatever analogy of English can be brought to bear when he says that anyone, failing to catch a name, would ask properly "A greater poet than who?" rather than whom.[44]   But Murray[45] and most of his followers carefully state that the objective case is required after *than* in this construction—which probably has never been used since, save as Baker illustrated it.

10.   *Possessive cases.*   The remainder of the discussion of case is an account of wavering applications of analogy and logic in the attempt to fix the formation of the possessive or genitive of nouns and pronouns and to determine the uses of the structure.   Ben Jonson's grammar states clearly that "the genitive plural . . . is all one with the plural absolute";[46] and his paradigms give no apostrophe in either singular or plural. No doubt this represented preponderant usage during the seventeenth century.   Morris notes that "the general use of the apostophe in the singular is not often found before the end

---

[42]*Short Introduction*, 1763 ed., pp. 159-60; not in the first edition.
[43]*Reflections*, 1770 ed., pp. 47-8.
[44]*Remarks*, 1779, p. 110.
[45]*Grammar*, 1800 ed., p. 172.
[46]*Grammar*, 1909 ed., pp. 86-8.

of the seventeenth century."[47]   Greenwood follows Wallis[48] in
stating that "the Genitive Case . . . ends, in Singular and
Plural Number, in *s* or *es*." His examples are "Man's Nature,
Men's Nature, the Churches Peace."[48a]   He adds, "If the
Substantive be of the Plural Number, the first *s* is cut off;
as the Warriour's Arms . . . for the Warriours's Arms," and
emphasizes in a note Wallis' argument that it is the *first s*
which is "left out for better Sound's Sake . . . . We have
really no distinct Genitive Plural."[49]   He notes, as do most of
the grammarians, the curious formation of group genitives like
"the Queen of England's Crown."[50]   We have seen that Wallis
uses the apostrophe in this construction and before the *s* in the
genitive plural.

The possessive singular form became fairly well established
in the course of the eighteenth century, but the plural was un-
fixed from the beginning to the end of the period, as the following citations will illustrate.   In the *Many Advantages of a
Good Language to any Nation,* a proposal for an Academy
(1724), we find *Mens Thoughts,* page 66, and *men's eyes,*
page 68.   Johnson's *Dictionary* (1755) has in the Grammar:
"Genitive masters, plural masters" in the paradigm, "always
written with a mark of elision *'s;* winter's severity."   It is
noted that "collective nouns" are similarly marked; the examples are "the multitude's folly" and "women's passions."   But
in the next column on the same page, he writes, "Plurals ending in *s* have no genitives; but we say, Womens *excellencies,*
and *Weigh the* Mens *wits, against the* ladies *hairs.*   Pope."[51]

---

[47]See Richard Morris, *Historical Outlines,* 1880, p. 81.
[48]Wallis discusses the possessive or genitive of nouns under "*Adjectiva
Possessiva.*" His specific rule is "*Fit autem à quovis Substantivo (sive
singulari sive plurali) addito s (aut es, si necessitas pronunciationis postu-
laverit)*"; his illustrations are *mans nature, Virgils poems.* Of the *substan-
tivum aggregatum,* he notes the placement of *s* at the end of the phrase; his
examples are *The Kings Court . . ., the King of Spain's Court.* This is the
first appearance of an apostrophe in his discussion. *Grammatica,* Oxford,
1674, pp. 69-71.
[48a]*Essay,* 1711, p. 52, 1729, p. 65.
[49]*Essay,* 1711, pp. 52-3; 1729, pp. 65-6.
[50]*Essay,* 1711, p. 54; 1729, p. 67.
[51]Johnson's *Dictionary:* the "English Grammar," *n. p.*

If it were not for the quotation, we might suppose that this statement applied to speech only. Johnson adds, "Wallis proposes Lords' house for house of Lords . . . the mark of elision is improper, for in the Lords' house nothing is cut off," and noting that confusion [apparently in pronunciation] would result between this and "the Lord's house," insists that "house of Lords" is better.[52]

Lowth follows Johnson's account of the derivation of the possessive from the Saxon genitive—though he gives it incorrectly as *is*, a fourteenth-century form—and comes to the same conclusion: " . . . we now always shorten it with an Apostrophe; often very improperly, when we are obliged to pronounce it fully; as, *Thomas's* book." He refutes the derivation from *his*,[53] as does Greenwood. Finally, "When it is a Noun ending in *s*, the sign of the Possessive Case is sometimes not added; as, 'for *righteousness* sake'; nor ever to the Plural Number ending in *s*; as in 'on eagles wings.' "[54]

J. Johnson's *Royal and Standard English Dictionary* (1762) introduces a variation popular with school-children today; the genitive, he says, is formed "by adding *'s* to the nominative . . . generally distinguished by prefixing an apostrophe before or over the *s*." If any critic had discovered this, he would have had "prefixing" to add to his lists of improprieties.

Priestley duplicates Lowth's account of the Saxon *is* genitive. "Sometimes the additional *s* is suppressed in writing," he says, "as in *Jesus feet,* more commonly by poets. Sometimes the apostrophe is wholly omitted, even after the plural number; tho' in that case, there is no other sign of the genitive case. *A collection of* writers *faults.* Swift's Tale of a Tub, p. 55. *After ten* years *wars.* Swift.

"When, in this and other cases, the terminations of words are such, that the sound makes no distinction between the genitive of the singular and of the plural number; as, *the prince's injuries,* and *princes' injuries.* Humes's Hist., vol. 5, p. 406.

[52]*Ibid.*
[53]Advanced in *Spectator No. 135.*
[54]*Short Introduction,* 1762, pp. 26-7.

It should seem to be better to decline the use of the genitive in the plural number and say, *the injuries of princes.*[55]   He counsels the same phrase construction in place of "the army's name, the Commons' vote" because of "harshness of the sound" with the genitive.

11.   Buchanan gives a clear example of the difference between precept and practice.   He states an explicit rule for the possessive singular, with many manufactured examples of "false syntax."[56]   But these examples were unnecessary trouble, as he himself writes "childrens time" (p. xvii), "readers judgment" [apparently singular], "forms sake" (p. 171).   Of the plural he says, "We certainly have a Genitive Plural, though there has been no Mark to distinguish it . . . *warriors arms—arms of the warriors.*"   He suggests an "apostrophe reversed, *warrior's arms*" as the sign for this.[57]

Mennye objects to the "improper omission of *s* in Moses', Phinehas', Felix'," but apparently allows it in "Peleus' son." He notes "too much stiffness and formality in using the apostrophe to form the genitive plural; as, on eagles' wings . . . of service to the reader only, not the hearer."[58]   He himself writes *children's hands, Lord's day, scholars* [apparently plural] *books. The Columbian Grammar* of 1795 gives the rule "by the addition of an *apostrophe,* sometimes with an *s* and sometimes without," especially in plurals.[59]   *The Complete Letter Writer,* 1793, a sensible compilation, says, "The English have but one case, that is the genitive, which ends in the singular and plural in *s* or *es* if the pronunciation requires it; as, Virgil's Aeneid, or the Aeneid of Virgil."[60]   No plurals are given as examples.   Priestley (1768 ed.)[61] first states the rules for substantives in the modern publishers' form, and Murray illustrates the convenience of distinction which the placing of the

[55]*Rudiments*, 1769 ed., pp. 68-9.   I have carefully reproduced the exact punctuation, including the sentence separation and *Humes's*, elsewhere, and in the 1768 ed., p. 69, *Hume's*.

[56]*Regular English Syntax*, 1767, pp. 124 ff., xvii, and 171.

[57]*Regular English Syntax*, 1767, pp. 124-5.

[58]J. Mennye, 1785, p. 76.

[59]*Op. cit.,* 1795, pp. 15-16.

[60]*Op. cit., p.* 50.

[61]*Op. cit.,* p. 7.

apostrophe makes in writing.[62]   But Webster in 1807 writes "thirty years reading."[63]   It is clear that the plural form was far from settled at the end as well as the beginning of the eighteenth century.

12. *The Art of Speaking* (1708) uses the apostrophe for a nominative plural, *Idea's*.[64]   Robert Baker censures this same error in forming plurals of words in *a, o,* and *s*:[65]   "For why should an Apostrophe be placed where there is no letter omitted?" he inquires.   Potter, in his criticism of Johnson, 1779, writes "superabundance of comma's," and "a nine days wonder."[66]   Bayly notes on the Latin analogy that "nouns of measure are either genitive or dative."   The apostrophe form was later established for most of these cases as a publishers' rule.

13. *Possessive pronouns or possessive adjectives.* The story of the forms for the genitive of pronouns, or possessive adjectives, is an extreme instance of how the eighteenth-century grammarians introduced confusion into usage, and of how usage in spite of them settled the matter quietly as it had formerly stood.   Wallis, in his 1674 edition, gave a table of pronouns, spelling these forms except *who's—its, yours,* and the like—as we do today.[66a]   This table was copied by Greenwood, J. Johnson's *Dictionary,* and others.   Nevertheless there was extreme uncertainty among grammarians throughout the century as to the forms of these words.   Lowth writes *your's, our's, her's, their's,* and explains "His (that is, Hee's)" and *whose* (that is, *who's*),"[67] but uniformly gives *its* as the possessive form.   Priestley writes in one place "its being reckoned" and in another "it's being impossible."[68]

[62]York (1809) ed., p. 81.

[63]Webster, *Letter to Dr. Ramsay,* p. 18.

[64]*Op. cit.,* p. 4, 36, etc. This was common in the period.

[65]*Reflections,* 1770 ed., p. 25. But see his insistence on an apostrophe where no letter is omitted, below § 15.

[66]Potter, p. 82 (1779). This confusing use of the apostrophe is still taught for the plurals of letters, figures, and sometimes of illustrative words [too many *and's*]. It can not be too soon got rid of in schools.

[66a]Cf. Wallis, *Grammatica,* 1674, p. 78. On p. 77: "*Whose* (vel potius *who's*)."

[67]*Short Introduction,* 1762, pp. 35-6 and 38. Greenwood, *Essay toward a Practical English Grammar,* 1711, p. 55, writes that "the Words *his* and *whose* are nothing else, but *hee's, who's,* by mistake."

He appears to be the first to attempt a principle of distinction, which obviously he does not follow, but which was quoted elsewhere: "sometimes these possessives have an apostrophe before the *s,* when they are found without their substantives, which gives them more the appearance of a genitive case. *That you may call her your's.* Fair American, vol. 2, p. 64."[69] Mennye gives precisely the opposite rule: "Possessive pronouns, without a substantive, should be used without the apostrophe," and corrects the same sentence as Priestley uses for his example.[70]   Both Baker's *Reflections,* 1770 edition, and Withers' *Aristarchus,* 1788, use *it's* with occasional exceptions throughout; but Baker's 1779 edition appears to have changed all to *its,* though I have not examined it in detail for this point.   Baker also writes *our's, her's, their's;* Withers in *Aristarchus* appears to spell these pronouns in the accepted fashion; but he has also "the authors name," "the Readers Attention."   Franklin's 1768 letter on a reformed way of spelling, as quoted at the close of Webster's *Dissertations,*[71] is concluded "Your's affectionately."

14. *Pronoun reference to a genitive.*   The logic of reference of a succeeding pronoun to a possessive was not greatly debated in this period.   Buchanan writes that "a pronoun cannot refer to Great Britain, in the phrase, 'the armies of Great Britain' " since the word is "a Genitive governed by Armies."[72] Other writers make the same objection to reference to a noun or pronoun actually in the possessive, but not on the score of ambiguity of meaning—solely on the logical-grammatical or authoritative ground of its "impossibility," perhaps by analogy with Latin.   Priestley, however, allows this construction, citing as correct "thy goodness, who art . . ."[73]; but he notes the possible ambiguity of "Disciples of Christ whom we imitate," and

Rudiments, 1769, p. 70 and p. 85.
Ibid., pp. 86-7.
English Grammar, 1785, p. 77.
Op. cit., 1789, p. 410.
Regular English Syntax, 1767, pp. 139-40.
Rudiments, 1769, p. 97.

remarks the "want of a distinction of numbers in the pronoun relative."[74]

Buchanan also notes that "*Of* being the sign of the Genitive Case, we cannot put it before a Noun with (*'s*)[75] for this is making two Genitives." The *Monthly Review,* in the criticism of Baker's *Reflections,* notes that he writes "an original of *Vandyke's* for *of Vandyke*";[76] but their distinction, though they do not explain it, is perhaps of meaning rather than form. One grammar quotes a curious over-refinement of double possession from Cowley's preface to his *Poems*: "Our own coarse cloathes are like to become us better, than those of another man's."[77]

15. *Genitive case before the gerund.* The first comment on this construction is a severe reprobation by George Harris, the author of the *Observations*:[78] "Another instance in which *s* is used as an Abbreviation without the least pretence for it: . . . Doctrine of a future STATE'S being taught; . . . equity of the Episcopal CHURCH'S being . . ." Lowth, who followed this writer in a number of points, spoke in his second edition of expressions like "the Rule's being observed . . . and "its being disregarded" as "anomalies to be rooted out."[79] His objection seems not to have turned upon the impropriety of putting "words for inanimate objects" in the possessive case; that stricture appears never to have occurred to the eighteenth-century grammarians, but was reserved for the subtlety of the nineteenth.[80] Lowth's objection was to making the verbal "amphibious" in both governing an object and taking a possessive, a construction that could not be "resolved" to "the being observed of the rule." Though he apparently says nothing on this point in the 1769 edition, he continues to hold

[74]*Loc. cit.*
[75]*Regular Syntax*, p. 124, *note.*
[76]Vol. XLV *o. s.* (August, 1771), p. 95.
[77]Cited in *Grammar and Rhetoric,* a volume of the *Circle of the Sciences,* 1776 ed., p. 214, *note.*
[78]*Observations on the English Language,* 1752, p. 23.
[79]*Short Introduction,* 1763, p. 105, note 1. Cited by Campbell and by Dr. Bryan. Not in the 1762 ed.
[80]Fitzedward Hall traces it to Coleridge, *Philology,* 5-6 *note.*

a like brief against the awkward phrases "the sending to them the light," and "by preaching of repentance."[81]   Priestley admits either possessive or accusative with the gerund, and elsewhere he shows the difference in meaning between "of my horse's running" and "of my horse running."[82]   Campbell, after turning the question this way and that, and noting that "the genius of the tongue permits" that these verbals be construed as nouns, concludes formally "that the idiom in question ought not to be entirely repudiated."[83]   Baker first stated a positive rule, that in "His words being applicable to the common mistake of our age, induce me to transcribe them," quoted from Foster, first, we should read *words'*, and second, *induces;* else "words . . . induce me to transcribe words" is nonsense.[84]

Webster is equally positive on this point, and we perhaps owe to him the dogma that the possessive must invariably be used in this construction.   He insists "This is the genuine English idiom . . ." and the "omission often changes the sense of the phrase or leaves it ambiguous."[85]   If he had been tentative, as Murray apparently was,[86] we might have been spared a great deal of dogmatizing on this subject.   But the grammarians of the nineteenth century did not in their usual fashion follow Murray in this matter; their "speech instinct" committed them rather to the more positive statement which they seem always to have preferred.

16.   *The subjunctive or conjunctive mood or mode.*   Before Dr. Johnson issued his dictionary, the idea that English has a subjunctive mode seems not to have been suspected.   Greenwood, in the *Royal English Grammar,* 1737, says that there are no moods in English, though he remarks later that the personal terminations are omitted and *be* is used in the passive after *if*

---

[81]*Short Introduction,* 1762, pp. 111-4.
[82]*Rudiments,* 1769, 122.
[83]*Philosophy of Rhetoric,* I, pp. 507-11.
[84]*Remarks,* 1779 ed., pp. 81-2 and 92.   A pencil note in the margin of the copy in the Library of Congress comments, "The first member of the sentence [i. e., the entire phrase?] is the nominative," but says nothing on the problem of verb-agreement.
[85]*Dissertations,* 1789, pp. 279-82.
[86]*English Grammar,* 1809 ed., pp. 271 and 273.

and the like.[87]   He notes the use of *were I* as an instance of inversion "when the verb is used by way of yielding or concession," but says nothing of its mood.[88]   James Harris, observer of Requisitive, Interrogative, and other modes in Greek, says specifically that English "is so poor in this respect, as to admit no Variation for Modes."[89]   J. Johnson states that there are no moods in English, but that "*be, be'st, were, wert,*" are generally used after *if, that, although,* etc.[90]

Dr. Johnson announced the "conjunctive mode," with the complaint that it is "wholly neglected" in his day, though "used among the purer writers of former times after *if, though, ere, before, till* or *until, whether, except, unless, whatsoever, whomsoever,* and words of wishing."[90a]   Lowth, following him, was thoroughgoing in his determination to ascertain the subjunctive, the only mode remaining distinct from the indicative in English.[91]   "Shall we in deference to these great authorities [Milton, Dryden, Addison, Swift, etc.] allow *wert* to be the same with *wast,* and common to Indicative and Subjunctive Mode? or rather abide by the practice of our best antient writers;[92] the propriety of the language, which requires, as far as may be, distinct forms for different Modes; and the analogy of formation in each Mode; I *was,* Thou *wast;* I *were,* thou *wert;* all which conspire to make *wert* peculiar to the Subjunctive Mode."[93]   He notes correctly that in the Subjunctive "the Verb itself in the Present, and the Auxiliary both of the Present and Past Imperfect Times, often carry with them somewhat of a future tense as, 'If he come tomorrow, I may . . .'   'If he should or would come, I might, would, could, or should, speak . . . .'   So that in this Mode the precise Time of the Verb is very much determined by the nature and drift of the Sentence,"[94] as indeed it always is.

[87]*Op. cit.,* p. 62.   *Essay,* 1711, p. 117.
[88]*Essay,* p. 210.
[89]*Hermes,* 1751 (1771 ed.), p. 148, *note.*
[90]*Royal and Universal Dictionary,* 1762.
[90a]*Dictionary,* 1755, the "English Grammar" *n. p.*
[91]See Bayly's remark on this, above, Ch. II, § 2.
[92]Compare here Bayly's statement, § 17, below.
[93]*Short Introduction,* 1762 ed., p. 52, *note.*
[94]*Short Introduction,* 1762 ed., pp. 54-5, *note.*

Lowth gives the usual list of conjunctions, adding *whether
—or,* which "seem in general[95] to require the subjunctive Mode
after them: . . . but by use they often admit of the indicative;
and in some cases with propriety."[96]   He notes, of examples
such as "if thou *be* the Son of God" and "though he *were*
divinely inspired," that the indicative would have expressed a
more proper religious certainty, and concludes, "The proper use
then of the Subjunctive Mode after the Conjunction is in the
case of a doubtful supposition, or concession."[97]   On the following page he notes, "*That,* expressing the motive or end, has
the Subjunctive Mode, with *may, might, should,* after it."
However, because their constructions do not fit precisely into
this rule, he censures Swift for writing "but that no modern
have . . ."[98] and Shakespeare for "That birds would sing, and
think it were not night,[99] though the latter is quite evidently
contrary to fact.   Lowth seems to have no mention of the subjunctive after verbs of wishing.

17.   Priestley gives in his catechetical grammar[100] the usual
list of conjunctions followed by the "conjunctive mode," and
later remarks: "Mr. *Johnson* assigns no conjunctive form to
the *preter tense:* but the analogy of the language forms seems
to require that both the tenses be put upon a level in this respect.—It seems to be used with propriety only when some degree of *doubt* or *hesitation* is implied; since when an event is
look'd upon as absolutely certain, though in speaking of it we
make use of the conjunctive particles, &c. the usual change of
termination is retained: to give a familiar example of this: we
should say, in pursuing a person, '*We should overtake him
though he run*'; not knowing whether he did run or no;
whereas, upon seeing him run, we should say, '*We shall overtake him though* he runneth, or *runs.*'"   He examines and
seems to reject the solution[101] later urged by Webster, that we

[95]In 1762 ed., *"properly"* for *"in general,"* (pp. 140-2).
[96]*Ibid.,* 1763 edition, pp. 154 ff. and *note.*
[97]*Ibid.,* 1769 ed., p. 178.
[98]*Ibid.,* 1762 ed., p. 143, *note.*
[99]*Ibid.,* 1769 ed., p. 111, *note.*
[100]*Rudiments,* 1769 ed., p. 16; p. 117.

have here an ellipsis for "should run," since that will not do for
the "preter tense" in irregular verbs like *drew*. Complaining
that the conjunctive form, "though our forefathers paid a pretty
strict regard to it, is much neglected by many of our best
writers," Priestley rates Addison's "If he chances to think right,
he knows not . . ."—a perfectly plain indicative—and notes inconsistent uses within the same sentence from Harris and
Swift. He concludes with an appeal to euphony or custom:
"Grammatical as this conjunctive form of verbs is said to be,
by all who write upon the subject, it must, we think, be acknowledged, that it sometimes gives the appearance of stiffness, and harshness to a sentence," citing "before that opera-
tion were performed" from *Tale of a Tub*.[102]

Buchanan notes that "conditional, doubtful, contingent, con-
cessive, and exceptive" meanings are expressed in the Subjunctive Mood, but the Indicative is "required for a more clear
and determinate Sense" when "no doubtful Supposition and
Concession" is indicated. He notes the same examples as does
Lowth, and adds others, where *wast* should be substituted for
wert, in Milton, Addison, Dryden, Swift. He adds later that
the mood does not depend on the conjunction used, but on the
sense.[103] The rest of the grammarians between him and Webster were satisfied to repeat the subjunctive rules of Lowth and
censure noted authors. Bayly, citing Ascham and the Bible
translators, notes that the "first English writers were more accurate than the Moderns,"[104] but that confusion of Moods and
Tenses was "frequently observable in every translation, particularly of the Old and New Testament."[105] Lord Monboddo[106] laments that since Milton's time the subjunctive is
"almost quite out of fashion," but notes that the unfortunate
defect is supplied by auxiliary verbs. That this was coming
to be preferred is suggested by Potter's criticism of Johnson.

[101]Probably suggested by Greenwood, *Essay* (1711), p. 144: "if he write =
shall write."
[102]*Rudiments,* pp. 116-21, *passim.*
[103]*Regular English Syntax,* 1767, pp. 80-1 and 95.
[104]*Introduction to Languages,* p. 100.
[105]*Plain and Complete Grammar,* 1772, p. 99.
[106]*Origin and Progress of Language,* 1774, IV, p. 122.

Of "he . . . had been the proper poet," he remarks, "Not to cavil at *had been,* for *would have been* . . ."; and again, "If our lexicographer had written, 'He sometimes retains *what would have been* more properly omitted'; instead of the jargon . . . 'were more'; it might have been as well or better."[107] Of "the world had wanted many an idle song," Clarke comments, "There is an absolute grammatical impropriety . . . *would have wanted* is alone correct. But . . . Mr. Pope was always so tenacious of Harmony and Sound that he would at any Time sacrifice Sense to it."[108]

Withers objects to "it were to be wished" and "I could wish" where there is no "Hypothesis or Reserve to justify" it, but approves it where the conditional clause is understood, in the sentence, "He has so provoked me, I could wish him dead."[109]

18. Webster's change of position on the entire matter of the subjunctive is the best possible illustration of his honest attempt to record the facts of usage. In the first edition of the *Grammatical Institute,* while he was still under the influence of Lowth rather than of Priestley and Tooke, he writes, "Conjunctions implying doubt or supposition govern the subjunctive mode," and gives the usual examples and paradigms.[110] But the edition of 1787 states that "if . . . am . . . were, may be . . . could be, etc." form the present subjunctive and "if . . . was, had been . . . might have been, etc.," the past. "The old form for past time *'if I were'* is obsolete."[111] The forms *be, have,* for the third singular present, commonly called subjunctives, he explains by stating that "the auxiliary sign is sometimes omitted in the future time" after conjunctions *"if, though, unless, except, whether"*[112]—a theory we have seen Priestley suggesting, but apparently rejecting.

Webster later develops this position in detail: " . . . by the construction of our language, no subjunctive mode is nec-

---

[107]Potter, 1779, pp. 88 and 101. In Temple's *Sketches* we find "if he would have," "if either of the Universities would have." (pp. 15-16.)
[108]*Rational Spelling Book,* 1796, p. 81.
[109]*Aristarchus,* 1788, pp. 48-9.
[110]*Grammatical Institute,* 1784, pp. 85-6.
[111]*Ibid.,* 1787 ed., p. 19.
[112]*Ibid.,* p. 48.

essary—in most cases it is improper—and what is the strongest of all arguments, *it is not used in the spoken language,* which is the only true foundation of grammar."[113]

He gives many examples of true indicatives rendered by the Bible translators as subjunctive and defended by Lowth, but insists that *"though* never requires the sujunctive mode," and of *if,* "where is the good English writer or speaker that uses the subjunctive after it?" *"Be* in the indicative is not now used by well-bred men." If it is not used in speech, he argues, it should not be used in books; and he comments on the efforts of teachers "to perpetuate differences between the written and the spoken language." "If . . . have" he notes as "worse than if . . . be."[114] This of course is inconsistent with his position that *be* and *have* are used as futures without auxiliary. "Whether he *is,"* Webster maintains, is "the correct form of doubt or uncertainty, because it is universal custom in our *spoken* language."[115] Finally, he reiterates strongly that "there is no subjunctive at all after conjunctions." *Be,* he contends, strictly belongs to the indicative, where it is "still good English, though considered vulgar," but . . . "is become so far obsolete, as to deserve no countenance," being either vulgar or pendantic —an interesting position if one can ravel it out.[116]

19. This extreme position in Webster's 1798 letter may be due to Tooke's radical influence; but it is more probable that he failed to explain that his attack is chiefly against the "present subjunctive" and particularly the form *be.* For in his *Dissertations on the English Language,* 1789, Webster is perfectly clear in explaining that "if I were, thou wert, he were" are "the present hypothetical tense of the subjunctive mode . . . not used in the indicative"; that *should* and *would* are sometimes present indicative and sometimes subjunctive with a future sense; and that all preterite tenses, including *might* and *could,* are "established by unanimous consent in practice"

[113]*Errors of English Grammars,* 1798, pp. 15-16.
[114]*Ibid.,* pp. 11, 13; See pp. 7-24 for the entire discussion.
[115]*Ibid.,* pp. 8-9.
[116]*Ibid.,* pp. 18-19.

as equivalents of a present subjunctive."[117]   Here Webster's discussion is closer to the facts of usage than are many current grammars. Of the "present subjunctive" of Lowth [*if he have, stand, be,* and the like] he notes that Addison uses it rarely, Swift often, so that his is a more formal style, and that the followers of Lowth, and especially Scotch authors, "lamed" by following him and Johnson, chiefly affect it. He notes how "stiff and even ridiculous" *if he cough* would be for the indicative in a passage from Addison, and sums up the matter by saying that, "however just Lowth's distinction between the modes may have formerly been, it is not warranted by the present idiom of the language."[118]

20. But, having thus settled the problem with due allowance for the force of custom and refuted the grammatical purists with vigor, Webster turns upon Addison and other standard writers and proceeds to revise perfectly good indicatives into what look suspiciously like present subjunctives; but these he labels future tenses, with *shall* "understood and easily supplied by the reader." Addison's "If any member absents himself . . .,"[119] and Prospero's "If thou neglectest or dost unwillingly . . ." are turned to *absent* and *neglect;* he does not tell what to make of *dost,* but apparently it would according to his principle be *do*—not subjunctive but elliptical future.[120] Similarly, though he admits that in the "hypothetical present subjunctive tense" *were* and other preterite forms are correctly used with an infinitive for the future, and that the present in English "hath often the sense of the future,"[121] quoting Lowth's *Introduction,* yet he denies countenance to quite clear instances of a precisely similar construction: "Suppose they marched up . . ." "if they foraged . . ." and "if I dedicated . . ."—the last from the dedication to the *Spectator*: "The sense is future, and therefore *should march, should forage . . . should dedicate* would have been more correct" or "accurate."[122]

[117]*Dissertations,* 1789, pp. 231-2 and 263-70.
[118]*Errors of Grammars,* pp. 17 and 24; *Dissertations,* pp. 244-9, *passim.*
[119]*Spectator No. 9.*
[120]*Dissertations,* 1789, pp. 241-2.
[121]*Ibid.,* pp. 250-1.
[122]*Ibid.,* pp. 278-9.

For his "hypothetical" or subjunctive present *were,* Webster notes, "in conversation, we generally hear *was*; 'if I *was* in his place'; 'if he *was* here *now.*' &c. and I observe that modern writers are copying the general practice,"—with a quotation from Bolingbroke. "Both these forms have such authorities to support them, that neither can be considered as wholly incorrect; they are both English. But custom will eventually establish the latter, *was,* as the hypothetical form of the substantive verb. It is now almost universally used, except in books; and the tide of general practice is irresistible."[123]

21. In expanding his notion that *was* represents with *were* a present hypothetical or subjunctive form, Webster gives a paradigm that equals that of William Ward[124] in its cool reconstruction of the language—this time out of the vulgar speech. For the past time, affirmative, he gives: "If he had or was yesterday—uncertainty. If he *had have*[125] or had been yesterday—certainty that he had not, or was not." On this Webster has the footnote: "This tense is not admitted to be good English; yet is often used in Speaking; the *have* being contracted or corrupted into *a, had a written,—had a received.*" And similarly for the negative, "had not have."[126]

22. Webster might have found more support than he apparently supposed for *was* as a subjunctive if he had looked carefully, in books of the eighteenth century, save by "Johnson and Lowth and their Scotch followers, who learn the English language grammatically."[127] The following examples, gathered without special search, will perhaps sufficiently establish this:

. . . as if *Sun* was of the *Male Sex* . . . as if *Church* was of the *Female Sex.*

Greenwood, *Essay,* 1711, p. 57.

If you *was* to send to your haberdasher for a hat, you might receive . . .

Connoisseur, Jan. 22, 1756.

[123]*Ibid.,* pp. 268-9.
[124]See Chapter VI, § 23, above.
[125]The italics are not Webster's.
[126]*Dissertations,* p. 269.
[127]*Ibid.,* p. 248.

If I was to reduce my own private Idea . . . , I should call
it . . .

> L. Temple, *Sketches,* 1758, p. 4.

It would be better, if its severity was alleviated . . .

> *Ibid.,* p. 67.

As solemn and sublime . . . , as if he was a Seraph or an
Arch-angel.

> *Ibid.,* p. 67.

Temple was so correct a writer that he used Mobility for the
vulgar *mob.*

> Suppose I *was* to say—Light is a body . . .
> Harris, *Hermes* 1751 (1771 ed.), p. 78.

In this book, four modes and two subclasses are distinguished.
It has also:

> It were to be wished, he [Milton's Corrector] had been as wise.[128]
> *Ibid,* p. 60.

> . . . happy would it be for the modern world, if the picture
> had not its likeness in modern times, but *was* confined to the decline
> of . . .
> Nash's Notes to *Hudibras,* 1794 (Appleton, 1853 ed., p. 252.)

> . . . dare used without *to* after it "as if it was an auxiliary verb."
> Priestley, *Rudiments,* p. 132.

Campbell of course used *were,* even extravagantly:

> We should hardly say that a house were richly furnished; I am sure
> we could not say that it were well furnished, where we found . . ,
> *Philosophy of Rhetoric,* I, p. 479, and elsewhere.

> Dr. Johnson declared . . . that if he *was* to publish another
> edition of his dictionary, he would introduce . . .
> Webster, *Errors,* 1798, p. 22.

But Webster prefers forms like "Would the limits of this

[128] In the Dublin edition of Lowth, 1769, appears this sentence: "If this method was adopted; if children were taught . . ." (*Short Introduction,* Preface, p. x) This apparently is not the Bishop's English. It is absent from the earlier editions and from the London issue of 1769 also. But he also writes, ". . . if the measure would have allowed . . " (London, 1769 ed., p. 35 *note.*)

sketch permit"[129] which are to be found less and less frequently elsewhere.

23. *In summary,* having seen the statements of grammarians and a sampling of the actual usage in one particular, we have a basis for understanding the cause of a phenonenon noted by Webster:[130] "There are few or no English authors [including many of the grammarians themselves], who seem to have adhered uniformly to any rule in the use of the verbs after the conjunctions. In consequence, either of ignorance or inattention, the most correct writers have fallen into inconsistencies, even in the same sentence." His examples of this last are from ¦Bolingbroke and Priestley   He might have added curious instances from Robert Baker the authoritarian,[131] from Swift and James Harris, quoted by Priestley, and from Milton and Addison, quoted by Lowth. Webster is particularly triumphant in accusing Priestley of an error "even on Lowth's principles," if not of downright impiety, in the expression "If reverence, gratitude, obedience, and confidence *be* our duty . . ."[132]

Webster is given thus at length because in his contradictions, dogmatic certainties, and both professions and practical denials of usage, he represents on this single topic the eighteenth-century reasoner upon language. His effort at observation and record of the language was more thoroughgoing and more honest than that of most of his contemporaries, but he was not sufficiently informed and scientific to arrive at a just description. The account of his attempts here presented shows clearly why he was less followed than were Lowth and Murray. They were more dogmatically sure, though just as frequently wrong. The eighteenth-century schools, and almost as fully those of the following century, wanted assurance and authority.

[129]*Letter to Dr. Ramsay,* 1807, **p. 18.**

[130]*Dissertations,* p. 249.

[131]"If this be the Case; if the Word was invented in the Nursery . . ." (*Reflections,* p. 36). "If one of these Houses happen to fall." (p. 123) "Notwithstanding the Word *regards* have no Nominative" [It has none] (**p. 116).**

[132]*Dissertations,* 1789, **p. 242.**

These confused applications to the problems of inflection, of authority, "reason and analogy," usage, and euphony, illustrate rather well the state of thought upon these matters in the eighteenth century. A further collection of similar attempts to solve problems of concord or agreement follows in Chapter XII.

CHAPTER XII

VARIOUS SOLUTIONS OF PROBLEMS OF CONCORD

When we pronounce Judgement on a Plurality of Objects, the Affirmation ought to be plural, in Conformity to the Plurality of Ideas in the Mind. The Analogy is natural and elegant. And by this Mode of Diction, People of Education are distinguished from the illiterate Multitude.

Withers, *Aristarchus,* 1788.

CHAPTER XII

VARIOUS SOLUTIONS OF PROBLEMS OF CONCORD

1. The varying discussions of verb-subject agreement begin with James Greenwood's rules: that the subject of the singular number "if it comprehend many particulars" may take either a singular or a plural verb, evidently according to the meaning; and that "Sometimes the Verb may be put into the Singular Number, when there are two Substantives; as, *His Justice and Goodness was great*: But then here, *was great* is left out in the first Sentence; as, *His Justice was great and his Goodness was great.*"[1]

The former rule, for collective nouns, is accepted and repeated without question by all the grammarians examined except Withers, who attempts to explain when such nouns are singular, when plural.[2] John Clarke's *Rational Spelling Book,* 1796, says stoutly that the plural verb for a noun of multitude like *mob* is "false English" since there is "but one mob." But as he himself wrote "Such kind of expressions are . . ." it is not necessary to take his rule too seriously.[3]

2. *Verbs with compound subjects.* Greenwood's rule for subjects joined by *and* or in a series met varied favor, but opposition to it was not elaborated and exalted into a dogma before Withers' *Aristarchus* (1788). That Greenwood represented a considerable body of usage will be evident to anybody who observes the list of "violations" by standard writers in the later grammars which tried to introduce a rule of strict logic.

Even the Bishop of London allowed that "sometimes, after an enumeration of particulars, the Verb follows in the Singular Number, and is understood as applied to each of the preceding

[1]*Essay,* 1729 ed., p. 229.
[2]*Aristarchus,* pp. 89-95.
[3]*Op. cit.,* pp. 83-4; pp. 80-1.

terms." He gives as examples quotations from Hooker, and the Bible verse, used by several grammarians later as a bad example: "Sand and salt, and a mass of iron, is easier to bear . . ."[4]

3. *Logic of concord.* One phase of this problem is introduced by Priestley's comment, ". . . if the subjects of the affirmation be nearly related, the Verb is rather better in the singular number." In his examples the portion in roman type is what Priestley would emphasize: *"Nothing but the* marvellous and supernatural hath *any charms for them."* The second is from Dr. Johnson: "Idleness and ignorance [considered as kindred dispositions, and forming one habit of mind] *if* it be *suffered to* proceed, &c." The matter in square brackets is Priestley's; he does not give the verb of the main clause. He continues:

"If the terms be very nearly related, a plural verb is manifestly harsh; though it may be thought to be strictly grammatical. *His* politeness and obliging behaviour were *changed* . . . Hume's History, vol. 6, p. 14, *was* would have read better."[5]

Robert Baker admits, of "Justice and honor requires," that a singular verb "may perhaps be allowed, where those Nominatives have the same, or nearly the same, Signification: but not else. This [instance from Melmoth's *Cicero*] is therefore bad English."[6]

It would have contributed to the gaiety of eighteenth-century grammar if Robert Baker had discovered, in the review of his first edition, the following violation of principles so firmly enunciated by the author and no doubt subsc ibed to by his critics: ". . . a general knowledge of grammar . . . and a familiar acquaintance with its terms and their eanings seems to be an essential qualification . . ."[7]

4. William Ward gives almost Greenwood's rule: "A verb

[4]Lowth, *Short Introduction*, 1763, pp. 111-113 and *note.*
[5]*Rudiments*, 1769, pp. 185-6.
[6]*Reflections*, 1770, pp. 93-4.
[7]*Monthly Review*, XLV o. s. (August, 1771), 90.

of the singular number may be considered as first applied to one, and then to another of the substantives singular, which are joined by copulative conjunctions"; he adds the same example as did Lowth.[8]

Bayly is equally liberal, or more so; when two subjects stand before a verb, he says, "The verb is usually made plural, but may stand singular by situation next to one noun singular, or by being taken distributively." His first example illustrates that the conjunction *but* was not accepted as a preposition in the eighteenth century: "nothing but verses *is* or *are* wanting." The others, "Then David goeth, and Samuel," or "Then goeth David and Samuel," and "I am wicked, and my people," apparently differ considerably in acceptability in cultivated usage.[9] Bayly's philosophy leads him still further, to stating that "since the verb expresses one action though the agents be many, it may stand singular with a nominative case plural"[10]—an appeal evidently to the "entity" of language. He gives no examples of actual usage here. In the same place he anticipates Jespersen by noting that our language has no particular need for verbs which are "respecters of persons"[11]— that vary to agree in person with their subject.

5. That usage itself was confused need hardly be illustrated; the same Dr. Salisbury who labored so hard over *had rather*, himself writes, "In well framed sentences there is both agreement and government,"[12] evidently considering these synonomous or complementary ideas; and he escaped being cited for it in any grammar examined in this study—though Withers, an unsparing opponent, had read his pamphlet. Lowth himself wrote, "for here is a Noun, and a Pronoun representing it . . ."[13]

Harrison allows the singular verb for "allied subjects."[14] But this was the last word of liberalism for some time; in 1788

[8]*Essay on Grammar*, 1765, p. 455.
[9]*Plain and Complete Grammar*, 1772, p. 65.
[10]*Ibid.*, pp. 31-2.
[11]The phrase is Jespersen's not Bayly's.
[12]*Two Grammatical Essays*, 1768, p. 8.
[13]*Short Introduction*, 1763 ed., pp. 105-6 *note*.
[14]*Rudiments of English Grammar*, (1782) 1787 ed., pp. 36-7.

Philip Withers made a devastatingly logical attack on this position. Apparently his *Aristarchus* was not reprinted more than once (in 1822), but its influence must have been pretty vigorous among the writers of grammars, for not only his ideas, but even his phrases and examples are copied well into the nineteenth century. He considers that "GRAMMATICAL CONSTRUCTION constitutes the first Excellence of Style"; this is his interpretation of Swift's "proper words in proper places."[15] And his distribution of emphasis is clear from the fact that almost precisely half his book (214 pages) is devoted to VERBS. Of this portion, one hundred pages (Section II) are taken up with the agreement of verb and subject.

Many of his strictures and citations have appeared in their due places earlier in this study. Of compound subjects he writes: "It is a received Opinion among some Grammarians, that any two Nouns, which express synonymous Ideas, may be used in Construction with a Verb singular. But if the Ideas are synonymous one of them is unnecessary; if they are distinct, Reason and Analogy demand a plural. In either case it is a Blemish in Composition."[16] He expressly denies the authority of the classical languages, which no doubt had influenced the authorities who defended the form.[16a] To custom or cultivated usage he makes no reference, but solely Reason and Analogy support his rule. Needless to say, he is positive in insisting that "One and One ARE two" is alone permissible. As noted above, he had a large and enthusiastic following of logicians and grammarians.

6. Withers, however, admits the correctness of "Temperance, Justice, Fortitude, IS a Virtue" provided "there is no—AND— in the sentence" and he makes the same provision for a series of infinitives. "But observe," he adds, "the Admission of— AND— between the Infinitive Modes renders the Construction ungrammatical. . . . even when the Attribute may be affirmed of each Noun separately, and on that account if the—AND— be

Aristarchus, p. 136.
Aristarchus, p. 40.
See above, Ch. IV, §4.

omitted, it is always more *safe* and frequently more *elegant* to insert it. . . . But take particular Notice, if one of the Nouns be plural, it is indispensably necessary to use a Verb plural, though there be no—AND—in the Sentence, and though the Noun which immediately precedes the Verb be singular."[17]

Withers falls into a trap of his own making when, commenting on "Not to believe rashly, IS the SINEWS of Wisdom," he remarks: "The Student will readily perceive that— *not to believe rashly*—convey an Idea which needs no Definition, and that the Expression, *Sinews of Wisdom* is, in it's Nature, metaphorical and obscure. He will, therefore, make *Sinews of Wisdom* the Subject of the Proposition, and exchange —IS—for—ARE."[18] Both in his correction and in his own government of the verb *convey* Withers is apparently guilty of a misapplication of analogy. Withers codifies the principle he is here following under two rules: Of two substantives joined by a verb, "If one of the terms be singular, and the other plural, place the plural Term before the Verb, and make the Verb correspond with it in Number. E. G. 'The Wages of Sin are Death.' " This contradicts his argument in favor of making the "Idea which needs Definition" the subject. And "When two, or many, Infinitives connected by—AND—are one Part of the Proposition, and a Noun singular the other Part, place—IT —before the Verb, and make the Verb singular. E. G. It is the Prerogative of Virtue, to dread no Eye, and to . . ."[19]

7. Following him, Alexander[20] and Murray[21] insist on the plural verb for subjects joined by *and* or in series. But in Murray's elaborate system there is a curious exception, which no other grammarian of the eighteenth-century seems to have observed, "Every man and every woman was," "Everything heard, and everything seen, is." Murray notes also the subject really one, of the type "That able scholar and critic is . . ."[22]

[17]*Aristarchus*, pp. 53-7 *passim*. See his metaphysical justification of this, Chapter II, § 2, above.
[18]*Ibid.*, pp. 87-8.
[19]*Aristarchus*, pp. 125-7.
[20]*Grammatical System*, 1794 ed., p. 27.
[21]*English Grammar*, 1800 ed., p. 122.
[22]*English Grammar*, 1809 ed., II, p. 322, *note*.

8. As we shall observe later,[23] Webster in the early editions of the *Grammatical Institutes* formulated an ironclad rule on this point covering "verbs, pronouns, and nouns"; but he changed its wording to "may" instead of "must" in his 1804 issue, and in a note in the Appendix gave about the same justification as Greenwood had offered for variations—namely, elliptical construction.[24] Webster also made what appears to be the first clear defence of *need* as a third person singular, explaining that this is the form for the auxiliary use of the verb. He did not mention *dare*.[25]

9. *Subjects with neither, either.* Lowth censures Addison for writing "as either of these two qualities *are* wanting." But while he objects to a double negative in two sentences from Bacon and Clarendon, of the pattern "neither the King nor the Queen were not at all deceived," he says nothing of their verb-agreement.[26] Priestley writes, "Faults, with respect to number, are often made by an inattention to the proper meaning of *or* and other disjunctive particles." Of his illustrations, two are of phrases with *as well as*.[26a] Potter, the critic of Johnson, wrote, ". . . concluded that David or Charles were personifications."[27]

Baker makes an exception to the usual rule in favor of subjects themselves plural thus joined, and illustrates it curiously by: ". . . strange accounts. Are either of them impartial? No, neither of them are." He is correct in remarking that when the subjects are one singular, one plural, "it seems most natural" to make the verb plural.[28] But Withers rends Dr. Blair for a sentence on this order: "There was much Genius in the World, before there WERE Learning, or ARTS to refine it." The capitals are Withers'. His comment on this is characteristic in tone and in a complete overlooking of the real issue: "It is far from my Intention to give Offence,

[23]In § 21.
[24]*Institute*, 1804 ed., pp. 32 and 95.
[25]*Ibid.*, p. 96.
[26]*Short Introduction*, 1762, p. 150 *note*.
[26a]*Rudiments*, 1768, p. 190.
[27]Potter, 1779, p. 57.
[28]*Reflections*, 1770, pp. 55 and 122-3.

when I speak of the Diction of *Englishmen*. I am fully convinced of the Universality of Truth, and the illimitable Nature of Reason. I disdain to countenance national Distinctions in the Republic of Letters, that glorious Republic . . . Yet,—Dr. Blair will pardon the Remark—no *Englishman* of liberal Education would ask, ARE Milton OR Virgil good Poets? Nor say—in the world WERE Homer OR Hesiod, before the Laws of Poetry were formed into a System."[29] Withers' other instances of this point, also from Blair, are similarly argued—he says that the most illiterate rustics south of the Tweed perceive the difference. Blair had written,[30] of "archbishop Tillotson and Sir William Temple," ". . . neither of them are remarkable for precision"; "An ostentatious, a feeble, a harsh, or an obscure Style are always faults"; and "What the Heart or the Imagination dictate." Withers also takes this occasion to trample on Johnson's term "DISJUNCTIVE CONJUNCTION—Monstrous Association of Ideas! Can mortal imagination conceive what is meant?"[31] But the battle of terminologies is outside our purpose.

10. *Agreement with a modified subject.* The plural verb with a subject modified by a phrase was generally treated to merely arbitrary logical condemnation instead of analysis of its meaning. Temple had already corrected on an errata page the verb in his sentence, "The music of these islands seem to agree . . .,"[32] so that we know writers were conscious of this principle before the grammarians paid heed to it. Priestley notes that misagreement of verbs and subjects occurs because words connected with the proper subject mislead and introduce confusion. Instead of chronicling errors, however, he remarks, "It is not necessary that the two subjects of an affirmation should stand in the very same construction, to require the verb in the plural number. If one of them be made to depend upon the other by a connecting particle, it may, in some cases,

[29]*Aristarchus*, p. 86.
[30]*Lectures*, I, 177.
[31]*Aristarchus*, pp. 59 and 82-5.
[32]*Sketches*, 1758, pp. 29 and 86.

have the same force, as if it were independent of it." His instance is from Hume, but he could easily have collected from contemporary grammars alone examples from various periods of English, including Goldsmith, Swift, and Addison, to make a quite sound buttressing of his principle by custom.[33]

Robert Baker says of the phrase "were blended true Dignity with Softness of Manners,"—"very common both in English and in French; and it must be owned that in many Places it appears easy and natural. But in many others there is an Uncouthness in it, the Violation of Grammar being too palpable."[34] This does not help us to any extent; we only know that sometimes we can evade the authorities with this construction. Murray, as might be expected, is strictly logical and allows no exceptions; he treats this form under two different rules for concord of subject and verb, and each time remarks conclusively that the nouns governed by prepositions "cannot be at the same time in the nominative and objective case,"[35] and so cannot help govern the verb.

11. *Special instances of collective nouns.* Priestley censures, in Smollett's *Voltaire,* "The number of inhabitants were not more than. . . ." This construction causes a special difficulty which the grammarians did not resolve by noting that *number* is a collective noun with either singular or plural meaning. Thus Nash, in his notes to *Hudibras,* wrote "There was a great number of slaves in Sicily," and Muray corrected "The number of the names together were" to *was,—* both admissibly. But Murray objected to the entirely correct sentence "A number of men and women were present," and Alexander to "Now here are a number of immediate duties"; and textbooks and syllabi still continue to correct this form.

Priestley notes the "harshness" of writing "The peasantry goes barefoot—the middle *sort* makes use. . . ."[36] A similar difficulty in resolving problems of agreement arise in "nouns of multitude" like *kind* and *sort.* The author of the *Many*

[33]*Rudiments,* 1769 ed., p. 186.
[34]*Reflections,* 1770, p. 117.
[35]*English Grammar,* 1809 ed., pp. 208-9 and 210-12.
[36]*Rudiments,* pp. 187-8.

Advantages and numerous others wrote without question "those best kind of beauties."[37]   Robert Baker first gave what appears to be a correct description of the state of current American usage in this matter: "Of this sort of men *is,* or *are,*" he wrote, "As for me, I prefer *is*—but either is much less offensive than *these* (or *those*) *sort*,"[38] which he notes as frequent in Warburton's *Divine Legation.*   Webster condemns "these kind of informations" from *Spectator No. 428,* but a few pages later writes, "This sort of verbs is purely Saxon; they are often . . ." —a quite natural construction.[39]   Indeed, there is little question that "This kind of men are" is accepted in standard English today, while *these kind* and *those sort* are reputed uncultivated at least in the United States.[39a]   The attempt to solve both problems by means of the same rigid logic, largely a project of the nineteenth century, has met with little success.

12.   The discussions as to proper verb and adjective agreement with singular nouns in *s,* like *means, pains, news, mathematicks,* add nothing new,   Webster was no doubt right in saying that "a mean" was purely fabricated and "scarcely used by any author from Chaucer to Lowth"; though the latter bravely mentions "Hooker, Sidney, Shakespeare," he gives no citations,[40] whereas Webster has pages of them for *news, pains,* and the rest.[41]   Murray further supports this position by noting that Johnson, who was dubious, and Lowth, who condemned it, both used the form in substance when they wrote "By means of something" (*Idler*) and "by means of some additional connection" (Lowth's *Introduction*), linking *means* with a singular.[42]   Acceptance seems to have been general of "a great many men," noted as curious by Ben Jonson, and of "many a," which, Murray explains, "refers to many individuals

[37]*Op. cit.,* 1724, p. 37.
[38]*Remarks,* 1779, pp. 100-101.
[39]*Institute,* 1804 ed., pp. 40 and 45.
[39a]For the contrast between American and British usage in this and pronoun agreement, as in other matters, see George H. McKnight, "Conservatism in American Speech," in *American Speech* I (October 1925) 1-17.
[40]*Short Introduction,* 1762, p. 120, *note.*
[41]*Dissertations,* pp. 201-214, and *note.*
[42]*English Grammar,* 1800 ed., p. 131.

separately, not collectively considered"—which seems to make it easier to swallow. "This many years," censured by Lowth,[43] nevertheless continued to be used. The only other protest was by the author of the *Observations,* who condemned as improper "in a few days, never a one, many a time, every five years," and a number of equally substantial idioms.[44]

13. Apparently the word *there* beginning a sentence was sometimes vaguely felt to be a substantive and to govern. Priestley says, ". . . when the particle *there* is prefixed to a verb singular, a plural nominative may follow without a very sensible impropriety. There *necessarily* follows *from thence,* these plain and unquestionable consequences."[45] This looks like an example of Priestley's own manufacture. Campbell wrote, ". . . the reader will find that there hath been several instances of this kind," but corrected it to *have* on his errata page.[46]

14. The problem of concord in the phrase *as follows* or *as follow* after a plural substantive greatly agitated Baker[47] and many others. The whole argument is summed up by Murray in two pages of note-type, including Campbell's contention for its construction as an impersonal verb and Tooke's for the explanation by logic of *as* as a relative pronoun meaning *which.* Murray inclines to Tooke's side.[48]

15. The meticulous insistence with which Lowth and others corrected Pope for violations of "agreement with the pronoun *thou,*" in places where the emendation would introduce unwieldy words such as *touched'st* and *defend'st* and quite distort the meter, arises from considerations of logic and fidelity to an imagined perfect past.[49] But this did not prove a profitable quarry, as the supply of faults was soon exhausted. Lowth remarks that *hath* and *doth* belong properly to the "ser-

[43] *Op. cit.,* p. 120, *note.*
[44] *Observations on the English Language,* 1752, pp. 21 and 25.
[45] *Rudiments,* 1769, p. 191.
[46] *Philosophy,* I, 89 and 512.
[47] *Remarks,* 1779, pp. 2-3 and 60. Baker is for the singular construction.
[48] *English Grammar,* 1809 ed., p. 206-8.
[49] *Short Introduction,* 1769 ed., pp. 67-9, 119 *note,* 171-2 *note.*

ious and solemn style,"[50] and in the article on Language in the first edition of the *Encyclopaedia Britannica,* 1775, we find, "We have changed *loveth, moveth* into the more modish forms of *loves, moves;* instead of *doth* and *hath,* we now make use of *has* and *does."* As in holding to the second-person singular *st* endings and to *ye* long after they have disappeared from ordinary use, some of the grammarians and rhetoricians gave indeed a solemnity and archaic dignity to their style; but they suggest also their remoteness from the language spoken and naturally written in their time.

16.   Lowth was apparently the first to attack *you was* an "an enormous Solecism: and yet Authors of the first rank have inadvertently fallen into it."[51] He does not explain why it is wrong, but Priestley and Withers base the conventional form on the analogy with *you are,* citing errors by Blair among others.[52] Only Webster holds out, giving *you was* in his paradigms—though admitting *you have* and *you are* "to be construed as singular verbs when we address one person." In defending this position he is, as often, slightly inconsistent: In the 1789 *Dissertations* he notes that in conversation *you was* is generally used, and adds, "Notwithstanding the criticisms of grammarians, the antiquity and universality of this practice must give it the sanction of propriety; for what but practice forms a language? This practice is not merely vulgar; it is general among men of erudition who do not affect to be fettered by the rules of grammarians, and some late writers have indulged it in their publications."[53] In the 1798 letter he simply remarks, "In the substantive verb the word has taken *you was,* which practice is getting the better of old rules, and probably will be established."[54] That Webster was wrong as to the trend of this form, but at least partly right as to the fact of its usage in his own day, is supported by Wyld's statement on *you was:* "This habit was apparently passing into disrepute at the begin-

---

[50]*Short Introduction,* 1769, p. 69 *note.*
[51]*Short Introduction,* 1769, pp. 67-8 *note.*
[52]*Aristarchus,* pp. 38-9.
[53]*Dissertations,* pp. 233-4.
[54]*Letter on the Errors,* p. 25.

ning of the nineteenth century."[55]   He notes it was not used by
the better-bred in Jane Austen's novels.   If I am not mistaken
it appears at least once in Lamb's letters.

17.   *Pronoun agreement.*   Lowth says practically nothing
on this topic, being much concerned with establishing what he
considers the proper meaning of *either* against the use of the
Bible translators.   Priestley is very clear that two singular
nouns joined by *or* must be referred to by a singular pronoun,
and gives the usual lot of examples, including a questioning of
Dr. Johnson himself for his use of *them* to refer to an academy.
A choice instance of a "concealed error" of this type is ferreted
out of Swift's *Proposal for Correcting* by Blair: ". . . why
our language is less refined than *those* of Italy, Spain, or
France."[56]   There was naturally rich hunting for this sort of
error, in the eighteenth century as later, and Addison was even
more than usually in request for faulty sentences.   The following from John Oldmixon's answer to Swift's letter to
the Earl of Oxford, though not cited by the grammarians, would
have been interesting for the purpose, as the "correct form"
would undoubtedly be ambiguous: ". . . that everybody loves
Flattery as well as himself, and Will take any Thing kindly that
is said in their favour."[57]

18.   *Adjective-agreement.*   Lindley Murray has a similar
problem of agreement to propose in objecting to "a beautiful
field and trees."   This "is not proper language.   It should be,
'Beautiful fields and trees'; or 'A beautiful field and fine
trees.' "[58]   This is clearly a "concealed grammatical error," the
misagreement of *a* and the plural noun.   Akin to this, and reminding one of Campbell's objection to "christian and sirname," is Priestley's detection of "confusion in numbers" in:

[55]*Hist. Mod. Colloq. English*, p. 356.

[56]*Blair's Lectures*, I. 447.

[57]*Reflections on Dr. Swift's Letter*, 1712, p. 33. I found a remarkable instance of "correctness" in a child's story of being ducked while in swim-
ming. "When I came up, everybody was laughing at me, but I was glad
to see *him* just the same." This was written in a seventh-grade English
class without anyone's correction or suggestion of the form.

[58]*English Grammar*, 1800 ed., p. 173. What would Lowell and other nineteenth-century discriminators of words say to *fine* here?

"Words consist of *one* or more *syllables,* syllables, of *one* or more *letters*."[59]

19. Robert Baker, alone in the eighteenth century so far as discovered in this study, made objection to the use of a pronoun "as a Relative to the indefinite Noun *One*.[60] . . . The *One* here is not the Unit in Number. It has the Sense of the *On* in the French Tongue, from which it is taken, and does not suffer a relative pronoun. . . . No person of tolerable taste would endure" *she* or *her* in this use, and "the Recurrence of the word *One* is not offensive" in: "One can't possibly help . . . Let one make what Use of one's Reason one will, one is still highly pleased."[61] Which is, obviously, a matter of taste. The recurrence of the "entity" principle is interesting.

20. It would not be difficult to demonstrate that the minute attention to agreement, particularly of pronouns, had little effect on the writers of the period following; probably quite as many cases of reference of *they* and *their* to words like *person* and *one* and *everybody* could be discovered in an equal number of pages of Jane Austen or Walter Scott and of Addison or Swift. And though the matter was brought to sharp focus and fully attended to by the critics of the succeeding period, there is good evidence that British usage is still about equally unfettered in the manner. The greater conservatism of American writers, as usual, has led them to follow this rule more carefully.[62]

21. *Predicate nominative agreement.* The problem of "two nouns of different number connected by a verb" caused much logical perplexity. The usual rule, first given by Martin, was that the verb "agrees with the nearest word." His examples were "nothing is wanting there, but Charms," and "Riches are often a Snare to Men."[63] As we have noted, Withers alone attempted, in fifty-eight pages of closely logical reasoning, a

[59]*Rudiments*, pp. 193-4.
[60]The word *one* was considered a noun by Withers and others who still capitalized all nouns. Any pronoun referring to an antecedent was described as "relative."
[61]*Reflections*, 1770, pp. 23-4.
[62]See McKnight, *op. cit., American Speech I*, (October, 1925), 1-17.
[63]*Introduction to English Language and Learning*, 1754, p. 118.

distinction between subject and predicate nominative in this construction, and refuted Harris' contention that the subject is always first in the sentence.[64]   But nobody seems to have paid any heed to this sustained effort, and Webster's grammars give the rule, following Harris, ". . . the verb more elegantly agrees with the first."

Probably from a sense of necessary parallelism, it came to be considered that the predicate nominative must likewise agree in number with the subject.   Priestley thought it necessary to explain that when one said, "They are a good apple," it was to be understood as meaning "They are a good kind of apple."[65] Robert Baker was very conscious of his necessary concord. He tells us we may say "they are every one of them my friends," but that "every one of whom I have experienced to be my friends" makes *every one* plural and is wrong; it must be *friend.*[66]   Webster had stated positively in his first and subsequent editions that "Two or more nouns singular connected by a copulative conjunction must have *verbs, pronouns* and *nouns* agreeing with them in the plural number.[67]   Evidently he felt that this did not agree with his third rule, quoted in the preceding paragraph, which regulates as to a verb joining words of different number; for in the 1804 edition this had been altered to "may have"; but the italics and the inclusion of the word *nouns* in the rule left things much as they were. Murray held to the rigid idea and as usual dominated most of the nineteenth-century grammars.

22.   By a similar logic Lowth was greatly disturbed by the phrases " 'tis they, 'tis two or three," as likewise "a person . . . so much your betters," in the *Battle of the Books*.   The expression, "though pretty common and authorized by Custom, yet seems to be somewhat defective."[68]   Priestley, though in general even less inclined to censure, condemns, "It is wonderful, the very trifling accidents, which . . ." quite parallel with

[64]*Aristarchus*, 1788, pp. 57-115.
[65]*Rudiments*, p. 62.
[66]*Remarks*, 1779, pp. 50-51.
[67]*Institute*, 1784 (1st ed.), pp. 29 ff; 1787 ed., p. 29; 1804 ed., p. 33.
[68]*Short Introduction*, 1762 ed., p. 120-1, *note*.

the example quoted by Lowth.[69]   Campbell, noting that John-son said the phrase "has yet an appearance of barbarism," pur-sues it through eight pages of analysis, and concludes that "those critics, who though both ingenious and acute, are apt to be rather more scrupulous on the article of language, than the nature of the subject will admit," had here followed a false trail, and that the translator was wrong who had scrupulously written "they are they which . . ."[70]

This concludes the examples of attempts to solve by various theories the problems of concord in English.   Like the preced-ing instances of problems of inflection, these have illustrated applications of most of the appeals which were examined earlier in this study, though in these cases "reason and analogy" pre-dominated, and less reliance was put upon usage or historical considerations; of euphony apparently no application was made to questions of agreement.

[69] *Rudiments*, pp. 190-1.
[70] *Philosophy*, I, 497-504.

CHAPTER XIII

THE RESULTS AND VALUE OF EIGHTEENTH-CENTURY CRITICISM

It appears to me, therefore, to have been not unhappily remarked that it is one thing to speak Latin and another to speak grammar.

Quintilian, *Institutes.*

Hence most students of rhetoric, when they have fallen into these inexplicable labyrinths, have, as being fettered by the inflexible restrictions of rules, lost all power of action, even that which they ought to have from their own mind, and, keeping their eyes fixed on a master, have ceased to follow the guidance of nature.

Ibid.

. . . men, speaking the proper language of their country, i. e., according to grammar-rules of that language, do yet speak very improperly of things themselves.

Locke, *Essay on the Human Understanding*

CHAPTER XIII

THE RESULTS AND VALUE OF EIGHTEENTH-CENTURY CRITICISM

1. *Summary of observations.* Several clear conclusions as to fact are possible from the data presented in this study. There was a great and increasing interest in problems of language in the eighteenth century, and particularly in the last third of the century. This interest was directed largely toward philosophical considerations of the nature and origin of language, the possibilities of a universal grammar, and the desirability of remodeling English toward the ideal of a complete and consistent language by principles of logic and order. The emphasis was on matters of correctness and precision, with only minor attention to merely utilitarian questions of clarity or force in the communication of ideas.

The authors of grammars and rhetorics and the critics of language based their rules and proscriptions on a number of theories as to language which have been here grouped as follows:

1. Language as an entity requiring conformity to its nature, since it is a mirror of actuality.
2. The authority of the grammarian's or the critic's *ipse dixit*.
3. The arbitrament of universal grammar and universal reason, which became in effect that of the Latin analogy.
4. The conflicting ideals of (a) analogy of forms in the language itself and (b) the need of differences in form for all possible differences in relations of ideas.
5. The authority of absolute logic—precision in matters of syntax and of word-choice.
6. The etymology of words and the history of the language as determiners of usage.
7. The authority of good custom, defined as national (pure, not

foreign or provincial), reputable (proper as opposed to vulgar), present, and further circumscribed by numerous canons of exception, such as beauty and the various principles described in Numbers 3-6 above.

It has been repeatedly emphasized in this study that other matters than correctness and logical precision were considered by rhetoricians and critics in the eighteenth century. Temple and others speak of being understood as the first virtue of writing. Archibald Campbell and Thomas Edwards, scourgers of Johnson and Warburton, stand out in the eighteenth century as critics who kept their attention upon the characteristics of a style good because genuinely fitted to its purpose. But these ideals were lost to sight in a mass of minutely logical exceptions; or rather, the belief of the eighteenth-century critic that clarity is actually promoted by subtle discriminations in wording and in structure, prevented any perspective in their view of actual problems. The main emphasis on correctness is illustrated in the statement of Michaelis: "Scrupulous attention to language, sometimes called grammatical pedantry, [is] a point of very great importance to human knowledge,"[1] and that of Webster ". . . it is inexcusable to sacrifice *propriety* to any consideration whatever."[2]

2. *The value of the century of emendation.* What did the main proponents of correctness accomplish in the eighteenth century? There is no question that the interest in problems of language, which they no doubt in part created, had useful effects in causing greater popular appreciation and respect for the mystery or craft of using English. The students who in the eighteenth century devoted incalculable toil to problems of correctness in English were gentlemen of lesiure like Robert Baker, Esq., politicians out of favor like Horne Tooke, barristers and bishops and college dons unencumbered with exacting duties, and Scotchmen and Irishmen anxious for distinction, who in previous centuries would probably have disputed about the classics or theology, but now turned to their

[1] *Dissertation,* 1769, p. 77.
[2] *Grammatical Institute,* 1784, p. 60.

own language as a respectable and needy field for their endeavors.   They brought to this work a certain liberalism in
philosophy, which made them willing to propagate the ideals of
gentlemanly culture, but an even stronger admiration of regularity and order and exact logic.

What was the result of their activity in reforming the
English language?   It has been generally assumed that they
did efficient service in regularizing a speech still full of an uncertainty inherited from the Middle English period.   But Dr.
Winship points out that Wm. Byrd's diary, 1732-3, is literate in
both spelling and grammar; that these standards were sufficiently clear in his day for whoever would take the trouble to
discover and follow them.[3]   Morris gives no account of changes
in inflection after 1700.[4]   Similarly, Wyld notes that in manu-
scripts and books "after the first decade of the seventeenth century" the "very instructive spelling . . . and . . . dialectal fea-
tures . . . are increasingly hard to find. . . . Orthography and
grammar are uniform and stereotyped" by the end of that
century.[5]   Extreme as this perhaps is, and modifiable by other
statements of Wyld's own, it is nevertheless clear that the style
of Addison and his contemporaries not only does not so "offend
against every part of grammar" as Swift, to point a moral, assumed, but is in point of correctness little farther removed from
the good gractice of today than that of writers a century later.

There is no doubt that the huge labors of the grammarians
were somewhat influential.   They hastened the gradual process
of bringing the "provincial usage" of Scotland and the like,
and particularly the class dialects, into line with the accepted
standard—though whether any particular standard form is a
loss or a gain must be a matter of opinion.   But their accomp-

[3]*Cambridge History of American Literature*, I, 10.   The *New English Dictionary* marks 18th- and 19th-century uses (8 and 9) as *Current English*.
[4]*Historical Outlines of English Accidence*, 1872.
[5]*Hist. Mod. Colloq. English*, (Unwin, 1920), p. 162.   His apparently contradictory statement that "the general diffusion of [Received Standard]
among the higher classes cannot be assumed "much before the end of the
eighteenth century" is probably to be understood particularly of pronunciation, of which he is speaking in the preceding paragraph, and of the per-
sistence of dialect forms.   (*Ibid.*, 103, cited by Fries in "Common School
Grammars," *P. M. L. A.*, XLII, 223.)

lishment in this regard is clearly comparable to Dr. Johnson's for spelling: it was rather diffusion of a standard already clear among literary men than that rectification of the best practice which obviously they purposed to accomplish. As might be expected, the correctors were most influential on matters of written form, details which are attended to in revision and are the staple of editorial style-books; no doubt we owe to them—to Lindley Murray in particular—the rather superfluous apostrophe in the possessive plural of nouns. On the contrary, the possessive pronouns or possessive adjectives, after a century of the greatest conflict and uncertainty, were returned to precisely the condition in which Wallis discovered and described them. The dubious and wavering practice of the eighteenth century, however, still reflects itself in the half-educated spellings *it's* and *her's;* it is probable that much of this difficulty would never have become so acute if the logical grammarians had not given it their confused attention.

Upon other matters of revision of writing, the opinions of these grammarians and critics had some effect. It is doubtful whether much of their attention to minute discrimination between words, which we have noted as the heritage of the critical emenders, has been of significant value to thought or expression. Rarely can one assume, in any but a small audience of like-minded purists, that words used in an elaborately exact and differentiated sense will be so precisely understood. The only safety, as Locke reminds us, is in definition. On the other hand, in spite of their arbitrary statements of right and wrong and their exclusively logical rather than rhetorical consideration of the problem, the grammarians' attention to sentence structure has no doubt had useful effect.

3. We cannot perhaps better sum up the achievement of this period than in the words of the grammarians and critics themselves. They had started confidently at the beginning of the century with the recommendation that one's own language be learned by rule, as Latin or other foreign tongues must be

learned.[6] They had been at first less concerned with grammar than with other sorts of logic and matters of vocabulary; but when Bishop Lowth, particularly, proceeded to list the grammatical errors of admired writers, the hunt was up, and large numbers of gross violations were collected and condemned.

Usser, in 1796, wrote most confidently of results in reforming the English language: ". . .the successive labours of the learned . . . have investigated its nature, remarked its peculiar idioms, and reduced it to grammatical precision."[7] Or if not so confident, and aware that "English is not taught" well and that "nobody cares" sufficiently about correctness, the critics nevertheless felt that most of the necessary scientific knowledge had been accumulated, and only application was needed; *The British Grammar* quotes from Turnbull's *Observations on a Liberal Education* a complaint of the neglect of English studies and the following logically complete plan for a remedy: One daily exercise in schools should be "to write a page of English, and after that to examine every Word by the Grammar Rules; and in every sentence to give an account of the English Syntax and Construction."[8]

The achievement of the grammarians during the eighteenth century is most accurately presented by Webster in the Preface to the 1804 edition of the *Grammatical Institute*. Whereas his first edition had praised Lowth as "well acquainted with the origin and genius of the language"[9] subsequent doubts and contradictions had disturbed his faith:

When a Lowth, an Ash, and a Priestley differ from each other in opinion, the curious inquirer has no resource but to look for satisfaction in the state of the language itself, as it has been exhibited in the best writers and in general practice.

Grammatical Institute, 1804 ed., preface pp. iii-iv.

[6]Richard Johnson, 1706, preface, *n. p.* A. Lane, cited by McKnight, *Mod. Eng.,* 291-2.
[7]*Elements of Grammar,* p. iv.
[8]Buchanan, *British Grammar,* 1784 ed., pp. xvi-xvii; *Regular Syntax,* 1767, p. xxiii. This practice is also strongly commended by Bayly, *Plain Grammar,* p. 96.
[9]*Op. cit.,* 1784, preface, p. 4.

In the *Dissertations,* he says:

> Lowth . . . has criticized away more phrases of good English than he has corrected of bad . . . by arbitrary rules substituted phrases that have been rarely, or never used at all.
>
> *Dissertations*, 1789, p. 287.

And in the 1807 letter he reiterates:

> But of the *doubtful points* [in grammar] . . . not half of them have been correctly settled by Lowth and his followers, and I have no hesitation in affirming, that the grammars now taught in our schools, *introduce more errors than they correct.*
>
> *Letter to Dr. Ramsay, p. 28.*

Even a casual view of the arguments on almost any point in this study gives confirmation of Webster's view. Of course he himself was fully persuaded that he was in the way to rectifying all that at once; but the dissatisfactions and contradictions went on just as hotly in the nineteenth century as in the eighteenth.

4. It might be suggested that a further and more thoroughgoing application of the grammarians' own logic, if indeed their efforts could have had any appreciable effect upon the spoken language, might have resulted in useful betterment. For instance, as we have noted, the great majority of regular verbs, with the same form in preterite and past participle, might well have suggested a plain analogy, instead of a need for differentiation, for the forms in the few strong verbs. If analogy had been followed, we might now have fewer cases of divided and anomalous forms such as those of *ring* and *lie.* Again, if the grammarians had adopted Bayly's suggestion, in which he anticipated Jespersen, that there is no need in English for verbs to vary for person, a perfectly simple regularizing might perhaps have been effected in the third person singular of the present tense for all verbs save *be.* And so we might suggest further applications of their "reason and analogy." But they had too many principles to appeal to, and did not center their attention on any one practicable idea. It is hardly probable that they would have affected practice greatly, but

they might have stood less in the way of normal simplifications actually in process in their day.

Their activities appear in perspective to have been a prodigious raising of issues already laid, and of points irrelevant and insignificant. The burden of proof is clearly upon whoever would maintain that much important accomplishment was a result of their labors, and the materials for discussion are, it is hoped, impartially displayed in the chapters of this study. The glossary in Appendix I lists eighteenth-century opinions on over three hundred grammatical and logical issues. Of this total of prescriptions, in spite of the violence of censure quoted in the preceding chapters, less than a dozen condemned types of construction (noted in the glossary by **) are actually regarded as illiterate or popular usage today. In fact, a better point-score than that of these rhetoricians and grammarians could certainly have been achieved by pure chance.

Of the forms effectually banned, a number, already long dead, were exhumed in the eighteenth century solely for critical obloquy. Such cases are clearly the confusion of *ye* and *you* and the mixture of *thou* and *you,* and probably the use of *which* referring to persons. Other condemned forms were sporadic and passing errors, or positive creations of the grammarians, like *teached, methoughts.* In certain formal aspects of literary revision such as precise parallelism in sentence structure and sequence of tenses, and in printers' forms like the apostrophe in the possessive plural, a few more points were established. All this makes no creditable total record for the century of laborious grammatical criticism, and it illustrates well the useless precaution of purists. An exact count of the actual usage in books at the beginning and at the end of the eighteenth century and today might show more conclusively just what effect their efforts had on literary practice.

If this had been the end of the grammatical furore—if the grammarians had passed with the emenders—the result upon the practice of writing and particularly the practice of schools today would not be so unfortunate as it is. But the work of the grammarians had only begun. The nineteenth century was to see a yet completer inundation, with the stimulus of the Kantian categories and of half-digested ideas out of Indo-Germanic philology. And with all this addition, whole heaps of the prejudices, taboos, and prescriptions of eighteenth-century writers were carried entire into the books of writers who followed them, so that a majority of their ideas, based as most of these were in metaphysical and illogical concepts of language and usage, may nevertheless be found today earnestly and convincedly taught in schools. A cleaning out of this ancient purist muddle is suggested as essential before we can do any effectual teaching of composition.

5. *The correct style.* The grammarians and rhetoricians developed their own neo-classical conception of style—minutely logical, pure, precise, heavily formal and circumlocutory. It is best observed in their own writings. An instructive comparison is that between the robuster, more individual and irregular expression of Swift and Greenwood, and the formal parsable style of Johnson and Campbell. The grammarians' style grows out of their theories quite naturally. It is sufficiently obvious that "national" expression tends to exclude all flavorful local speech as well as foreign idioms; that purity and propriety, pursued to their logical conclusion of majority use only, as these writers pursued them, must result in stereotyped and flat, general expression. "If you must write like everybody else, it is useless to take up the pen."[10]

The place of correctness is clear in a sound theory of expression such as Locke formulated.[11] It is by no means the first and foundational requisite, as the eighteenth century regarded it; its sole function is the necessary but subsidiary one of preventing opaqueness in the medium of communication.[12] It has comparatively little to do with clarity directly, and little to contribute even to force and energy, or to beauty. But it may serve to prevent obstruction of communication and distraction of attention. Whatever form of expression is once used is, ob-

[10]A. Albalat, *L'art d'écrire* (Colin, 1909), p. 57.
[11]See the quotations in Ch. II, §§ 4 and 5 of this study.
[12]See Locke's *Essay*, Book III, Ch. XI, § 11.

viously, possible to be used, whatever its deviation from established formulas. Whatever will pass for the most part unregarded by a cultivated reader belongs to the "area of negligible variation,"[13] and has nothing to do with the genuine problems of effective communication. By definition it belongs to what Harold Palmer calls "Plain English . . . that style of vocabulary and composition that constitutes [the major part] of any connected speech or text in English," which raises no problem of usage, "gives no clue as to who or what the speaker or writer is," and calls no attention from the idea imparted to the form.[14] But whatever calls attention to itself as a variation, causing scorn or amusement or even admiration, or making the reader stumble, is bad in so far as the writer wants to secure first and chief attention to the ideas he has to express. This may happen to apply, with any given audience, to Wilson's inversions of the usual order for "not only—but also," quite as much as to *these kind* or *he ain't*.[15]

We need specific studies of what hinders comprehension in reading, for various classes of persons both children and adults. The resulting data would be of the utmost importance both for teaching reading and for improving practice in writing. They would no doubt confirm the importance of a writer's or speaker's mastering the organization of his material, not on merely logical, but rather on rhetorical or on psychological principles; they would show that structure of sentences and choice of words, but more particularly failure to define words clearly, are matters of serious concern. But it is doubtful if many problems of conventional correctness would present themselves in such a study of the aids and hindrances to comprehension.

[13] G. P. Krapp, "Standards of Speech and their Values," *Modern Philology* XI (July, 1913) p. 58.

[14] "English, Plain and Coloured." Supplement No. 41, *The Bulletin for Research in English Teaching*, Department of Education, Tokyo, n. d.

[15] In a recent study of usage, such a Wilsonian sentence was rated, by 26 philologists, on precisely the same level of illiteracy with *these kind*, and but little better than *lay down* and *leave me come in*: "Current Definitions of Levels in English Usage," *English Journal*, May, 1927 (XVI, 345-59). See above, Ch. VI, § 2.

6. The "area of negligible variation" may be thought of as surrounding a comparatively small body of formal offences which do seriously obstruct communication. In the attention of cultivated readers, various conventionally proscribed expressions, such as "like I do," probably appear now in one, now in another of these two fields. The occasion, the speaker or writer, the subject, the purpose, the audience—all help to determine the place of any form at a given time. In general, the more cultivated and cosmopolitan the critic, the smaller is the area of "flagrant error" which he notices and is offended by, the larger the region of negligible variation, spreading imperceptibly into the wide continent of altogether acceptable speech.

It should of course be specifically stated that every one has the right and privilege of drawing where he pleases this boundary between unacceptable forms and permissible variants. As Lounsbury remarked, if one dislikes any expression, that provides him an excellent reason for not using it, but a poor reason for requiring anybody else to eschew it.

Moreover, the whole matter being one of effect, the problem is, what effect does one want to produce? If one of formal dignity and importance, many forms that suggest themselves will be barred as too free and informal; this standard of the "serious and elaborate performance," incidentally, is what the eighteenth-century critics, and most later handbook-writers and teachers, appear to have had in mind throughout their discussions. If, as is more often the case, the effect desired is of well-bred ease, the area of negligible variation correspondingly expands over a great part of the forms previously rejected. If on occasion one wishes to represent the usage of an illiterate person, as Mark Twain did in writing *Huckleberry Finn,* the area of proscribed forms shifts to take in the whole range of terms required for the serious and formal occasion. That this representation of illiteracy is a difficult feat is suggested by any study of literary dialects.

In fact, probably all that anyone can safely attempt to do with his language is to represent himself as he actually is—

marked with speech habits middle western or southern; cultivated or illiterate; interestedly attentive to words, or scornful of them and of forms generally.   Shibboleths of social élites cannot be learned seriatim as the grammarians and compilers of "ten thousand errors" assume; language habits are a matter of deeper cultivation, rooted strong in early feelings, prejudices, and habits of thought and conduct.

In the eighteenth-century studies here summarized, and always in the view of the grammarian or critic or teacher of limited outlook and information, the area of variation which may be permitted as unimportant tends to shrink, and that of reprehended "errors" to expand.   With few and minor exceptions here and there, mainly in Priestley, variation was not countenanced in any of the studies of language here analyzed. Campbell's elaborate scheme had only the narrowest and most inconspicuous place for it.[16]   Indeed, the search for expressions to proscribe was incessantly carried even into the realm of altogether accepted usage.   We have noted that Campbell would have nothing to say for the "colloquial idiom"; apparently he confused it with vulgar or illiterate speech.   The whole aim of these writers was to enlarge and round out neatly the area of disapproved speech, by logical analysis and refusal of all exceptions and anomalies, and to delimit it by a sharp line from the acceptable.   While actually this boundary is shifting and irregular, differing for different persons, purposes, occasions, they wanted to make it smooth and invariably logical.   An expression objected to in one case must in their view be objectionable in all cases.   If *this kind* is right, *kind are* must obviously be wrong.   Errors also lurked concealed, but discoverable to their diligent search, in the most inoffensive constructions such as "a field and trees" or "christian and sirname," and must be diligently haled out and condemned.

The result was, naturally, that specific hindrances to communication were constantly set up by an excess of zeal to make it serve its purpose better.   Quintilian recognized the same tendency in the activities of grammarians.   He speaks of their

---

[16]*Philosophy*, I, 372-3.

holding to "analogy" with "a most unpleasantly perverse attachment to exactness," and of the "contemptible absurdities" of the etymologists.   He notes that "attention to words leads chiefly to a *circulatoria volubilitas*"[17] and adds, ". . . It appears to me, therefore, to have been not unhappily remarked that it is one thing to speak Latin and another to speak grammar."[18]   This Locke usefully supplements with the statement "that men, peaking the proper language of their country, i. e., according to grammar-rules of that language, do yet speak very improperly of thing themselves."[19]

7.   The best illustrations of these contentions are conveniently found in the productions of the eighteenth-century critics of language themselves, as they are excerpted in these chapters. In the latter part of the century we come upon an increasingly painful correctitude, a frequent resort to circumlocutions and repetitions, an elaborate precision, "a barren Identity of Expression," as Withers puts it.   All this suggests what was no doubt the fact, that these writers, fearful of censure by critics of their ilk, examined their productions word by word and phrase by phrase, giving "an account of the English Syntax and Construction," in order to render everything perfectly parsable.   Apparently criticism had indeed gone too far, as Campbell feared while he drove it farther, and their language had come out "injured in copiousness and nerves," flattened by circumlocution.   Wyld, noting this change in eighteenth-century style, but attributing it entirely to the rise of the Middle Classes, says: "Pope and his generation still kept the sparkle, along with the ease of the seventeenth century . . . the sober decorum of Richardson . . . exhibits the correctitude of Middle Class propriety in speech and conduct . . . typical of a habit of mind and mode of expression which were gaining ground." He notes "a reaction in favor of the regular and solemn style of pronunciation and grammar . . . a falling off of

[17]*Institutes*, X, I, § 8.   See also I, ch. vi, §§ 17, 32, 39-42, 45; VIII Introduction, §§ 12-24.

[18]*Ibid.*, I, ch. vi, § 27.

[19]Locke's *Essay*, Book III, Chapter XI, § 24, (1751 ed., p. 244).

the quality of prose style among the generality of writers after the third quarter of the eighteenth century." So, he adds, Miss Austen's characters "converse."[20]

That a humdrum correctitude was the literary ideal toward which purity, propriety, precision and the rest were tending is suggested by the work of many late eighteenth-century critics. Wyld rightly adds, "the style of Literature is rooted in the life and conversation of the age. From these sources alone can prose renew its life from generation to generation."[21] Categories and principles which contemptuously disregarded the "colloquial dialect," and censured whatever was not altogether regular and logically exact even in standard authors, had little to contribute to such renewal; they rather tended to make it impossible. If the writers of the romantic period and later had not shown the same disregard for the theories of language which so thickly beleaguered their way, as for the rest of neo-classical criticism, they might have found themselves writing like Campbell or William Ward.

If, on the contrary, more attention could have been given, in the eighteenth century and later, to remedies for the real difficulties in communication which Locke listed, there would have been plenty of work to occupy the highest capacities of mind. Effectiveness of communication in Locke's view is not an affair of logical precision, extreme differentiation of words or inflections, or consistency in etymology. It depends chiefly on defining terms and illustrating them fully, detecting fallacies hatched by wrong uses of words as of logic, and using expressions only with intent and consistent heed to their meaning. We must add to this the idea, suggested by Berkeley, that it is also necessary to recognize and check, in both speaking and attempting to understand, the tendency to use terms "to raise some passion" rather than to convey clear ideas. If we include this differentiation, we have the outline of a fundamental grammar such as Ogden and Richards present.[22] Their

[20]Wyld, *Modern Colloquial English*, 1920, p. 185-8.
[21]Wyld, *loc. cit.*
[22]*The Meaning of Meaning*, (Harcourt, 1923), Chapter V, Appendix A, and pp. 205, 212, 257, 261-3 and 353-7.

techniques of translating and expanding symbols constitute a rigorous discipline, no doubt at least as useful for the training of the mind as the logicizing which Blair so highly praised. For obviously, learning something of the mastery of a living and indefinitely adaptable medium, and of its adjustment to the thought and passions of men in actual communication, calls for a more difficult sort of mental activity than following precise and invariable logical prescriptions. The attempt to develop mastery of language by the memoriter process of the rule-books is of a piece with the whole superstition that rote-learning produces knowledge and therefore power. If the attention of students of language in the eighteenth century had been turned in the direction which Locke indicated, rather than to a comparatively empty concern with correctness, their influence upon the actual use of the language as a means of communication and social control would have been different and probably more considerable, and such studies as this might have had a quite different content.

8. *Some practical considerations.* As we have noted, a great part of the prescriptions assembled in this study are still repeated in handbooks and style-sheets and the like today. The fact that they were in general developed out of quite false theories and conceptions of the nature of language is not, therefore, so important as the fact of their vitality and continuing influence. It has been observed that they were not for the most part evolved in schoolrooms, and forced upon the outside world by subtle forms of academic pressure. On the contrary, rules and theories of this sort are a perennial growth of every sort of curious observation of language, and are only a form of the criticism of manners and customs which goes on constantly in every society. Though most of those here discussed are recognizable as current in similar books and lists today, perpetuated by a century and a half of imitation, fresh forms of purism are constantly being created on the same or like principles and propagated with fresh enthusiasm.

The business of the student of language is to take account of such prescriptions as facts of significance in his study, important facts like any other set of human feelings and notions manifested in norms of conduct and in behavior.   Knowing more fully their origin and history, he may be better able to deal intelligently with the facts and discover their bearings. He will be not more, but rather less inclined to attempt changes in language, whether in the direction of simplification in spelling or grammar or of efforts toward protecting an assumed purity of the vernacular.   He will, in fact, be led to realize the fixity of patterns of tradition in the feelings about English and the usage of English by adult persons.   Conscious that most matters of so-called correctness are related slightly to clarity and intelligibleness of communication, and most largely to demarcations of social difference and grouping, he will in general be content with observing and understanding these phenomena.   His own effort will be toward increasing the precision of his instruments for noting and recording both the facts of usage and the nice gradations of effect secured by slight variations of form.   He will naturally appreciate the more, as he explores further in these areas, the often subtle effectiveness of fine shades in tone secured by observance of received conventions, the distinction, rather than the distinctions, which a speaker or writer may evidence by the use of words in awareness of their history and associations.   He will see more clearly that such conscious dealing with the medium of communication, and never in any case blind obedience to rules of correctness, alone can make a style.[22a]

In one problem it is possible that the materials of this study may prove of more direct value.   The rules of the eighteenth-century grammarians and purists and of their followers, we have noted, still appear in force in our schoolbooks and courses of study.[23]   In so far as any of these represent actual social discriminations, and reflect the feelings of the people whom the graduates of our schools will live and work among, such rules

[22a] This point is well presented in Dr. Canby's editorial "Pure English" in the *Saturday Review of Literature* for Sept. 22, 1928 (vol. V, No. 9).

[23] See Fries, "Rules of the Common-School Grammars." *P. M. L. A.*, XIII, pp. 221-237.

are probably significant and need to be known. The fact that
objection to a form is based in false logic, or in mere ancient
and ignorant prejudice, has nothing to do with the case; so
long as feeling against a usage in fact exists, young people need
to know this as protection against the prejudice which its use
may arouse against them. A case in point is the form *ain't*,
which has plenty of history and analogy as well as simple practical usefulness to support it, but nevertheless appears to be
considered, at least in this country today, a mark of illbreeding.
Precisely the same is true of *you was,* which is anciently reputable, analogical, convenient, but which is now unanimously condemned as illiterate.

9. On the other hand, literally thousands of proscriptions in
school grammars, handbooks of correctness, lists of errors, and
style-sheets are mere figments of the critical imagination.[24]
A huge proportion of them, like the "ipsedixitisms"[25] of
the eighteenth century, are special creations of the maker of the
list or handbook, or of someone whom he copies. Others,
ancient and historic by repetition, have no closer relation to the
facts of cultivated usage. So long as these rules are confined
to a single business or editorial office, they concern only the
small group whom they there restrict. But when they get into
schools, their potential harm is enormous. They foster dis-
gust with the idea of decent English expression, which they
confuse hopelessly with the vulgarity aptly called "schoolmas-
tered language," and they lead to inhibition of ordered speech
and writing, in children whose normal difficulties in expressing
themselves are great enough without their unnecessary and

---

[24]A friend of mine, a linguistic scholar and a writer of literature of the
first order, has suffered, in his proofs from one of the oldest and most distinguished publishing houses, such drastic and unintelligent revision as to
remind one of Bentley's Milton or Blair's strictures on Swift. Such phrases
as "This difficulty, due to . . ." have appeared altered to "because of";
poetical but unusual words like *aery* have been turned nonsensically to
eery, and *get* portentously and inappropriately made over into *obtain* according to the style-book. His proofs did not, like Mark Twain's, return
"a mush of concession," but his labors in defending his right to express
himself in his own English took time from more fruitful labors and
irritated him endlessly.

[25]Fitzedward Hall's name for them.

baffling burden. Notable examples are the usual small, meaningless distinctions of parts of speech, which in real use are fluid and almost without compartments, the false "logical rules" of case and concord, and the absurd purisms in wording which are the staple of much English teaching. Investigation into the facts of cultivated usage, of the feelings which various expressions do actually arouse, and consequently of the forms most essential to be mastered, is proceeding in various directions and will gradually be made current among teachers and writers of textbooks.

10. Meanwhile, we know quite definitely the rather small area of grossly illiterate forms against which there is genuine and strong consensus of feeling among reasonably cultivated persons in this country, and we can concentrate attention upon these with some hope of success. Probably forty or fifty type errors in grammar, for example, constitute the total of such forms that need to be attacked as seriously hampering in ordinary social and business relations; it is unlikely that more than this number exist in the speech of children of American descent. So-called "misuses of words" are flagrantly bad in even smaller proportion. Where distinctions of meaning do exist, the exigency of actual situations will put a speaker right; but most announced distinctions are quite imaginary. At any rate, practically none of those made with determined positiveness in the eighteenth century, and still copied diligently into language books, have apparently either credit or value in cultivated use today.

Certainly the very conservative larger dictionaries may be trusted to delay acceptance of an expression long enough. Once it is entered there as "colloquial," that is, acceptable for all informal uses by cultivated people, it should be unquestioned in such use. And informal occasions, for both speech and writing, are practically the only ones which most children in grades and high school will ever encounter. Neither textbooks nor courses need be wrested from their true purpose to fit any pupil for improbable occasions of writing inaugural addresses or funeral sermons; those who need these sorts of skill will learn them elsewhere, later. Yet it is the English of the quite formal, literary occasion which most school texts and courses apparently describe and teach. Often more than half the expressions in the handbook "glossary of errors" will be found accepted in even the sternest lexicons. When purists' dicta are examined in the lump, their credit is even worse, as we have seen of the mass of eighteenth-century rules presented in this study and summed up in the glossary (Appendix I).

Our school courses and texts in English need thorough revision in light of the facts of language history and of current usage. Only in this way can we stop perpetuating gross misconceptions about the language. Only so can we hope to make some gain in the highly difficult business of helping children to master the first stages of that long and interesting craft, the simple, effectual use of English in speech and in writing.

APPENDIX I

The advocates of each expression cited are given in the right-hand
column, its opponents on the left.

† preceding a name or list of names indicates that the writer, in
advocating or condemning a given expression, apparently misinterpreted the trend of usage; †† that his proposal or dissent never
probably represented actual usage.

* marks the names of those who apparently represented correctly
the fact and trend of a given form; ** that they may possibly have
influenced a change in usage.

19C indicates that, so far as this study has explored, there was
no objection in the eighteenth century to a given expression, but
that it has suffered attack by later purists.

Explanations and references are usually given in full in the
sections of the study, here indicated by Roman numerals followed by
Arabic numbers.

Arabic numerals alone or followed by decimals refer to the divisions
of this glossary itself.

Occasionally references are made direct to Johnson's Dictionary
(Johnson), editions of 1755 and 1785, to the New English Dictionary
(N. E. D.), and to Fitzedward Hall's books (Hall *Phil.* and *Mod.
Eng.*) and McKnight's *Modern English in the Making,* listed in the
bibliography in Appendix II C, below.

It is important in examining this table to note the wise abstention
from attack and the rarer defence of actual usage, particularly by such
men as Priestley and Johnson, rather than to give exclusive attention
to the quibbling niceties of judgment of which the account is chiefly
composed.

The table is divided into twenty sections, with subdivisions, as follows:

1. Differentiation of Parts of Speech
   1.1 Adjective and Adverb
   1.2 Substantive and Adjunct
   1.3 Verb and Other Parts of Speech
   1.4 Transitive and Intransitive Verb

1. DIFFERENTIATION OF PARTS OF SPEECH

1.1 ADJECTIVE AND ADVERB—II.9, V.13, AND VIII.6

1.11 Adjectives as adverbs

> agreeable to, comfortable with, consistent with. See previous to
>
> exceeding II.9, V.13, IX.3

Lowth

Defoe
Priestley
Bible translators

Murray allowed *exceeding clearly*

> extreme jealous V.13

Priestley
Bible translators

> godly V.13, IX.12

††Lowth

Johnson
Priestley
Campbell
Webster

heavenly, homely—see godly, lowly

ill

19 C. See Hall *Phil.*, 83   *Johnson
and *n.*

is like (for *likely*), *like enough*
19 C   Johnson

lively—see *godly*

lowly V.13, IX.12

†Johnson—proposes *lowlily*—no   Johnson—gives *lowly* as adverb
   citation   Webster
(See Poe's "Virginal Lillian")   Campbell

miserable poor V. 13
                                        Priestley

not near so accurate IV.3, V.13
                                        James Harris
                                        Defoe

previous to V.14, VI.23, XI.1
†Baker   Webster

prior V.14
††Baker (advocated *priorly*)
††Johnson has *priorly*—not in 1755 ed.

safe, arrive VI.13
                                        *Baker

silly—see *godly, lowly*

slow V.13, IX.12
††Johnson   Milton, etc.

some few III.4
†Monthly Review   Baker

soon V.13, IX.12
††Johnson quoting
  More (*soonly*)

suitable to V.14, XI.1
†Lowth   Bayly
                                        Webster

See *previous to*

1.12 Adverb as adjective V.14, X.6

above X. 6

19 C   Withers (used)
                                         Harris

look apishly, leoninely
                                         Harris

placed as nearly as possible to
                                         †Withers

look meanly
                                         †Johnson

manner was thus
Baker   Swift

sound harshly
                                         Murray

then government V. 14
19 C   *Baker
                                         Harris
                                         Murray

was there V. 14
19 C   *Murray

arrive safe previous to, etc. under 1.11

1.2 SUBSTANTIVE AND ADJUNCT V.10

1.21 Substantive as abverb

noways

Johnson—used by "ignorant barbarians"   Webster

some better, few, III.4
Burn , 1786, p. 220   "Standard Writers"
Monthly Review   *Baker

that, this as adverbs
19 C   *Webster

1.22 Substantive as adjective, V.10

yesterday's (adj.) V.14
                                         *Murray

1.23 Adverb as substantive

in no wise V.3

†Campbell

since when, by then X.4, V.14*n*

Priestley   Murray
Baker
Not in Johnson

whereof, whereby XI.1

*Johnson
Bayly

worth their while X.4

†Priestley   "Standard Authors"
Johnson
See N. E. D.

from thence, whence, see *Redundancy,* 8.0

1.24 Adjective as substantive

everlasting V.10

††Campbell
Priestley

former, latter

††Lowth (1763)
Not in Johnson

a modern X.4

Potter

one IV.6, XII.19*n*

* Johnson
Priestley
Withers

plenty V.10

Priestley   "Works of considerable merit"
Campbell

See N. E. D.

the same X.6

19 C   Bayly
Johnson

whether—see DUAL NUMBER, 3.4, below

Johnson
Murray

1.3   VERB AND OTHER PARTS OF SPEECH

1.31   Verb coinage

See F. Hall, *Mod. Eng.*, 40 and 285*n*

smoothen

Johnson—"bad"   N. E. D.

womanize

Johnson—"not used, but proper"
See N. E. D.

1.32   Substantives and adjuncts as verbs or verbals

anguishing IX.4

†Baker

See Hall *Mod. Eng.* 71-2 and *n*

compete X.8

†J. Johnson

had like to have V.10

*G. Harris   "Greatest part of our writers"
Johnson

had rather, had better V.10, IX.14, X.4

††Salisbury	Withers
Johnson	Johnson in *Rasselas*
Lowth	Priestley: "had better have been
Campbell	made"

had as lief

†Salisbury   Priestley
Campbell IX.14   Johnson (Shakespeare, etc.)
See Hall, *Mod. Eng.* 238

honeyed

†Johnson (See Hall, *Mod. Eng.* 70*n*)   Johnson (*honeying*)

notice V.10

†J. Johnson   Shaftesbury
Franklin (*Mod. Eng.* p. 285*n*)   Johnson (*noticed, unnoticed*)

patient (verb) III.7

Johnson (Shakespeare)

premise V.11

Lowth   Swift

1.4 TRANSITIVE AND INTRANSITIVE VERB V.11, 12

was amounted to

†Mennye   Swift

were appealed V.11

††Mennye   Swift
                                                Johnson

Priestley queries

were asked
Priestley queries

beholding for *beholden* V.12, VIII.16 *note*

†Campbell   Sidney
Lowth   Dryden, etc.
Johnson "very corrupt"

forfeit (trans. use) V.11

†Mennye

Priestley queried

ingratiate with him V.11

Mennye   Bentley
Baker

Priestley tentative

lay for *lie* IV.6, V.11, VII.7, X.9, XIII.4

**Baker
Webster
Bingham

is lain down, III.2

†Baker (but accepts *is risen*)

lay me down

††Coote

lay for VII.7

                                                *Johnson

learn for teach X.8

*Johnson, 1785, ("now obsolete")   Johnson, 1755 (syn.)
J. Johnson   Spenser
                                                Shakespeare, etc.

is forging, printing, V.12

Hornsey
Johnson "vitious corruption" for "a-building"
  See *Mod. Eng.* 224 ff. on the current form, "is being built"

to be let X.3, 6

††Withers

overlay VII.6   See *lay for lie*

am mistaken V.12, VI.23

††Lowth   Withers
Johnson
Welsted

owing to V.12

†Johnson   Dryden
Lowth
Campbell

premise with IV.6

Lowth   Swift

Priestley tentative

repent him of IV.6, V.11

†Mennye   *Johnson

Priestley tentative

resemble them V.11

†Swift
†Nash (Notes to
   Hudibras, 1793)

19C   *set for sit* VII.7
                       See Hall *Phil* 108n[2]

Johnson

sneering him V.11

*Z. Grey (VI.14)
Nash notes

wanting

††Lowth   Swift, etc.

was split upon by V.11

Lowth   *Campbell
                                     (matter of clarity)

stumble him V.11

Priestley (queries)   Monboddo

are swerved V.11

Mennye   Johnson
                                     Lowth

teach—see *learn*

wanting V.12 (see *owing*)

†Lowth   Addison
                                                   Johnson

1.5 PREPOSITION AND CONJUNCTION
except

19C   Johnson

like V.10

19C.   Neither used nor mentioned in 18C. grammars

without V.10

*Tooke   Webster
Johnson (colloquial only)   Lord Mansfield
                                                   Congreve and stand-
                                                   ard authors of 18th
                                                   century

but V.10, XII.3, 4

††Murray
    Priestley   (regarded as conjunction only)

1.6 MISCELLANEOUS DIFFERENTIATIONS
a-bed, a-fishing V.12

††Hornsey

as follows VI.13, XII.14

††Kames awkwardly writes *what follows* (*Elements* II, 24, 41, etc.)

different than VI.12

Baker
Willich

See Hall *Mod. Eng.* 82*n*, and N. E. D.

different to III.6, VI.12

Baker prefers *from*

excepting as preposition

††Johnson "not proper"

if for *whether* X.10

††J. Johnson

more, and more evident

††Objected to as adverbs in "double function"

no, with *whether . . . or,* V.3, 11

††Bingham
Campbell

such . . . . as VI.13

††G. Harris	Johnson
John Nott	Standard Authors

See Hall *Mod. Eng.* 199*n*, 213*n*, and 256

that after *greatest* and *same* XI.2

Priestley

that as a relative V.8, VIII.6

††*Spectator Nos. 78 and 80*	Johnson
G. Harris	

see § 2.0 below

themselves and families X.5

Baker

No eighteenth-century stricture against *myself* as a personal pronoun

very pleased, etc.

19C.   See Hall *Mod. Eng.* 54-5 and *n.*

withal as preposition XI.6

††Buchanan   Shakespeare, etc.

you as impersonal VI.1

†Priestley	Addison
Parr	Johnson
	Fox

2. DIFFERENTIATION OF GENDER

Discussed by Greenwood, Harris, Lowth, etc.

that for *who* V.8, VIII.6

††Addison and Steele
Buchanan
George Harris
Lowth (tentative)
Hornsey (tentative)

which for *persons* II.8, V.8

*Most grammarians	W. Ward (used)
	Webster
	Beattie

who for *which* II.8, V.8

†Murray   Johnson and
Buchanan   standard authors
Hornsey
Priestley

See Hall *Phil.* 8n

whose as genitive of *which* V.9, VIII.6, IX.20

††Lowth   Johnson
Buchanan   Bayly
Baker   Harris
Withers   Blair
Webster (1798)   Murray (preferred
Hornsey   because shorter)
                                           "Standard authors"
Priestley divided in opinion
Cf. Hall *Phil* 6-7 and *n; Mod. Eng.* 348.
See Gerund—below, 3.23

"Shifts" in Gender V.7
'tis these, they, two or three

††Campbell
Johnson

3. SUBSTANTIVE DECLENSIONS

3.1 CASE, NOMINATIVE AND ACCUSATIVE XI.4

3.11 Substantives in double function VI.2, 4; XI.4

††Lowth
Baker
Murray
Campbell
See Parallel Structure, below, 7.0, *Concealed Error* 9.5

3.12 Case of pronouns after prepositions, etc.

between or *told you and I* IV.6, XI.5

**Priestley and   A. Campbell—cites
    most grammarians   "Contemporary
Walpole   novels"
Chesterfield   Wycherley
Monthly Review and *Critical Review*

3.13 Case in predicate

it is me IV.6, XI.5

†Lowth

Baker (cites Congreve—is dubious)

Campbell

Murray

*Johnson (Hall *Mod.
Eng.* 199*n.*)

Priestley

"Standard authors"

it is us, him, etc. XI.5

Priestley defended *us,* but used *we*

Baker

if it be I XI.5

Priestley

3.14 Accusative invariably after infinitive XI.2, 5

Lowth

Subsequent grammarians divided

3.15 Other personal-pronoun cases

my father and him have IV.6, XI.5

*Priestley (suspects French influence)

Walpole

"Contemporary novels"

Chesterfield

woe is me VIII.1

*Bayly

methinks, methought VIII.5, IX.10, 14

†Temple

Lowth

Campbell

Johnson

methoughts VIII.5

*Lowth

Campbell

††Addison

See *N. E. D.*

3.16 Nominative and accusative who

who should I meet, who is it for? IV.4, XI.6

†Lowth

Buchanan

Hornsey (confused)

Bingham V.11

*Webster

Priestley

"Standard authors"

Bayly dubious

whom do men say that I am, whom he thought was III.3, XI.7

Lowth	Locke
Baker	Bayly
Webster	Webster
Baker's anonymous critic	

      Se Appendix of Jespersen's *Philosophy of Grammar*

head of whoever had XI.7

Priestley dubious	Hume

3.17 You as nominative VIII.9, 11; XII.15

Lowth, Campbell, differentiate	Johnson "now established"
	*Campbell uses *you* nom.

3.18 Case after as and than XI.8

"Same case after as before"

           †Bayly
           Buchanan
           Hornsey (confused)
           Harrison
           Ash

"Accusative always when verb not repeated" XI.8n
           †Buchanan

"Accusative as for preposition"

Lowth	Priestley cites Smollet
Campbell	Withers

      W. Ward allows either
      See Hall *Phil.* 5 and *n²*

"Case governed by omitted construction" XI.8

Withers (sees fallacy)	Lowth
Bentley	Buchanan
	Campbell

3.19 Nominative Absolute IV.5

†Bentley	
	Lowth cites Milton
	Bentley (reverses
	himself)

3.2 POSSESSIVE FORMATION VIII.7, XI.10-15

Present rules for singular possessive of nouns first formulated by Greenwood, 1711; for possessive plural by Priestley, 1768 (?). Usage throughout the eighteenth century confused and divided.

See *Ulysses his bow*—in *Spectator* No. 135, August 4, 1711

††G. Harris, Baker (VIII.7)

cf. Hall *Mod. Eng.* 355, ff. *n.*

3.21 Double Possessive: "of Van Dyke's" XI.14

†Buchanan   Baker
Monthly Review   Cowley

3.22 Possessive adjective and pronoun

without apostrophe XI.13

†Baker, 1770   *Wallis (except *whose*)
Lowth   Greenwood
Franklin   Baker, 1779
Withers, etc.   J. Johnson
                                        Johnson
                                        Ward

Priestley attempted a distinction, reversed by Mennye. Confusion was extreme, and few observed the principles they stated.

ours, yours VIII.12

††G. Harris: "*s* form makes nonsense"—alternative not given
Webster noted historical facts as to *ourn, yourn*

his self, their selves V.3

Lowth (reversed himself) 1767   ††Lowth 1762

3.23 Accusative with gerund VIII.7, XI.2, XI.2, 15

rule's being observed VI.23, XI.2 and 15

Baker   G. Harris
Webster   Lowth
G. Harris
Lowth (*its being observed*)
          Campbell allows either; Murray tentative;
          Priestley makes distinction in sense

this's being done VIII.7

*G. Harris

3.3 PLURAL FORMATION VIII.4, X.4

apostrophe plural XI.12

*Baker   †Locke
                                         †*Art of Speaking*—etc.
                                         frequent usage at beginning of century

acquaintance—see § 19.1, below

chickens
††J. Johnson (after Greenwood?)

enow—plural of enough IX.15 and *n*
†Johnson (no examples)
Priestley
Campbell
Withers: "polite auth-
ors now use *suffi-
cient* with the plural"

geniuses
††Gray

See Hall *Phil* 3*n*

cowen and *sowen*, plurals VIII.4
††Lowth

specie (sing. of species)
†Swift

specieses (plural)
††Monboddo

ten pound, four wheels chaise, etc, see § 6.2, below.

3.4 ATTEMPTS TO PRESERVE THE DUAL NUMBER V.16

alternative for two only V.16
†19C.
Goold Brown's use for several not corrected in a number of
meticulous anonymous corrections in his 1851 *Grammar*, Wisconsin University Library

between for *among* VII.3, 9

†Johnson (admits usage)
                              Johnson quoted by
                              Boswell
                              Neither stricture nor
                              observance in
                              Trusler, etc.
See N. E. D.

superlative degree for two only V.16
†Murray   *Priestley
Campbell (queried)   Walpole (XI.5)

each other for *several* V.16

†Baker   *Johnson "whether of two or
            of a greater number"

another for *one of two* V.16

†Murray

either, neither, for *two only* V.16
            †Murray
See F. Hall *Mod. Eng. N. E. D., etc.*

whether as dual pronoun V.16
            †Murray

4. FORMS FOR COMPARISON OF ADJECTIVES AND AD-VERBS

Irregularities regretted by Lowth, Murray, etc. VIII.4, IX.2 and 12

least VIII.4
††Wallis, Lowth (should be *lest*)

4.1 DOUBLE COMPARISON, V.4, VII.10-11

*Lowth (permitted to noble poetry)   Johnson
Mennye

most highest V.4

Mennye   Lowth (for Diety only)

worser
*Lowth   "Standard authors"
Johnson

lesser VII.10; IX.2, 12 (Cannon 3)
††Johnson (admits usage)   "Standard Authors"
Lowth

4.2 COMPARISON OF INCOMPARABLES

chief, extreme, perfect, round, VII.11; IX.12
†Dr. Parr   Fox
Murray   Lowth
                             Johnson
        See *Mixed Comparisons,* below, § 14.

4.3 ANALOGICAL FORM OF ADVERBS V.3

afterwards, backwards, homewards, thereabouts, etc.
    preferred by Campbell on analogy principle

5. VERB-CONJUGATIONS

5.1 PRINCIPAL PARTS OF VERBS V.6; VII.6, 7

Argument for differentiation by Johnson, Priestley, Mennye.
See Hall *Mod. Eng.*, 104*n*, 208*n*, *Phil.* 100*n*.

5.11 Past participles distinguished from preterites V.6

beat

Webster (dropped—1804 edition)   Lowth (as alternative)
Mennye (regrets *en* lost)

See *N. E. D.*

bore IX.18

*Lowth   "Writers of note"
Buchanan

bound

†Webster prefers *bounden*   Lowth
    but drops it in 1804 ed.

broke

**Lowth
Mennye
    en "almost hopelessly lost"; so for *drove, spoke, took, stole, wrote*

burst

                                                  †Lowth gives alternative
                                                      bursten
                                                  Mennye

cling, clang, clung

                                                  †Lowth

drove—see *broke*

eat

                                                  Allowed by Lowth, Mennye,
                                                      Hornsey. *See* beat
                                                  A. Campbell has "have ate"
                                                      (*Sale*)

gotten

Obsolescent in 18th century England   †Practically all grammar-
                                                      ians favor; both *got*
                                                      and *gotten* in Johnson

holden

†Webster

holpen

†Bayly

knewen
Ironically suggested by Withers with
founden and *weren*, IX.18

lien

††Lowth
Campbell (alternative)
Webster (dropped,
1804)

See *lay* for *lie*

is lain down
†Baker (he accepts *is risen*)

loaden

†Swift
Webster

showed

†Johnson—"justified
only by custom"

sitten VIII.9
Campbell   ††Lowth (Dr. Middleton)
Webster
Johnson gives *sit* as past participle with *smit, bit, writ*
See F. Hall *Phil.*, 65, for R. G. White's insistence on
sitten, shew, gotten

slidden VIII.11

†Campbell
Webster

spitten

†Webster

spoke
*Lowth   Withers defends
(*Arist.* 372 ff.)

stricken (beside *struck*)
†Bayly

stridden

†Lowth
Bayly

took

Priestley   Defoe, etc.

washen

                                            Hornsey

went IX.18
Withers says "*gone* is more usual but not more proper"

wreathen, writhen

                                            †Hornsey

wrote IX.18

**Lowth   †Withers
Buchanan   †Johnson—gives
Webster   "written, writ, or
                                               wrote" as P.P.

5.12 Preterites

Doubtful, obsolescent, or merely invented forms V.6

abid

                                            ††Bayly

clang

                                            †Lowth (almost obsolete)

beat

                                            Hornsey

holp

                                            †Bayly

raught for *reached*

                                            †Johnson

sate

                                            †Johnson

stroke or *strook*
(from *strike*)

                                            Bayly

swang

Lowth—*swung* only   Johnson and later
                                               dictionaries

swam, swom, or *swum*

Johnson
*Lowth (except *swom*)

wan (preterite of *won*)

†Hornsey
Johnson

wrang

†Hornsey

5.13   Weak Preterites used or Advocated, V.6

beseeched

Johnson

blowed

†Colman and Thornton

catched V.6, X.6

Baker   Hornsey
*Withers—"not well bred"   Walpole
                               Johnson—"catched
                                 or caught"

falled, knowed, rised

††G. Harris (laments
passing)

teached

Johnson (obsolescent)

5.2   BE AS INDICATIVE, XI.18

†Webster defends

5.3   PRESENT FOR PRETERITE

says VI.24
Withers—queries: allows to historian   *Harris
                                             Walpole XI.5

See *Consistent Tenses* 13.0 below

5.4   SUBJUNCTIVE FORMS, XI.16-23

Existence of moods in English denied before Johnson's *Dictionary,*
1755

5.41 Be, come, have, as present subjunctive, XI.16-21

Webster, 1787 and later denied,
but confusedly

Johnson
Lowth
Bayly
Priestly
Webster, 1784, etc.

Priestly notes, but finds "stiff"

5.42 if . . . had-a XI.21

†Webster

5.43 if . . . was (contrary to fact) XI.20-23

†Webster, 1784

*Webster, 1789
Greenwood, and most
other grammarians
and standard authors
used

5.44 if . . . were as preterite subjunctive XI.16-23

*Webster, 1787
"Obsolete as past subjunctive";
used for present and future.
He later preferred *was, should,* etc.

Campbell, most grammarians

5.45 would as subjunctive form in principal clause XI.17, 22 and n, 128

Priestley
Johnson
Monboddo
Webster (XI.22)

Johnson
Temple
Clarke (censures Pope)
†Webster
Potter

5.46 Mixture of moods XI.17, 23

Priestley
Webster

Blair VI.8
Priestley
Harris
Swift
Bible tr., etc.

5.47 wert subjunctive only XI.16, 17

Johnson (used in indicative)   †Johnson
Campbell   Lowth
                                          Buchanan
                                          Webster

See F. Hall *Mod. Eng.* 77-9 and *n*, 361-2.

Subjunctive after *wish* not mentioned

Active and Passive Voice (See 1.4, above)

6. PROBLEMS OF AGREEMENT

6.1 OF VERB

6.11 Precedence of Persons in Agreement IV.4, 5

W. Ward   †Lowth, Murray, etc.,
                                          give usual rule

6.12 Obsolescent Forms Required I.1, VIII.9, 11; XII.15, XIII.4.

st and *dst* forms
Priestley   †Lowth
"Standard authors"   Baker
                                          Murray

Thou and *you*, mixed use of I.1, VIII.9, XIII.4
Baker
Lowth
Buchanan

Hath, Doth, Conducteth VIII.11, X.3, XII.15
Lowth ("serious and solemn style only")   †Bayly
1st ed. Britannica, art.   Campbell
   "Grammar" notes "obsolescent"   Blair

See *loved,* below, 18.2

6.13 Dare, Need, V.3. VIII.6, XII.8

Webster   ††Campbell—*s* necessary
                                          by analogy
                                          Baker

6.13 Collective nouns singular only IV.5; XII.1, 11, 12

*Greenwood, Priestley, Fell   ††Clarke
Ward, Withers, distinguish
according to meaning

neither VI.4, XII.9

Baker   Withers
Blair   Baker

See § 6.15, below

number always singular XII.11

Bible translators   ††Alexander
Standard Authors   Murray

See Hall *Mod. Eng.* on Fox's use

none—singular only

19C.   †Johnson
                                              Baker says either singu-
                                              lar or plural, not both.
                                              Priestley and Murray
                                              allow either

the one are

                                              Baker—cf. 1770 ed.,
                                              pp. 122-3 and 68.

half a score more . . . . are III.4

                                              Baker

sort, kind, XII.11, XIII.6

Baker (preferred singular verb only)   *Swift (plural)
                                              *Priestley (singular
                                              "harsh")
                                              Clarke VII.4

"Nouns of measure" either singular or plural
                                              *Bayly

See §s 6.18 and 6.2, below

6.14 Compound subject always plural II.2, IV.4, XII.2-8, XII.21

*Greenwood (allowed singular)   Baker (qualifies)
Shaw (Latin analogy)   Colman
Ward   Alexander
Lowth (sometimes permissible)   †Withers
Priestley   Webster, 1784
Bayly   Murray
Webster, 1787 (qualified)
Monthly Reviewers
Johnson
Salisbury (used)
Harrison
Blair

See Hall *Mod. Eng.* 612*n*

Verb agrees with the first word of a series
G. Harris

Verb agrees with the nearest word
Martin
Withers attempts elaborate logical distinction XII.5

6.15 Singular subjects connected by "disjunctives" must have singular verb XII.9

Lowth (fails to censure in Clarendon)	†Lowth
	Priestley
Blair (used repeatedly)	Baker
Baker (notes exception)	Withers
Potter	Murray
A. Campbell	Johnson

F. Hall is dogmatic here (*Mod. Eng.* 199*n* and 292*n*) but cites Johnson and his admired Newman and Macaulay See § 9.5, below

6.16 Verb-agreement with you

you have IX.20 *n*
Anomaly for singular, accepted by custom—Murray

you was IX.6, XII.16, XIII.4

**Lowth	Blair
Priestley	Webster
Withers	Standard Authors of eighteenth century

See F. Hall *Mod. Eng.* 209*n*

6.17 Modified singular subject always singular XII.10

Standard Authors	†Baker
	Murray
	Temple

Priestley judicious, 1768 ed., pp. 184-5

6.18 Miscellaneous cases

there are XII.13

Priestley (permits plural)

See Campbell's erratum, *loc. cit.*

as follows, concerns, regards, XII.14

††Tooke   Campbell
Murray   Baker attempts a distinction

s singulars—*means, news,* etc. VIII.6, IX.14, XII.12

††Lowth, 1769   Priestley
Baker   Murray, citing Lowth
Johnson (cites Standard   and Johnson
   Authors using "not very   Webster
   grammatically")   Campbell
Webster, 1784   Standard Authors

See F. Hall *Mod. Eng.* on *remains, pulse,* etc.
See adjective-agreement, § 6.2

what have been said

Lowth   Britannica
Blair   Webster
Campbell   Standard Authors
                                               A. Campbell, *Sale,* p. 93

6.2 OF ADJECTIVE V.3, VIII.6, IX.14 CANON 9, XII.11-12, XIII.5

a great many, a few, many a VIII.6, XII.12

††G. Harris   Murray
                                               Lowth
                                               Campbell

a woods, a ways
19C.   See N. E. D.

every five years XII.12

††G. Harris

five year, ten pound V.3

J. Johnson
Baker

means, a or *this* IX.14, XII.12

††Lowth   Webster
Johnson (admitted use)   Murray (cites Johnson
Campbell   and Lowth)
                   See Hall *Phil.* 2-3

these kind, sort XII.11, XIII.5

Lowth, 1769 ed.   *Many Advantages*
Baker   —18 C. usage
Murray

See § 6.13, above

this many years XII.12

†Lowth

6.21　Instances of "extraordinary correctness"　V.3

degrees of doctors of divinity, a four-wheels chaise,
several hues and cries, a twenty-guns ship

*Baker

6.22　Instances of "concealed errors"

a beautiful field and trees XII.18

††Murray

cutting polysyllables into one IX.15

††Campbell　See VI.4

a house and an orchard VI.11

†Murray

one or more letters, etc. XII.18

††Priestley

6.3　OF RELATIVE-PRONOUN IX.12, XI.2, XII.14

I am the Lord, that make, etc. XI.2, etc.

Bayly (*Intro.,* 1792)　　　　　　　Lowth (either)

one of those who was

Baker

thou who are IX.12, Canon 3

Bayly

See *as follows,* § 6.18

6.4　OF PERSONAL PRONOUN XII.11, 17, 20

they, their with singulars XII.11, 17, 20

Priestley　　　　　　　　　Swift
Blair　　　　　　　　　　　Oldmixon XII.17
Murray　　　　　　　　　　Johnson
　　　　　　　　　　　　　Standard Authors of
　　　　　　　　　　　　　　18 C.
　　　　　　　　　　　　　Lowth (used)
　　　　　　　　　　　　　Farro (X.1)

he, she, with *one* XII.19

†Baker

6.5 OF PREDICATE NOMINATIVE—MISAGREEMENT IN NUMBER WITH SUBJECT XII.21

'tis they, these, two or three

††Baker
Murray
Webster, 1784
Lowth
Johnson

Priestley (logical explanation)
Webster, 1787, modified

See Hall *Mod. Eng.*, 40*n*
See Gender, § 2.0, and Parallelism, § 7.5

6.6 MISCELLANEOUS CASES OF AGREEMENT

a person so much your betters XII.22
every one . . . my friends
our language . . . less refined than those XII.18

†Lowth
Baker
Blair

Swift

7. PROBLEMS OF PARALLELISM III.4n; VI.2, 21; XII.21; XIII.4

7.1 SHIFTING DEGREE OF COMPARISON VI.2

††Buchanan (VI.2)

Greenwood
Lowth
Webster
Spectator
Campbell

7.2 BOTH BY SEA AND LAND, ETC.

19C.

Baker
Campbell
Greenwood
Lowth
Bayly
Webster
Mennye

7.3 PARALLELISM WITH CORRELATIVE CONJUNCTIONS . . NOT ONLY, EITHER, NEITHER, ETC., III.4n, VI.2, 21 (eratum) XIII.5

Baker (erratum) Parr
Campbell Baker
Fox
Baker
Monthly Review
Lowth
Bayly
Mennye

7.4 AND WHICH, AND WHO VI.2

19C. †Lowth (bis)
Blair

7.5 PREDICATE NOMINATIVE VI.2, XII.21

is when, reason is because, etc.

Baker Baker (used)
Lowth Lowth
Mennye Greenwood
"Our greatest authors"

See § 6.5, above

7.6 SHIFT OF RELATIVE VI.2

†Priestley Standard authors

7.7 ACTIVE AND PASSIVE TOGETHER

†Baker, 1770

7.8 PARALLEL VERB STRUCTURE VI.2, 4

can or ought to conciliate, etc.

††Dr. Parr Fox
††Campbell Lowth
Webster
Baker

See *Substantives in Double Function,* above, 3.11, and *Concealed Errors,* 9.5

7.9 PARALLEL CONSTRUCTION WITH THAN

No other answer than by VI.2, 9

†Baker
Murray

8. PROBLEMS OF REDUNDANCY

"Circumlocution" advocated VI.8, 11

*Withers	Blair
Campbell	Bayly
Monboddo, citing Milton, etc.	Mennye

approved of IX.12

†Campbell

as yet

†Johnson: "seems redundant"

but however

Swift, etc.

for to be seen

19C.

Lowth
Bible tr., etc.

from hence, thence, whence III.6, VI.3, IX.3

†Johnson

Johnson (used)
*Baker
Priestley
Withers
Swift

have got (possession) X.6

††Withers

Johnson

it is very true what he says IX.4, III.6

Warburton, defended
by Baker

"a juice, whereof whoever drinks, that person . . ." XI.7

††Priestley—counsels "another verb"

kind of a, sort of a III.6

Baker

old veteran XI.5

Monthly Reviewers   A. Campbell

that needlessly repeated VI.3, 11

*Baker

that there, this here VIII.12

†Webster defended as
ancient usage

"the bringing to them of the light" VI.7, XI.15

Lowth
Webster (discriminates)

†Baker (bis, in errata)
Johnson
Greenwood

"an expression of . . ." VI.3

†Baker (bis)

the same X.6

19C

Bayly

whatsoever III.4

††Geo. Harris
Monthly Reviewers

Baker

9. ELLIPSIS, "IMPROPER" VI.8, VII.4, X.4

Cf. Hall *Mod. Eng.* 261 and 272n

9.1 OF ARTICLE III.2; VI.7, 11; IX.1, 15

††*Oxford Magazine*
Baker
Mennye—censuring

Withers
Bible translators
"Standard authors"

Ward notes acceptance by usage.
Murray makes distinction in sense
See *Poem, the,* § 16.1, below

koran for *alcoran* IX.15

†Campbell

9.2 OF RELATIVE, VI.8-11, X.3, XI.1

9.21 Accusative relative VI.8-10

†Lowth ..
Monthly Reviewers
Blair
Bayly
Addison, *Spectator,* Aug. 4, 1711

*Baker
Fell
Blair—cited by
Withers
Campbell

Murray makes a distinction

9.22 Of nominative relative XI.1

Baker (guarded)

9.23 Of relative plus preposition VI.8, 10

†Murray   Swift
Lowth   Addison
                                    Oldmixon

9.24 Of antecedent of relative VI.8

                                    †Campbell
                                    Milton

9.25 Of relative and verb VI.9

††Murray   *Withers—"elegant"
Blair

9.3 OF PREPOSITION VI.9, VIII.5

†Murray, Campbell, Buchanan censuring   Milton, etc.

write me, each other VIII.5
†Baker   *Lowth (see *methinks,*
                                        3.15)
                                    Johnson
                                    Campbell
            But cf. Baker's *take me up too much time* III.4

9.4 MISCELLANEOUS CASES

Ellipsis of as VI.10
Campbell   *Spectator*
Monthly Reviewers   Swift
                                    Baker

Ellipsis of that (substantive clause)
                        *Fell

Those required before relative (inverted rule?) VI.10
                                    †J. Johnson

"*Voice of the Lord, walking* . . . ." VI.6
Ellipsis supplied by Bayly—no censure

dare say, or *go, help carry on* X.8
†Priestley ("Scotch")

9.5 CONCEALED GRAMMATICAL ERRORS—V.3, 11; VI.4; XII.18

  book that has, is, or shall be published VI.4
Campbell
              Christian and sirname IX.15, Canon 2
††Campbell   Addison

     compassionate and condole with his friends VI.4
††Parr   Fox

      cutting Polysyllables into one IX.15, Canon 2
††Campbell   Swift

             loves not plays, as thou dost VI.4
                                            *Lowth

          neither has he, nor any others VI.4
Baker

        take the same measures that I have
††Campbell   *Guardian No. 1*

                whether or no V.3, 11
††Campbell   Johnson, cites
Bingham   Standard Authors

        always have and still do use VI.4
                                            Webster

See *Parallelism,* § 7, *Substantives in Double Function,* 3.11,
Adjective-noun Agreement, 6.2, *Double Negative,* 12, etc.

10. PROBLEMS OF REFERENCE

10.1 DANGLING VERBAL VI.6

*Baker, 1770   Lowth
Kames, vol. II, p. 40   Bayly
                                      Bible tr.
                                      Standard Authors

10.2 PRONOUN REFERENCE TO GENITIVE OR SUBSTANTIVE AFTER OF XI.14

Buchanan   *Priestley (good
Monthly Reviewers   unless ambiguous)
                                   Cowley
                                   Baker

10.3 PRONOUN REFERENCE TO CLAUSE OR SENTENCE VI.5

††Baker

Warburton
Standard Authors
*Ussher
*Murray, etc.

10.4 PRONOUN REFERENCE TO ONE, XII.19

†Baker

11. PROBLEMS OF SENTENCE ORDER VI.16-22, X.8

11.1 SPLIT CONSTRUCTIONS VI.16

General principle, Kames, vol. II, pp. 53, 61

11.11 Split verb VI.16

††Priestley (allows exceptions)

*Webster
Harris
Newton
Standard Authors

11.12 Preposition separated from noun VI.17

††Blair
††Withers

11.13 Participle from adverb VI.17

††Baker

11.14 Split Infinitive VI.18

19C.

Rare use
Campbell (bis)

11.2 STEREOTYPED ORDER VI.19, X.8

"A man's every feeling"

†Dr. Parr (vol. I—p. 616)   *Fox

born and bred

†Withers VI.19

best part he plays IX.14n

††Baker

milk and bread, butter and bread X.8

†J. Johnson ("Scotch")

neither read nor write VI.19
††Baker
Withers

pretty enough girl X.8
††J. Johnson

rushing torrents and descending rains VI.19
††Webster   Addison

so well a bred man VI.17
Baker

11.21 Only, preverbal placement of III.4n, 14; VI.21, XI.1

††Baker (slovenly)	*Baker (euphony)
Lowth	"Standard authors"
Blair	Swift
Buchanan	Campbell
Campbell	Johnson
	(See *narrate,* § 19.1
	below)
Withers	Monboddo
	Brightland

11.22 Not, "misplaced" III.4n, VI.21, IX.5, 1

19C.	Baker
	Blair
	Michaelis, etc.

11.23 Four last years VI.20; four first canons, VIII.11

19C.	*Swift
	Z. Grey
	Trusler
	Campbell

11.24 Post-placed preposition VI.22, IX,12, XI.2

*Lowth (mildly)	Lowth
Priestley (by implication XI.2)	Ward
Blair, Hornsey—on ground of	*Bayly
force and pleasing construc-	Fell
tion only	Murray
	A. Campbell

12. DOUBLE NEGATIVES (See IV.4) VI.14, VIII.16

London Review in 1864 laments passing
(See F. Hall *Mod. Eng.* 270, 279-80)

**Lowth	Lowth (M. E. 270)
Johnson	Bentley
Withers	Addison and "standard
Campbell	authors" throughout
Mennye	18th century
Clarke	Withers
Upton	Priestley
Baker	Z. Grey

12.1 NEITHER AND OR VI.14

Lowth   Withers
Priestley—*not*—*nor* more emphatic

12.2 NEVER SO VI.14

††Greenwood	Priestley
Lowth	Lowth (Hall *Mod. Eng.*
Johnson	270) Cf. *Ibid.* 119*n*
Campbell's anonymous annotator	Campbell
	Addison, Bible transla-
	tion, etc.

13. TENSE SEQUENCE

Consistent tenses demanded VI.24

Swift	†Priestley
Campbell	Baker
Priestley	Villiers
Harris	
Webster	

14. MIXED COMPARISONS VI.15, XI.8 and n

as old, or older than, etc.

†Campbell	"Standard authors"
Priestley	
Withers	

12.3 NOT SO . . . AS, X.7

†Mennye

"fairest of her daughters"

Campbell   Milton

15. MISCELLANIES OF SENTENCE STRUCTURE

15.1 "LOGICAL RESOLUTION OF STRUCTURES" V.14, VI.12 AND 23, XI.2, 8, AND 15

                              ††W. Ward
                              Withers (*as, than,* etc.)
                              Lowth
                              Baker

15.2 WHERE AS RELATIVE IX.9

a protestation where, same course where
Priestley ("foreign importation")
See *that, as, if, whether,* etc. (1.6), *who, which* (2), "omitted relative," (9.2)

15.3 LOGICAL ABSURDITIES

pure limpid stream when foul with stains VII.4
††Campbell   Addison

talks all the way upstairs to a visit, VII.4
††Campbell   Addison
Webster

seven ladies, every one prettier than another IX.14
††Campbell   Addison

however difficult or impossible VII.12
Monthly Reviewers   Baker

however heavy X.7
††Dr. Parr ("inaccuracy")   Fox

if thou certainly return VII.12
                              Bible tr.

if peradventure he can, VII.12
                              Bible tr.
See *Subjunctive,* 5.4

sings a good song IX.14, and *note*
††Campbell
Baker

understand her meaning VII.12

††Baker: "absurd"

16. PURISM IN WORD CHOICES

16.1 LOGICAL DISTINCTIONS

abandon, forsake, etc., distinguished, VII.3
†Trusler
Mrs. Piozzi

affection IX.9
Campbell (foreign importation)   Johnson

attain for *obtain, procure* III.7
††Webster   Johnson

beside for *besides* VII.9
19C.   *Johnson
Lowth
N. E. D.

between—among (See 3.4 above)

between every pillar VII.9
†Baker   F. Hall *Philology,*
22n, (De Quincey,
etc.)

can for *may* VII.3, VII.6 and *n.*
†Johnson distinguished   Johnson—*may,* sense
3—"to have power"
Not in Trusler

choose for *make choice of* VII.3
†Trusler   Johnson

See F. Hall *Mod. Eng.,* 220 and *n.*

couple
19C.   Swift
Hickey, etc.
Johnson, sense 2

See Hall *Phil.,* 92

discernible taste or smell VII.4
†Webster

cf. Webster's "palpable nonsense,"
"ears cannot but revolt"

each for *every*

Johnson—"rare except in poetry"   Hall *Mod. Eng.*, 229-
                                                   30 and *n.*

each other
See Number, Dual, 3.4

either for *each* III.6, XII.17

Lowth   Johnson
                                                   Baker

enow, enough IX.15, Canon 3
See Plural, 3.3

expect it was X.9

†Webster—"absurd"

famous for *infamous*

†Baker, 1779, p. 9—"nothing of   Congreve
lively antithesis"

farther—further

19C.   *Johnson

fatigue—weary VII.6

††Blair (distinguished)   *Johnson (synonymous)
Hornsey

fewer (see *Less*)

flee—fly VII.7, IX.2

Baker   Standard Authors
Johnson—admits "now confounded," but,
     in 1785 ed., "a barbarous corruption"
††Withers (still another distinction attempted).

hung for *hanged* VII.6

†Priestley   Priestley's paradigm
Lowth   Johnson—no dis-
Dryden ("animal . . . hanged")   tinction
                                                   Hickey, etc.

ill—see *sick*

kind "misused" for *sort* VII.12 and *n.*

††Priestley   Johnson (synonyms)
††Monthly Review   Baker

lay for *lie* (see 1.4, above)

less for *fewer* VII.10

†Baker

lesser (See 4.1, above)

light a pipe VII.4

††Fenning   Clarke

may—see *can*

nowadays IX.2

††Johnson—"perhaps bar-   *Campbell
barous," but "common and
used by best writers"

obstructed for *deterred* VII.5

††Webster   Johnson

pair of bars, stairs IX.19

Webster—"very absurd", but "better
admit than fall foul of custom"
    Johnson gives only "two of a sort, couple, brace"

past for *by* X.9

††Webster—"nonsense"   *Johnson

past for *after*

†Webster—"half after" more correct   Hoadley, 1773, "as
                                              the modern English
                                              now is"

                    See Hall *Mod. Eng.* 124

people for *persons* VII.3

††Trusler   *Johnson

the poem (for poetry in general) IX.15, Canon 3

††Campbell

propose for *purpose* VII.12 and *n*, X.9

†Baker—"French"   Blair
Webster
Withers

                    See N. E. D.

relatives for *relations* VII.5 and *n*

"Certain precise gentlemen"   *Johnson—synonymous.
Geo. Harris   Swift, etc.
                                            Withers

reply and *rejoin* VI.24

†Johnson—distinguishes
†Withers

seem and *appear* III.6

††Trusler's distinction   *Johnson

set for *sit*—See 1.4, above

sick for *ill* VII.3 and *n*

*Johnson—synonymous   ††Trusler—imaginary distinctions
                                ††Webster

sort—see *kind*

stanza—see *verse*, § 17.1, below

together for *successively* VII.4

††Campbell   *Spectator*
                                Johnson: "without
                                    intermission"

unloose VIII.16

††Campbell   Standard authors
Johnson "a word perhaps barbarous and
    ungrammatical"

unravel

††Campbell   Pope
                                Johnson

want—see *wish*, 18.1, below

weary—see *fatigue*

will for *shall* V.15, X.8, 9

†Wallis   Fell
Ward   Withers
Lowth
Priestley (qualifies: 1768 ed., pp. 128-32)
Withers (X.6)
Webster (qualifies)
    Johnson: "difficult to show or limit signification"—
        "I shall" = "I am resolved," etc.
See §s 18.1, 19.1

16.12 "Misuses of prepositions" VII.8, X.8

e.g. "reduce to their power,"
"fell into their cognizance," etc.

See McKnight *Modern English in the Making*, p. 403

Lowth   "Standard authors"—
Blair   Swift, etc.
Murray

16.13 Distinction between words of place and of motion VII.8.

above—below—See *up, down*

after—behind

†Baker   *Johnson—synonymous

be—a verb expressing motion VII.8
                                         *Baker

in—into VII.8 and *n*

†Baker   Wilkins (unrecognized
                                         —17th century)
                                         Tooke
                                         Johnson (adv.)

there—thither VII.8

†Baker
†Ward

up—down for *above, below* VII.8 and *n*

††Baker   *Johnson—place or motion

16.2 OBJECTIONS TO FIGURATIVE EXPRESSION AS AGAINST "PURITY, SIMPLICITY, ELEGANCE, AND PERSPICUITY" (CAMPBELL)

See McKnight *Mod. Eng.* p. 327-8 on Greenwood's criticism

bolstering up an argument X.4

†G. Harris   Hooker
Johnson "now somewhat coarse and obsolete"   South

cast about for X.6

†Withers   Bacon
                                         Bentley
                                         Johnson

cannot for my heart XI.5

Monthly Review   Shakespeare
                                         A. Campbell
                                         Johnson

        curry favour IX.14, Canon 9

†Campbell   *Johnson—"rub down with flattery, scratch in kindness"
                                           Shakespeare

        chaulking out a way X.4

†G. Harris   Shakespeare
†Withers   Dryden
                                           Johnson

           cut a joke

Chesterfield: "lowest of vulgarisms"
Withers

      "a dog in a dancing school" X.5

Baker's critic   Congreve
   "too common" for address to King   Baker

        driving a bargain X.4

†G. Harris

       handling a subject X.4

†G. Harris   Johnson

     hammering one's brains III.4

†Monthly Reviewers   Baker

      having a month's mind

Campbell

    hold long in one mind III.4, IX.14, Canon 9

†Monthly Reviewers: "vulgar"   Baker
Campbell   Johnson

      leave in the lurch X.6

                                     Addison, Butler, etc.
†Withers   "A lady of name in the republic of letters"

       passion flags X.6

†Withers   Dryden
                                         Swift
                                         Johnson

     pitch upon III.4 and *n*; X.6

††Monthly Reviewers   Baker
Withers   Johnson

Blair
"Standard authors"—
Butler, More, Dryden,
etc.

shift for themselves X.6

†Blair   Swift, etc.
                                Johnson

swallow contradictions X.6

†Withers   Johnson (like uses)

17. PRESENT USAGE: HISTORICAL CONSIDERATIONS and ETYMOLOGY Ch. VIII.

17.1 ETYMOLOGICAL DUBIETIES

accedence VIII.14
                                ††Milton
                                ††Bayly, 1772
But Bayly had used *Accidence* in 1771

aversion from VIII.14, IX.11
†Lowth   *Campbell
†Johnson   Withers
                                Murray
                                "Standard authors"—
                                Clarendon, Swift,
                                etc.

beholden for *indebted* VIII.16
†Campbell (*beholding* . . . still more exceptionable)

circumstances, under
19C.

Not in Johnson; *in, by,* etc. are given

contemporary (noun and adjective) for *cotemporary*
†Baker   *Johnson
Warburton   Locke quoted for
†Webster (cotemporary)   both noun and adj.
Boyle   Bayly
Campbell

demean X.5

†Baker

Richardson
*Johnson: "lessen, de-
base"—cites stand-
ard authors

See F. Hall *Phil.* 105-6n

dislikeness IX.3

*Priestley

Locke

entirety

†Taylor, 1797

*Johnson—*entierty*
Bacon

See F. Hall, *Mod. Eng.* 43

ingenuity, etc. VIII.13, IX.12, Canon 3

††Baker (*suggests ingeneity*)
Monboddo
Campbell (prefers *ingeniousness*)

Johnson (has also
meaning [and word]
ingenousness)

methinks, methought. See § 3.15, above

mutual VII.3, VIII.15

†Johnson—but cites, without stricture
†Baker

Shakespeare
Bentley, Sterne, etc.
H. Walpole
Not in Trusler

presentiment VIII.15

††Baker—"Should be pre-sensation"
Johnson has *presension*

prosecute, persecute IX.18
*Withers insists etymology reversed, but accepts.
Johnson defines both "persue" (not in *Dict.*); gives
usual distinction

verse, stanza VIII.15

†Baker

*Johnson—"a line . . .
a piece of poetry"

substract IX.12, Canon 4

Campbell

††Insisted on by John-
son as "common
word," French ori-
gin—no examples.
Lowth

See *sherbet* and *punch*, etc., IX.7, note 44

17.2 "NEOTERISMS" SUSPECTED NEW COINAGES AND MEANINGS

advice IX.7n

††Campbell   Johnson

See § 18.1

callt IX.11

Apparently devised by Campbell to show the power of usage in
its condemnation

exit

†Parr—"A vile word"   *Johnson cites standard authors

falsify (make proof against weapon) IX.5

Dryden
Hughes

feeling for *tenderness*

Garrick   Johnson

Hall *Mod. Eng.* 122

humour, humourist, (in later sense) VIII.10, IX.4

†Congreve   *Johnson
Priestley ?   Lowth
                                                            Baker

informalities IX.3

†Priestley   Hume
Not in Johnson

lest, least VIII.4

*Johnson   ††Wallis
                                                            Lowth   (*least* for *lest*)

mechanist IX.3

Priestley   Johnson in *Rasselas*
Not in Johnson *Dictionary*

naturalness IX.3

††Priestley—"disagreeable"   Dryden
                                                            Addison
                                                            Johnson

nervous IX.7n

†Campbell   Hickey, etc.
Johnson attributes newer meaning to
  "medical cant"

self-love IX.15

†Campbell   Johnson
                         Shakespeare

shallest IX.11
See *callt*

subject matter IX.10

††Temple   Johnson
                         Dryden, etc.

swerve IX.10

†Temple   Johnson

turtle IX.7n, X.7

†Campbell   Johnson "used among
                         sailors and gluttons
                         a tortoise"
See *Class Dialects*, 18.1. McKnight has interesting examples
    in *Modern English in the Making*, p. 413

17.3 OBSOLETE WORDS AND MEANINGS

authoress

†Priestley (obs.)
  Not in Johnson
      See Hall *Mod. Eng.* 187f., *n.*

betwixt IX.10

Temple   Johnson

encroach IX.10, 14

†Temple   Johnson
                         Campbell

froward IX.10

Temple

inculcate IX.10 and 14

†Temple   *Campbell
                         Johnson

jeopard, jeopardy

†Johnson
  "a word not now in use"

kinswoman

†Miss Carter, 1754,   *Johnson
   "old-fashioned"

learn for *teach* (See 1.4)

livelong

†Taylor, 1797,   Not in Johnson
   "growing obsolete"
                    F. Hall, *Mod. Eng.* 126

poetess

Priestley (obs.)   Johnson: "a she poet"

purport IX.10, 14

†Temple   *Campbell
                                                 Johnson

vouchsafe IX.10

†Temple   Johnson

vulgar (in etymological sense) X.6

†Blair   Swift and 18th cen-
                                                   tury authors
                                                 Johnson—both senses
                                                   given

wittol IX.10

                                                 †Temple—old, but
                                                   necessary
                                                 Johnson

womanhood

†Johnson—obs.
   See excellent lists of the sort in McKnight, *Modern English*
   pp. 413-15, and Hall (out of Bentley, *et al.*) *Mod. Eng.* 116 ff.
   and *n.*

17.31 Stock Phrases condemned as "obsolete" IX.14 (canon 8)

by dint of

†Campbell   Addison
                                                 Johnson
              had as lief (See 1.32)

moot point

†Campbell

not a whit

†Campbell　　　　　　　　　　　　"no whit" repeatedly
　　　　　　　　　　　　　　　　　in Johnson

pro and con
†Campbell, "air of vulgarity and cant"

See *con* in *Class Dialect,* 18.2

17.32　Old-fashioned Elegance

female X.4

Warburton　　　　　　　　　　†Warburton's critics
　　　　　　　　　　　　　　　Johnson

tasty X.4
Not in Johnson　　　　　　　　　†Potter
(See *hath, conduceth,* and *st* and *dst* forms above, 6.12)

18.　REPUTABLE USAGE:　CLASS DIALECTS (Chapter X)

See Miscellanies of Logic, 15.3, Dougle Negatives, 12.0, Figurative
Expressions, 16.2, New Words, 17.2, etc.

18.1　"LOW" WORDS

advice as information IX.7n
†Campbell　　　　　　　　　　Johnson—"chiefly
　　　　　　　　　　　　　　　　commercial"

as I take it III.4
Monthly Review: "vulgar"　　　　Bacon
　　　　　　　　　　　　　　　Locke
　　　　　　　　　　　　　　　Baker
　　　　　　　　　　　　　　　Johnson

aye X.4
†Greenwood　　　　　　　　　　Johnson
Buchanan

anyhow X.4
†Priestley
Not in Johnson

assets
†Mrs. Piozzi

banter IX.7

†Swift, *Tatler*, Sept. 26-8, 1710

Johnson—"barbarous word, without etymology"

bigot IX.7

*Campbell—"arisen among the rabble," but "nobilitated by usage"

cash

†Mrs. Piozzi   Johnson

catch for *overtake* X.6

†Withers—equated with   Johnson
"none of your jaw"

See 5.13, above

chickens X.4

††J. Johnson (after Greenwood?)
"error of the vulgar"

dumbfound

†Campbell
Johnson "a low phrase"

exit

†Parr—"a vile word"   *Johnson—cites
standard authors

fib

Johnson "cant word among children."

flippant IX.7

Johnson, "a word of no great authority"
*Campbell

fop IX.7

Johnson
*Campbell—see *banter*, *bigot*

flimsy IX.7

Campbell: "from cant of manufacturers," but accepted

for all that X.4

†Priestley

See Hall *Phil* 48n²

helter-skelter

†Campbell   Johnson

hold for *continue*
See 16.2

hurly-burly

†Campbell

I look upon it as—III.4

Monthly Review   Baker

I say
Monthly Review "inelegance"

jackalent X.7

†Webster   Shakespeare
                                                     Johnson—defines as
                                                     "simple, sheepish
                                                     fellow"

jiggumbob

Webster   Shakespeare

most an end for *most commonly* X.5

Baker   Milton, etc.
"almost disgrace the mouth
of a hackney coachman"
          See Hall, *Modern English,* 211 and *n*

my Lord Bedford X.4

Priestley—"too familiar"

parma-citty X.7
Webster (probably vulgar pronunciation)

nervous—see Neoterisms, 17.2

penman III.3

†Baker's anonymous critic   *Johnson
                                                     Baker

punch IX.7n

††Johnson   Campbell
     "cant word"

somehow X.4

†Priestley

Johnson (gives as *adj.*)

themselves and families X.5

Baker

turtle—see 17.2

will for *shall* X.6

†Withers—"vulgar error." See § 16.1

wish for *want* VII.6

Johnson—synonymous
Hornsey—(elegance?)

without any more to do III.4

Monthly Reviewers
"vulgar"

Baker

wording

Wilkes

(Hall *Mod. Eng.*, 123)

write me, each other VIII.6

††Baker—"especially by people in trade"

yea for *yes* X.4

*Greenwood
Buchanan (see *aye*)

Johnson

18.2 CONTRACTIONS

ado for *to do* X.3

††G. Harris

Johnson

See *to do*—III.4 (above, 18.1)

an't X.3

Withers

A. Campbell, etc.

con

†Johnson—"despicable cant" for *contra*

does for *doeth* VIII.11, X.3, and XII.15

††Bayly

don't for *do not* X.3

††Bayly
Not in Johnson

No specific condemnation for *it don't*, etc.

fix't X.3

Swift   *Art of Speaking*
                                                  Bayly

fledg'd X.3

Swift   *Art of Speaking*
                                                  Bayly

Swift wrote *enter'd*

han't X.3

**G. Harris   Johnson (no apostrophe)

has for *hath* VIII.11, X.3, XII.15

††Bayly ,etc

See 6.12, above

heard for *heared* X.3

††Bayly

i'n't it?
See Hall *Mod. Eng.* 236 and *n*

it's X.3

††Monthly Reviewers   Baker, etc.
††G. Harris
Buchanan (preferred *'tis*)
Campbell

to be let X.3, 6

††Withers
Must be *to be lett*

leads for *leadeth,*
loves for *loveth,*
moves for *moveth,* X.3, XII.15

††Bayly

lovéd X.3

††Hornsey   F. Hall, *Phil.*, 51*n*.
"Educated Clergymen" . . read lovéd

maynt X.3

††G. Harris

mob IX.15, Canon 1; X.3

††Swift   Campbell
Temple (XI.22)   Johnson
Wilkes   Standard Authors

on't for *of it* III.6, IX.15, Canon 3

*Campbell	Johnson
Baker	A. Campbell

penult X.3

†Campbell	Blair
Not in Johnson	

prais'd X.3

Hornsey

pro and con IX.14

See 17.31, and *con,* above

rebuk't X.3

Swift	*Art of Speaking*
	Bayly, etc.

shan't X.3

†G. Harris	
Not in Johnson	

'till X.2, 3

††Swift	*Art of Speaking*
	Bayly
	Johnson (without
	apostrophe)

'tis III.4, X.3

††Monthly Review—"barbarous"	Baker
††G. Harris	Buchanan }
	Campbell } prefer

won't X.3

†Hornsey	Without apostrophe in Johnson

19. NATIONAL USAGE

19.1 REGIONAL DIALECTS—SCOTTICISMS PARTICULARLY

See J. Johnson's list (X.8) and Word Order, § 11.2, above, etc.

acquaintances X.8

††J. Johnson—Scotch plural	Johnson—either plural

ax for *ask* VIII.12

	†Webster—American
	usage.

oy for *past* X.9

Webster

compete X.8

†J. Johnson—Scotch
Not in Johnson

dare say, go
See 9.4

have done, not *am done* V.11n and X.9

Webster—U. S.
Bingham

goot, gude, and *gueed* IX.11

Campbell

if for *whether* X.8

†J. Johnson—Scottish

Hume
*Johnson

learn for *teach* X.8

J. Johnson—Scottish

lies (ship) X.9

†Webster—calls
"American usage"
Bingham

narrate

Johnson—"a word only used in Scotland"

See Hall, *Mod. Eng.* 120-1 and *n.,* 275n[3]

nothing else X.7

†J. Johnson—"Scotch"

Shakespeare
*Johnson

on a sudden

†J. Johnson—"Scotch"

on, not *of, a Monday* X.9

†Webster—U. S.

ourn, yourn—see 3.2, above

half past six X.9

†Webster—prefers "American use", *after*

past—see *by*

purpose, not *propose*

†Webster—U. S.

See 16.1

proven X.8

†Johnson
Not in Johnson

the omitted before superlatives
†*Oxford Magazine*—"Scotch"

this here, that there, VIII.12

Withers et al.   †Webster
Scottish or Irish

will for *shall* X.6, 8, 9

†Webster—never heard in American usage!
Most grammarians—"Scotch or Irish"
See 16.1, above.

19.2 FOREIGN ANALOGIES OPPOSED—LATIN AND FRENCH IDIOMS REPUDIATED, ESPECIALLY BY PRIESTLEY AND G. CAMPBELL

cf. Hall *Mod. Eng.* 127n^3

affection IX.9

†Campbell (importation)   Johnson

impracticable roads IX.9

†Webster   This is not in
Campbell   Johnson
"Latinism"   N. E. D.

integrity IX.9

†Campbell ("Latinism")   Johnson

See *entirety,* 17.1

it is me, etc. IV.6

†Campbell denies authority
of French analogy. See § 3.13

lay for *lie* IV.6

Baker suspects influence of *coucher*

See 1.4

my father and him have IV.6

Priestley—"French idiom." See 3.15

one as impersonal IV.6

*Priestley—though
French, acceptable

See 10.5, above

repenting him of IV.6
†Priestley—French

suite
†Priestley—objection to importation

a protestation where, etc. IX.9
See 15.2
Priestley

See IX.9 and Chapter IV, on the course of other appeals to foreign analogies; and sections above on Pronoun Case, 3.1, and Verb-subject Agreement, 6.1.

20. "IPSEDIXITISMS"—Dicta supported by no assigned or discoverable principle

as also III.4
Monthly Review   Baker

commute to III.2
Baker   Swift

compunctious visitings III.7
†Webster   Shakespeare
            Johnson

corresponsive III.7
†Baker   Swift
Webster   Shakespeare
            Johnson

it is very true what he says III.6
See 8.0

mistake many people lie under III.4
Monthly Review—"a vile phrase"   Baker

pelting rivers III.7
†Webster   Shakespeare
            Johnson

sowed or *sown* III.6
       *Baker—either

upon for *on the contrary* III.6 and *n*
Baker   Johnson
Potter

whatsoever
††Monthly Review
Inelegant

APPENDIX II—BIBLIOGRAPHIES

A. LISTS INCLUDING EIGHTEENTH-CENTURY WRITINGS ON THE ENGLISH LANGUAGE

GOOLD BROWN, *Grammar of English Grammars*, London, 1751, pp. xi-xix.

CHARLES C. FRIES, "The Periphrastic Future with *Shall* and *Will* in Modern English." *P.M.L.A.* XL., No. 4, pp. 963-1024. Bibliography, pp. 968-9.

*(K) ARTHUR KENNEDY, *A Bibliography of writings about the English Language.* Oxford, Harvard, and Yale University Presses, 1927. Numbers after (K) refer to items of this bibliography.

GEORGE PHILIP KRAPP, *The English Language in America.* Published for the M.L.A. by the Century Co., 1925. Bibliography, Vol. II, pp. 273-284.

ROLLO LAVERNE LYMAN, *English Grammar in American Schools before 1850.* Department of the Interior, Bureau of Education, Bulletin 1921, No. 12. Bibliography, pp. 154 ff.

THOMAS MARTIN, *Philological Grammar of the English Tongue.* 1824. In the Plimpton Collection. Contains a genealogy of English from the Hebrew. Catalogue of Grammars, pp. 265-71.

WILLIAM HARVEY WELLS, *Historical Authorship of English Grammar, a Circular Letter,* Chicago, 1878 (NYPL)

B. PUBLICATIONS DURING THE EIGHTEENTH CENTURY ON ENGLISH GRAMMAR, RHETORIC, AND CRITICISM OF USAGE CONSULTED FOR THIS STUDY— IN ORDER OF PUBLICATION

The place of publication is London where no other is specified.

The libraries where the books were found are marked:—Columbia University (C) and Teachers College (TC), Cornell University (Cor), Widener Library, Harvard University (H), Princeton University (P), Yale University (Y), the University of Wisconsin (Wis), the University of Michigan (M), the Library of Congress (LC), and the New York Public Library (NYPL).

1700

A. LANE, *A Key to the Art of Letters* . . . English Grammar. (Kennedy 5745. B.M. Cat.)

1706

RICHARD JOHNSON, *Grammarical Commentaries, being an Apparatus to a New National Grammar* . . . *Falsities* . . . *of Lilly's System* (C). A grammar directed wholly to Latin. This and Lane's grammar apparently were the first to make the suggestion that we should learn English by rule, as we do foreign languages.

1707

THOMAS DYCHE, *Guide to the English Tongue*, in Two Parts. 2nd ed., 1710 (NYPL).

1708

The Art of Speaking: written in French by Messieurs Du Port Royal: in persuance of a former treatise, intituled, The art of thinking. Rendered into English. Second (?) edition, 1708 (LC). The first English edition may be referred to in *Pepys' Dairy,* Dec. 6, 1668. Thorp's catalog No. 377 (1926) listed a 1676 ed.

1710-11

[JOHN BRIGHTLAND] *Grammar of the Englsh Tongue, with the Arts of Rhetorick, Logick, Poetry, etc.* . . The whole making a compleat System of an English Education.

Opposite the title page is "The Approbation of Isaac Bickerstaff, Esq. . . . Censor"; hence this book has been frequently attributed to Richard Steele. (See K 5755). The chief points are in doggerel rhyme, and there are copious notes. (H)

Third edition, 1714 (Wis), and "Fourth Edition, Corrected, 1721" (C), used for this study, are abusive of Greenwood for following the Saxon, and of *The English Grammar* for forcing "every thing to the Method and Form of the Latin and Greek."

1711

JAMES GREENWOOD, *An Essay Towards a Practical English Grammar;* describing the Genius and Nature of the English Tongue (TC). 3rd ed., 1729 (Wis).

This contains a good account of the history of English, translated from Wallis, with added texts from the eighth century to Spenser.

ADDISON, STEELE, and others *Spectators Nos. 37, 78* (May 30, 1711), *80, 135,* etc.

1711-12

JONATHAN SWIFT, *A Proposal for Correcting, Improving, and Ascertaining the English Tongue*: in a Letter to the Most Honorable Robert Earl of Oxford and Mortimer . . . . (C)

[JOHN OLDMIXON] *Reflections on Dr. Swift's Letter to the Earl of Oxford about the English Tongue* . . . February 22, 1711-12 (NYPL)
Attacks mainly on political grounds, approves the idea of an Academy and displays a fresh crop of crotchets.

See also Swift's paper in *Tatler 230,* September 28, 1710, "Polite Conversations," whose introduction objects to other contractions, etc., and "Letter to a Young Gentleman Lately enter'd into Holy Orders" (1721), etc.

1724

ANON. *The Many Advantages of a Good Language to any Nation;* with an examination of the present state of our own; as also an essay toward correcting some things that are wrong in it.
Proposal for an Academy, and suggestions toward analogy in spelling. observations on grammar and etymology, etc. (TC)

LEONARD WELSTED, *Dissertation concerning the State of Poetry* [See Hughes, 1735, below] (Reprinted in Durham).

1731

[JOHN CHAPMAN] *Remarks on a Letter to Dr. Waterland in Relation to the Natural Account of Languages, by Philobiblicus* Cantabrigiensis. Cambridge, 1731. (NYPL)
A heap of learned citations in 48 pages to buttress the Babel account of languages against "higher criticism."

1732

RICHARD BENTLEY, Milton's *Paradise Lost,* a New Edition.
The frontispiece is an engraved portrait of Milton, with the somewhat inappropriate motto "Nascuntur Poetae, non fiunt" (C)

1734

ANON. *Characteristicks*: or a Specimen of the worth and integrity of the most favourite authors of the present age. No. 1. (Y)
Attacks Bayle's *Dictionary* and Locke's *Essay* as subversive.

WILLIAM LOUGHTON, *English Grammar.* 2nd ed., 1735 (Wis).

1735

THOMAS DYCHE and WILLIAM PARDON, *New General English Dictionary* . . . compendious English Grammar (K 6225). 1740 ed. (C)

Grammar of only 9 pp., "only general *hints* and specimens, not a critical treatise" (Preface).

JOHN HUGHES, *Of Style*. Written 1698. (Reprinted in Durham.)

1736

ANON. *A Prospect of Oratory*: or, the Art of Speeching, deduced from the Manner of the Celebrated Serjeant Kite. Dublin.

Mock-classic rhetoric, arguing for anticlimax, obscurity, etc. (NYPL).

1737

JAMES GREENWOOD, *The Royal English Grammar*, containing what is necessary to the Knowledge of the English tongue, Laid down in a Plain and Familiar Way, for the Use of Young Gentlemen and Ladys. 4th ed. 1750; 9th, 1780.

Omits the Historical Preface and Critical Notes on the *Essay;* Adapts Matters to "the Understanding of the meanest Capacity, that they who never learnt any Latin . . . every Thing Easy and Familiar to the Fair Sex . . ." (C)

1740

THOMAS DILWORTH, *New Guide to the English Tongue*. Boston, 1771, Portsmouth, 1795 (H).

Thirty-six editions in America between 1747-1792. (K5777a, 5778)

1745

[JOHN NEWBERRY] (K) *Grammar and Rhetoric,* a volume of the Circle of the Sciences.

87 pp. on Tropes. 2nd ed., also 1746 (C).

1746

DANIEL FENNING, *Universal Spelling Book*. Wells says the English Grammar was added to the 5th ed., "about 1770." Part II of the 1787 ed. is an "easy and rational guide to English Grammar" (20 pp.). (H). Kennedy lists also "A *New Grammar,* 1771"—probably reprinted from the 4th (1770) edition.

JOHN UPTON, *Critical Observations on Shakespeare* (C)

1748

[THOMAS EDWARDS] *A Supplement to Mr. Warburton's Edition of Shakespear*. Being the Canons of Criticism . . . and Glossary (C).

The editions of 1750, 1758, and 1765 have Edwards' name, are entitled *The Canons of Criticism,* and begin with these; they have several additional canons, and some remarks on Warburton's treatment of Edwards in the note on Dunciad IV, 567, circulated for the purpose of "laughing [W.W] down to his proper rank and character" (Preface, p. 23, ed. 1750).

The Yale University catalogue notes of the 1750 edition: "Richard Roderick was the coadjutor of Thomas Edward in his 'Canons of Criticism'".

"Mrs Slack (GEORGE or A. FISHER). *The American Instructor*: or, Young Man's Best Companion, etc. 9th ed. Philadelphia, printed by Benjamin Franklin. 14th ed., London, 1757, called *The Instructor*, etc. (K, 5789, 5808). 1795 ed., apparently of the same work, called *The Pleasing Instructor* (C).

ANON. *An Answer to Certain Passages in Mr. W.'s Preface to his Edition of Shakespeare.* (C).

1750

[ZACHERAY GREY] *Free and Familiar Letter to — W. Warburton.* By a Country Curate (C)

1751

JAMES HARRIS, *Hermes*, or a Philosophical Inquiry concerning Universal Grammar.

The British Museum has the second edition, 1765. Citations in this study are to the third ed., 1771 (C). References are mainly to Greek and Latin grammars and to classical sources.

1752

COLLEY CIBBER, *Familiar Epistle to W. W[arburton]* (C)
[GEORGE HARRIS], *Observations upon the English Language.* In a Letter to a Friend.

The source or first record of many objections and prescriptions by Lowth and others. (Cor).

1753

JAMES BUCHANAN, *Complete English Scholar* . . . learning Grammar without Latin.

It proceds from one-syllable words to selections from the *Spectator*. Part III (78 pp.) is a catechetical English Grammar, with four pages on Syntax.

1754

D. FARRO, *Royal Universal British Grammar and Vocabulary.*

BENJAMIN MARTIN, *An Introduction to the English Language and Learning*, in Three Parts (H)

I. Alphabet (pronunciation and spelling) for 22 sciences
II. Rudimentary English Grammar (21 pp., 2½ on syntax)
III. Lessons on "all the sciences"

JOHN WARD, *Four Essays upon the English Language*
III. is on "The Use of the Articles," IV. on "The Formation of the Verbs, and their Analogy with the Latin" with a catalog of English verbs arranged in four conjugations. 1758 ed. (C)

1755

The Complete Letter-Writer . . . plain and compendious Grammar. New York. (Wis); 1793 ed. (NYPL)

Sensible introduction and many interesting examples of ancient and modern letters.

SAMUEL JOHNSON, *A Dictionary of the English Language* . . . History . . . English Grammar (Wis). Sixth ed. 1785 (C)

36 pp. of texts, from Alfred's Boethius Modern English; one page of the history of the language; 15 pp. of grammar; only twelve lines on syntax.

1756

THOMAS BLACKLOCK, *An Essay on Universal Etymology*: or the Analysis of a Sentence, Containing an account of the Parts of Speech, as common to all Languages. Edinburgh.

16 pp. notes, 6 in rhymed couplets on parts of speech, by a follower of James Harris. (LC)

GEORGE COLMAN and BONSELL THORNTON, "On the Abuse of Words," *The Connoisseur* No. 104, Jan. 22, 1756 (NYPL). Mainly on the misuse and overuse of "ruined."

1758

ANSELM BAYLY, *An Introduction to Languages,* Literary and Philosophical, Especially to the English, Latin, Greek, and Hebrew. Exhibiting at one View their Grammar Rationale, Analogy and Idiom. (C, LC). Bayly's *Accidence* (1771) seems to refer to a 1756 ed.

Part II treats Analogy and Syntax; Part III has Four Dissertations on sounds, "just writing", "just speaking," etc.

LAUNCELOT TEMPLE, *Sketches or Essays on Various Subjects.* Second Edition, Corrected.

"Of Language . . . Of Taste, Of Turgid Writing . . . and Florid Writing, Of Obscure Writing, Of Superannuated Words, Of New Words . . ."

Bound with Young (*infra*) and Akenside's Pleasures of the Imagination, as *Armstrong's Sketches.* (C)

1759

E. Young, *Conjectures on Original Composition.* Bound with Temple, In *Armstrong's Sketches;* very general observations. (C)

T. Sheridan, *Discourse . . . introductory to a Course of Lectures* on Elocution and the English Language. (TC)

1760

[James Buchanan] *The British Grammar,* or an Essay in Four Parts on Speaking and Writing the English Language Grammatically and Inditing Elegantly. 1784 ed. (TC)

Kennedy's proof for assigning this to Buchanan is adequate: *Modern Language Notes,* v. 41, p. 388.

1761-2

Joseph Priestley, *The Rudiments of English Grammar,* Adapted to the use of Schools; with Notes and Observations for the Use of Those Who have made some Proficiency in Language. 1768 ed. (Wis) and "A New Edition, Corrected, 1769" (TC) used for this study.

Priestley is the most intelligent and consistent follower of usage in this period.

1762

J. Johnson, *The New Royal and Universal English Dictionary,* to which is prefixed a Grammar of the English Tongue. 2 Volumes (C)

20 pages of grammar, with a valiant attack on Scotticisms.

Lord Kames, *Elements of Criticism.* 2 Vol. 1783 ed. (C); 1788 ed. (Wis)

Pages 18-82 of Volume II consider "The Beauties of Language with Respect to Signification," including much sentence doctrine. One of his examples of revision is ridiculed in Campbell's *Sale of Authors* (1767)

[Robert Lowth] *A Short Introduction to English Grammar,* with Critical Notes. Anonymous, as are the 1763, 69, etc. editions. (H)

A completely logical account, with leanings toward metaphysics and universal grammar and great admiration of Harris and Johnson. 1763 (Wis.); Dublin, 1769 (TC); 1769 (Wis).

Joseph Priestley, "Lectures on Theory of Language and Universal Grammar," *Works,* 1822, V. 23.

Thomas Sheridan, *A Dissertation on the Causes of the Difficulties which occur, in Learning the English Tongue.* London, 1762 (TC).

A plan for his grammar and dictionary.

JOHN TRUSLER *A New Guide to Eloquence;* being a Treatise of the proper distinctions to be observed between words reckoned synonymous . . . upon the plan of a French work of the same nature by the Abbott Girard. (Wis).

Dedicated to Lady Montague; translates the French preface, which argues the advantages of fixing a language and of becoming "somewhat difficult in our manner of selecting words." Synonyms given only through the letter A—"to be continued, if found acceptable to the publick." See 1766, below.

1763

JOHN ASH, *The Easiest Introduction to Dr. Lowth's English Grammar,* designed for the use of children under ten years of age. (C).

Second edition, 1766. A thorough-going compressed piece of grammatical logic.

1765

WILLIAM WARD, *An Essay on Grammar* as it may be applied to the English Language, in Two Treatises: One Speculative, being an attempt to investigate proper principles. The Other Practical, containing Definitions and Rules, deduced from the Principles, and illustrated by a Variety of Examples from the most approved Writers. (TC)

Large folio, 294 plus 260 pp.; attempts a complete logical explanation, but does not fall foul of usage; as illustrated in this study, (XI § 8) he fits logic to usage by various shifts.

WILLIAM WARD, *A Practical Grammar of the English Language.* York. (Wis) See 1767, below.

1766

JOHN BURN, *A Practical English Grammar,* Glasgow. 1786 ed. (Wis).

Conventional Lowthist; anticipates Campbell on *it's* and *'tis;* large areas of "false English" from standard writers.

JOHN TRUSLER, *The Distinction between Words* esteemed synonymous in the English language—from Abbé Girard's *Synonymes François.* (See 1763)

Second edition "with revisions and amendations," 1783. (C).

1767

JAMES BUCHANAN, *A Regular English Syntax,* wherein is exhibited the whole Variety of English Construction, properly exemplified. To which is added The elegant Manner of arrainging Words, and Members of Sentences, etc. . . . for private young Gentlemen and Ladies as well as our most eminent schools. (P) ; 1780 ed. (1st American) (Wis).

[ARCHIBALD CAMPBELL] *Lexiphanes, a Dialogue.* Imitated from Lucian, and suited to the present Times, being An Attempt to Restore the English Tongue to its ancient Purity, and to correct, as well as expose, the affected Style, hard Words, and absurd Phraseology of Our English Lexiphanes, the Rambler.

> Attributed positively by Boswell. Second edition, corrected, (1767 also) used for this study. (C, Wis).

——————*Sale of Authors.* A Dialogue in Imitation of Lucian (LC)

> This includes some criticisms of Lord Kames' *Elements.*

WILLIAM WARD. *A Grammar of the English Language.* In Two Treatises. The First, containing Rules for every Part of its Construction; with a Praxis both of True and False English, Shewing how the Rules are to be applied in resolving the True, and in rectifying the False. The Second, shewing the Nature of the several Parts of Speech, and the Reasons of every Part of Construction. York, n. d. (Wis).

> The examples of false construction are manufactured by introducing errors into sentences from the *Spectator,* etc.

1768

W. R. "Letters (I-IX) on English Grammar" in *Oxford Magazine,* (1768) inveigh against the Scots' corruption of English.

[WILLIAM SALISBURY] *Two Grammatical Essays.* First, on a Barbarism in the English Language, in a Letter to Dr. S [alter]. (NYPL).

> "Had rather" riddled in 25 pages of reason and analogy, though Latin analogies are spurned.

1769

JOHANN DAVID MICHAELIS, *A Dissertation on the Influence of Opinions on Language and of Language on Opinions* . . . Advantages and Practicability of a Universal Learned Language. (LC)

> The author was "Director of the Royal Society of Göttingen and Court Counsellor to his Britannic Majesty"; probably the translation from the original German is his own.

1770

[ROBERT BAKER] *Reflections on the English Language in the Nature of Vaugelas's* Reflections on the French; being a detection of many improper Expressions used in Conversation, and of many others to be found in Authors. To which is prefixed a Discourse addressed to His Majesty. (H)

The address proposed an Academy. The 1779 edition had Baker's name; the title was altered to *Remarks,* the Address was omitted, and the preface carried on controversy with the *Monthly Review* critics, Dr. Salter of the Charter-House, and Johnson. Campbell refers to "the author of the Reflections," Withers to "the ingenious Mr. Baker," and R. G. White praised him highly. This second edition, also used, has "almost double the number of remarks." (LC,NYPL, H)

1771

ANSELM BAYLY. *The English Accidence* (Plimpton Collection, LC). *Monthly Review* XLV, 87-96, (August, 1771). Review of Baker's *Reflections.*

1772

ALEXANDER ADAM, *Rudiments of Latin and English Grammar* (L) (W) Edinburgh ed., 1786, and American ed.. 1812, (NYPL)

ANON., *The Tutor;* or Epistolary Guide . . . New Introduction to English Grammar . . . classical purity ascertained, the Barbarisms . . . rejected. (NYPL)

ANSELM BAYLY, *A Plain and Complete Grammar of the English Language;* to which is prefixed the English Accedence, with Remarks and Observations on *A Short Introduction to English Grammar.* (TC). The *English Accedence* preceding the grammar has separate paging.

1773

ANON., *Grammar and Rhetoric*
20 pages of grammar, ½ page of syntax; manufactured "false grammar."

J. B[UCHANAN] First Six Books of *Paradise Lost* Rendered into Grammatical Construction. (C)

Not another Emendation, but a supplying of ellipses and righting of inversions at the foot of the page to form a prose version "more easily understood."

WILLIAM KENRICK, *A New Dictionary of the English Language* . . . to which is prefixed *A Rhetorical Grammar* (LC)

Interest mainly in pronunciation.

[JAMES BURNET] *Lord Monboddo,* Of the Origin and Progress of Language. Second edition with large Additions and Corrections. Edinburgh 1773-92 (C)

Six large volumes of conjectural and scriptural history of language, interspersed with some sound ideas about primitive languages derived from the *Jesuit Relations* and the like sources.

1775

JOHN ASH, *New and Complete Dictionary of the English Language,* to which is prefixed a Comprehensive Grammar (28 pages, 4 on syntax, 3 on ellipses). (C)

ENCYCLOPAEDIA BRITANNICA, or a Dictionary of Arts and Sciences . . . by a Society of Gentlemen in Scotland. First Edition, 1775, 3 vol. (C)
Article "Grammar," vol. II, pp. 728-45: "Language," Ibid. 863-80.

1776

GEORGE CAMPBELL, *The Philosophy of Rhetoric.* London and Edinburgh, 1776, 2 vol. (C)
Vol. I contains the chief discussion of usage, and the canons.

1777

JOSEPH PRIESTLEY, "Course of Lectures on Oratory and Criticism." In his *Works,* 1822, volume 23,

1778

JOHN HORNE. A Letter to John Dunning, esq. (NYPL)
Dated at "King's Bench Prison, April 21, 1778". A treatise on meaning and derivation of conjunctions, ridiculing Harris, Johnson, etc. Its origin in Horne's commitment on a count of "two prepositions and a conjunction, . . . as degrading as being brained with a lady's fan."
The basis for Horne Tooke's *Diversions of Purley,* 1786, the 1829 edition of which reprints it in full.

JOHN SHAW, *English Grammar,* 1780 ed. (H). Third Edition, 1787, (Wis) called "A Methodical English Grammar. Rules and directions for speaking and writing the English Language with propriety and accuracy . . . Epitome of Rhetoric." Aim stated to aid mastery of Latin.

1779

ROBERT BAKER, See *Reflections* (1770)

ROBERT POTTER, *The Art of Criticism;* as exemplified in Dr. Johnson's Lives of the Most Eminent English Poets (LC)
Harsh criticism, incidentally of the lexicographer's style.

1780

JOHN ASH, *Grammatical Institutions.* Philadelphia. Marked "reprint of a British Book which first appeared in 1766"; the latter is marked (in B.M. Cat.) "Another edition" of the *Easiest Introduction.* See 1763.

THOMAS SHERIDAN, *General Dictionary of the English Language.* 1785 ed. (C). Rhetorical Grammar prefixed.

1781

JAMES HARRIS, *Philological Inquiries,* in Three Parts (NYPL)

1782

[JOHN CALLANDER] *Deformities of Dr. Samuel Johnson,* selected from his Works. "A Narrative which aims at Simplicity and is ambitious to record the Truth." Edinburgh, 1782.

A long final note on *Lexiphanes* and the Scotch.

RALPH HARRISON, *Rudiments of English Grammar,* 1787 ed. (NYPL). Part II is on Syntax.

1783

JAMES BEATTIE, *The Theory of Language,* in Two Parts. I. Of the Origin and General Nature of Speech. II. Of Universal Grammar. New edition enlarged and corrected, 1787 (C).

THOMAS SHERIDAN, *Rhetorical Grammar.* Philadelphia ed. (C, Wis)

HUGH BLAIR, *Lectures on Rhetoric and Belles Lettres,* in Two Volumes. The 2nd American edition from the fourth of London, dated, 1793 (C).

1784

[JOHN FELL] *Essay towards an English Grammar*: with a dissertation on the nature and peculiar use of certain hypothetical verbs in the English language. (Wis).

Good description of the use of *shall* and *will.*

NOAH WEBSTER, *Grammatical Institute of the English Language.* Hartford. (NYPL,H)

Part II (1784) contained the "plain and comprehensive grammar, grounded on the true principles of the language." The changes in the successive editions of this book from 1787 to 1804 are in general creditable to Webster's openness of mind on this subject.

1785

CALEB BINGHAM, *The Young Lady's Accidence.* Boston.
>Only 50 pages, including 22 rules of syntax and 2½ pages of errors corrected. 1794 ed. (H)

J. MENNYE, *An English Grammar* . . . compilation, with observations explanatory and critical. New York.
>Speaks complacently of "a variety of barbarisms from the writings of great men" as warning examples, and has 34 additional pages of manufactured false syntax.

1786

HORNE TOOKE, *The Diversions of Purley.* 2 vol. Based on his *Letter to Dunning.* (See 1778). (C)
>An elaborate collection of data and guesswork on English etymologies, concerned principally with the classification of parts of speech. (C)

1787

G. NEVILLE USSHER, *Elements of Grammar and Rhetoric* . . . particulaly for Ladies' Boarding Schools. 2d ed. Exeter, 1796.

1788

C. COOTE, *Elements of the Grammar of the English Language* (M)

JOHN STIRLING, *A System of Rhetorick*
>Conventional treatments of tropes and the rest.

NOAH WEBSTER, *Rudiments of English Grammar.* Philadelphia.

PHILIP WITHERS, *Aristarchus,* or the Principles of Composition, Containing a Methodical Arrangement of the Grammatical Improprieties of Common Discourse, with Select Rules for Attaining to Ease and Elegance in Conversation &c. &c. (TC,Y, LC) 1822 ed. (Y, LC).
>Anything but methodical: mainly concerned with verbs, but also with metaphysical theories of meanings of letters and figures, etc.

1789

NOAH WEBSTER, *Dissertations on the English Language.* Boston.
>Five lectures, "with notes, historical and critical", containing most of Webster's theory of language; an Appendix "on a Reformed Mode of Spelling, with Dr. Franklin's Arguments on that Subject." (C)

1792

CALEB ALEXANDER, *Grammatical System of the English Language.*
Keen, N.H. 1794 ed. (H) ; Second ed. 1793 (Wis).

Authors from whom errors are quoted are not cited.

"The following grammar contains more rules of syntax, than any
one book that has been published on the subject" (a total of 28) ;
but five more are added in ink in the Harvard copy.

1790

JAMES GREGORY, *Theory of the Moods of Verbs.* Transactions of the
Royal Society of Edinburgh II (1790), Part I, pp. 193-250. (LC)

Very abstruse and theoretical, in the manner of Harris, Beattie,
and Monboddo.

1793

JOHN HORNSEY, *A Short English Grammar in Two Parts.* York, 103
pp., material from Lowth, Blair, Priestley. (TC)

1794

CALEB ALEXANDER, *An Introduction to the Speaking and Writing of
the English Language* according to Grammatical Rules. Boston.
(NYPL)

An exercise book only. Authors quoted for error not named.

V. J. PEYTON, *The Elements of the English Language.* Philadelphia.
In French, with "familiar dialogs."

1795

BENJAMIN DEARBORNE, *Columbian Grammar.* Vol. 4 of a System of
Education. Boston, 1795, (TC)

An "english grammar," following Lowth and dealing much with
pronunciation.

LINDLEY MURRAY, *English Grammar*, comprehending the Principles and
Rules of the Language. York.

The grammar which by its combination of the elements of conservative and authoritarian liking held the field for years. Murray's ideals were Blair's of mental discipline—accuracy and order—
"one uniform system," "harmony of expression," and "smooth and
voluble terms, easily committed to memory." Preface, 1800 ed.
(LC)

1796

JOHN CLARK, *Rational Spelling Book*. Part II. Complete, concise, and easy English Grammar. *"16th ed.,* revised by John Entick". (H)

Preface states: "Preceding authors have totally neglected examples of wrong English." Earlier editions not traced.

1797

DUNCAN MACKINTOSH AND HIS TWO DAUGHTERS, *A Plain Rational Essay on English Grammar* . . . Boston

Main interest in pronunciation; says *as* and *than* take the nominative both before and after them; still writes *it's* possessive (C)

P. STANNIFORD, *Short but Comprehensive Grammar*. Boston

In the appendix, "comprehending a list of Vulgarisms and grammatical Improprieties, used in common Conversation by Persons of different Societies," are 7 pp. of mispronunciations, 5 of grammatical errors, and 8 taken from the Bible and the Best Authors. (H)

WILLIAM GODWIN, "Essay on English Style". *The Enquirer*, 1797, pp. 369-70.

1798

SAMUEL HENSHALL, *The Saxon and English Languages,* Reciprocally illustrative of Each Other . . . and a New Mode suggested of Radically Studying the Saxon and English Languages. (NYPL)

Large selection of texts with interlinear translation into English; condemns the former method of translating round about through Latin. Acknowledges the learned services, and condemns the character of Horne Tooke.

A. F. M. WILLICH, *Three Philological Essays*: chiefly translated from the German of John Christopher Adelung . . . Concise history of English [82 pp.] with specimens from Caedmon on, [source German; he explains carefully that *ox* and *beef* are not synonymous]; Philosophical [Kantian] view of the English Language; comments on Johnson's "Dictionary". (LC)

NOAH WEBSTER, *A letter to the Governors . . . of the Universities . . .* on the Errors of English Grammars. New York. (NYPL; LC)

Very severe condemnation of all efforts to date.

1799

LINDLEY MURRAY, *English Exercises,* adapted to the grammar lately published . . . and Key to all. 4th ed. corrected. This reappeared as Volume 2 of the 1809 (York) edition.

1801

JOHN WALTER, *A Rhetorical Grammar* . . . Outlines of Composition. 3rd ed. Composition section, "with the most trifling alterations," follows Blair (C).

1807

NOAH WEBSTER, *A Letter to Dr. David Ramsay of Charleston, S. C.* . . . respecting the Errors in Johnson's and others' dictionaries. He notes (1) insertion of words neither spoken nor written; (2) mischoice of authorities ("the style of Sir Thomas [Browne] is not English"); (3) admitting low, vulgar, cant words, i. e., *jackalent* (Ash worst here) ; (4) want of just discrimination. (NYPL)

C. ADDITIONAL SOURCES OF MATERIAL

CHARLES SEARS BALDWIN, *Ancient Rhetoric and Poetic*, Macmillian, 1924.

BISHOP GEORGE BERKELEY, *Works*, Oxford, 1881 ed. "Commonplace Book"; "Alciphron, or the Minute Philosopher, Fourth Dialogue"; "Principles of Human Knowledge"; "Theory of Vision."

W. F. BRYAN, "Notes on the Founders of Prescritive English Grammar." *Manly Anniversary Studies in Language and Literature.* University of Chicago Press, 1923, pp. 383-93.

——————"A Late Eighteenth-Century Purist", *Studies in Philology*, XXIV (January 1927), 358-70.

JOSEPH BUTLER, *Works.* Gladstone's ed., 1896. Vol. 1. "Analogy."

W. H. DURHAM, *Critical Essays of the Eighteenth Century*, 1700-1725. Yale University Press, 1915. Contains Welsted's *Dissertation*, 1724, and Hughes' *Of Style*, 1698-1735.

CHARLES C. FRIES, "Rules of the Common School Grammars", *P.M.L.A.*, XLII, 221-37. See also "The Periphrastic Future" in Bibliography A, above.

——————*The Teaching of the English Language*, Nelson, 1927.

BASIL GILDERSLEEVE, *Essays and Studies.* Baltimore, 1890.

FITZEDWARD HALL, *Recent Exemplifications of False Philology.* Scribner and Armstrong, 1872.

——————*Modern English.* Scribner and Armstrong, 1873.

Memoirs of William Hickey (1749-1775) edited by Alfred Spencer. Hurst and Blackett, Ltd., Third Edition, 1919, pp. 1-150.

JAMES HUME, *A Treatise of Human Nature*, Oxford, 1896 ed.
——————*Principles of Morals.* Open Court, 1900 ed.

OTTO JESPERSEN, *Language*. Holt, 1922.

——————— "Notes on Relative Clauses" *S.P.E. Tract No. 24*. Oxford, 1926.

———————*Philosophy of Grammar*. Allen and Unwin, 1924.

G. L. KITTREDGE, *Some Landmarks in the History of English Grammars*. Ginn, 1906.

GEORGE PHILIP KRAPP, *The English Language in America*, M.L.A. and Century Co., 1925.

——————— Modern English: Its Growth and Present Use. Scribner, 1912.

——————— "Standards of Speech and their Value." *Modern Philology* XI (July, 1913), p. 58.

——————— The Knowledge of English. Holt, 1927.

Works of John Locke, fifth edition, 1751, vol. I. "Essay on the Human Understanding."

GEORGE H. MCKNIGHT, *Modern English in the Making*. Appleton, 1928.

———————"Conservatism in American Speech," *American Speech*, Vol. 1, No. 1, October, 1925, pp. 1-17.

J. MACKAIL, *Bentley's Milton*. Warton Lecture XV, *Proceedings of the British Academy* XI, Oxford (no date)

B. S. MONROE, "An English Academy." *Modern Philology* VIII, No. 1. (July, 1910), 107-122.

J. L. MOORE, "Tudor-Stuart View of the Growth, Status, and Destiny of the English Language." *Studien zur Englischen Philologie*, Halle, 1910, Volume LI.

RICHARD MORRIS, *Historical Outlines of English Accidence*. Macmillan, 1872.

C. K. OGDEN AND WALDO RICHARDS, *The Meaning of Meaning*. Harcourt, 1923.

HAROLD E. PALMER, *A Grammar of Spoken English on a strictly Phonetic Basis*. W. Heffer, Cambridge, 1924.

Works of Dr. Parr, 1828. Vol. I contains letters of Charles James Fox answering criticisms (not reproduced) by Dr. Parr.

JOAN PLATT, "Development of English Colloquial Idiom during the Eighteenth Century" *Review of Language Studies*, II (1926), 70-81 and 189-96.

C. DE F. VAUGELAS, *Remarques sur la Langue François (1647) avec des Notes par T. Corneille*, Paris, 1687 and 1738. Preface, pp. 1-94.

Joseph Vendryes, *Language,* translated by Paul Radin. Knopf, 1925.

Johannis Wallis, *Grammatica Linguae Anglicanae.* Oxford, 1653. Fourth, 1674, ed. (Wis)

John Wilkins, *The Mathematical and Philosophical Works* . . . containing "An Abstract of the Essay towards a Real Character and a Philosophical Language." London, 1708.

Henry Cecil Wyld, *History of Modern Colloquial English.* T. Fisher Unwin, 1920.

INDEX

Roman numerals followed by Arabic refer to chapters and sections of the study. Chapter titles are in capitals, those of sections in small capitals. Arabic numerals preceded by G refer to the sections and subsections of the glossary.

Dates in parentheses refer to the citations in the bibliography, Appendix II B, which are chronologically arranged.

Clarke, John, *Rational Spelling Book,* (1796) V.8, VI.14, VII.4, XI.17 XII.1
"classical", applied to English, VIII.8
CLASSICAL ANALOGIES, See Analogies, classical.
classical languages, reverence for, IV.3, XII.6
cling, clang, clung, V.6; G 5.1
Coleridge, Samuel Taylor, XI.15 *n*
COLLECTIVE NOUNS, SPECIAL INSTANCES OF VERB-AGREEMENT WITH, VI.5, XII.1, 11; G 6.13
Colloquial English, History of Modern, H. C. Wyld, I.1 *n,* V.6, VIII.8 *n,* XII.16, XIII.2, 7
Colman, George, and Thornton, Bonsell, *Connoisseur* (1756), cited, XI.22
"colloquial dialect, the" rejected by Campbell; IX.6, XI.8, XIII.7
Columbian Grammar, The, Benjamin Dearborne, (1795), XI.11
common and mutual, VII.3, VIII.15; G 17.1
Common School Grammars, C. C. Fries on the, I.1, XIII.2 *n*
common soldiers for *private men,* X.8
commute to, III.2, G 20.0
Compact, origin of language in, II.4, 6; IX.1 *n*; IX.18
comparative and superlative degrees, differentiation of, V.16
comparative philology in the eighteenth century, VIII.1 ff.
Comparison, Mixed, VI.15 and *n*
comparison of adjectives and adverbs, V.4, 16; VII.11, VIII.4, IX.2, 12, G 4.0
comparisons, analogy in, V.4
comparison of supposedly incomparable adjectives, VII.11, IX.12; G 4.2
comparisons, superlatives used for, V.4, 16; G 3.4
"compassionate and condole with his friends", VI.14; G 9.8
compete for *enter into competition,* X.8; 1.32, 19.1, G 20.0
Complete Letter Writer, The (1755), XI.11
compound subject, agreement of verb with, II.2, IV.4, XII.1, 2-8; G 6.14, 6.16
compunctious visitings, III.7; G 20.0
con (see *pro and con*), G 17.31, 18.2
"Concealed grammatical errors", V.3; VI.4, 11, 14, 15, 23; IX.15, Canon 2; XI.8, XII.18, G 6.22, 6.6, 7.8, 9.5
concord, Logic of, XII.3, XIII.9
CONCORD, VARIOUS SOLUTIONS OF PROBLEMS OF, CHAPTER XII
conditional clause, XI.17, mood of verb in
conduceth, VIII.11
conformity to ancient usage, IX.12, Canon 5
Confutacion of Tyndale, by Thomas More, discussed by Withers, VII.6 *n*
Congreve, William, V.10, VIII.10, IX.4, X.5, XI.5

fop, IX.7; G 18.1
for all that, X.4; G 18.1
for righteousness sake, XI.12
for to be seen, G 8.0
Foreign analogies determining English constructions. See Analogies, classical, French, etc.
forfeit as transitive verb, V.11; G 1.4
former as a substantive, G 1.24
forwards, V.3; G 4.3
founden, IX.18; G 5.1
"four first canons", etc., VI.20, VIII.11; G 11.23
four-wheels chaise, V.4; G 6.21
Fox, Charles James, letters of, VI.2, 4; X.7, 10
Fox, George, "A Battle-Door for Teachers and Professors to Learn Singular and Plural," I.1
Franklin, Benjamin, letter on spelling, quoted by Webster, XI.12
FRENCH, THE ANALOGY WITH, IV.6; VI.14; VII.7; IX.4, 9
French Academy, III.5, 6. See Academy, An English.
Fries, Charles C., cited, I.1, *n*; V.15; XIII.2 *n*
from hence, etc., III.6; VI.3; IX.3; G 8.0
froward, IX.10; G 17.3
further and *farther,* G 16.1
"future, elliptical", Webster on, XI.20
future tense, formation of, V.14, X.6, 8, 9; no inflection for, in English, IV.5

GALLICISMS, REPUDIATED, IV.6, VII.7
Garrick's company, criticized by Robert Baker, X.5
GENDER, DIFFERENTIATION IN, SOUGHT, II.7 ff.; XIII.4; G 2.0; gender, natural, advantage of, IV.4; V.7; gender of *whose,* V.8; G 2.0
GENERAL LOGICAL CONSIDERATIONS, CHAPTERS VI and VII
genitive case, before the gerund, VIII.7; XI.2, 15; G 3.23; *of* as sign of, XI.14; G 3.2; of groups of words, XI.10; for inanimate objects, V.9; VIII.7; XI.15; of nouns, II.2; III.8; V.9; VIII.7; XI.2, 3, 10, 12, 14, 15; G. 3.2; double, XI.14; G 3.21
GENITIVE CASE, PRONOUN REFERENCE TO, XI.14; G 10.2
"Genius of the Language, The", II.9; III.8; V.3, 13; VI.14; IX.3; XI.15
genre, X.2
gentlemen, language of X.1 ff.; XIII.2
Gentleman's Magazine, X.5 *n*
genuineness, IX.3
GERMANIC TEXTS AND GRAMMARS IN EIGHTEENTH CENTURY, I.6, II.6, VIII.1 f; G 17